"ONE OF THE MOST SHOCKING TRIALS IN THE ANNALS OF MODERN AMERICAN CRIME."

—*San Jose Mercury News*

PERFECT VICTIM
Christine McGuire and Carla Norton

"A BLOOD-CHILLING SAGA of the outer limits of human depravity told with admirable clarity and dispassion."

—William Wright
author of *The Von Bülow Affair*

"GUT-WRENCHING BUT HEART-WRENCHING TOO."

—*Kirkus Reviews*

"A POWERFUL INDICTMENT of hard-core pornography, a memorable lesson for anyone who has considered hitchhiking and a real-life look into the psychology of victimization."

—*Chicago Tribune*

"A FASCINATING PSYCHOLOGICAL AND LEGAL THRILLER."

—*South Bend Tribune*

"WILL HOLD THE READER SPELLBOUND TO THE VERY LAST PAGE."

—*Rave Reviews*

PERFECT VICTIM

Christine McGuire and Carla Norton

A DELL BOOK

Published by
Dell Publishing
a division of
Random House, Inc.

Quotes from *The Collector* by John Fowles used with permission of
Little, Brown and Company, Boston, Massachusetts.

The trademark Dell ® is registered in the U.S. Patent
and Trademark Office.

ISBN-13: 978-0-440-20442-8
ISBN-10: 0-440-20442-9

Reprinted by arrangement with William Morrow and Company, Inc.

Printed in the United States of America

Published simultaneously in Canada

August 1989

OPM 30 29

Dedicated to Colleen Jean Stan

This story is a reconstruction of actual events. The information given and crimes depicted are based on legal evidence, on statements and testimony given by those involved, on individual research, and on facts and personal experience related by the prosecutor of *People* v. *Hooker,* Christine McGuire. Given that the events occurred over such a long period, recollections of those involved sometimes varied, particularly in terms of chronology. Where discrepancies arose, the most plausible version was presented, based on the fallible judgment of the authors.

To help protect the privacy of Colleen Stan and her family, her maiden name has been changed to a fictitious name, Martin. Her mother's current married name is fictitiously given as Grant. And as a courtesy, the first names of Colleen's youngest half-sister, and Cameron and Janice Hooker's daughters and niece have also been changed.

— CONTENTS —————————

Hear me, O God, as I voice my complaint;
protect my life from the threat of the enemy.
Hide me from the conspiracy of the wicked,
from that noisy crowd of evildoers,
who sharpen their tongues like swords
and aim their words like deadly arrows.
They shoot from ambush at the innocent man;
they shoot at him suddenly, without fear.
They encourage each other in evil plans,
they talk about hiding their snares;
they say, "Who will see them?"
They plot injustice and say,
"We have devised a perfect plan!"
Surely the mind and heart of man are cunning.
But God will shoot them with arrows;
suddenly they will be struck down.
He will turn their own tongues against them
and bring them to ruin;
all who see them will shake their heads in scorn.
All mankind will fear;
they will proclaim the works of God
and ponder what he has done.

Psalm 64:1–9
As quoted from the Bible by Colleen Stan

PART ONE

Not Even A Scream

May 19–November 1977

I never let her see papers. I never let her have a radio or television. It happened one day before ever she came I was reading a book called *Secrets of the Gestapo*—all about the tortures and so on they had to do in the war, and how one of the first things to put up with if you were a prisoner was the not knowing what was going on outside the prison. I mean they didn't let the prisoners know anything, they didn't even let them talk to each other, so they were cut off from their old world. And that broke them down.

The Collector, by John Fowles

Nobody who has not lived in a dungeon could understand how *absolute* the silence down here is. No noise unless I make it. So I feel near death. Buried.

Miranda, *The Collector,* by John Fowles

1

Straddling the cool, green rush of the Sacramento River is a town too small and undistinguished to warrant a stop by most tourists. It's a long way from postcard visions of the West Coast—no beach-front condos, few flashy sports cars, not even a whole lot of freeway.

This sleepy metropolis is the heart and capital of Tehama County, a bucolic expanse of olive, plum, walnut, and almond orchards; a few busy timber yards; and rolling cattle range.

Red Bluff got its name from the russet bluffs that plunge to the edge of the Sacramento River, cut there by time, glowing nearly iridescent in the afternoon sun. When early settlers steamed up from San Francisco on big paddle-wheelers in the 1850s, they spied those cliffs and christened this town after them—but most of today's residents wouldn't know that, so little time do they spend on that swift, dangerous river.

It must be the cattle ranchers that give that Southwestern twang to this place. Never mind the California address, chewing tobacco is more popular than alfalfa sprouts. Men in cowboy boots, denims, and an occasional Stetson stride up the sidewalks, and more than a few pickups rumble down the streets.

They say that Red Bluff's annual Bull and Gelding Sale, held every January, is the biggest in the country. And Round-Up Week, "a celebration of the Best in the West," tops off the silliness of a cowchip-throwing contest, a whisker-growing contest, and a roving jail for unlucky locals wearing non-Western garb, with what is billed as "America's Biggest 2-Day Rodeo."

With those new fast-foot places and shopping centers sprouting up by the freeway, you'd think Red Bluff was booming, but in fact the population has only just crept past 10,500, and "going out of business" sales plague the older parts of town. The economy is depressed, the streets are quiet, the pace is slow. There's not much to do here on a Saturday night.

Like other small towns, Red Bluff is a place of few secrets; broken marriages, accidents, and affairs are big news. But it's a fine place to raise a family, a place where strangers still get a nod and a "hello" on the street, a place where old-fashioned values are upheld by the congregations of little churches that seem to stand on nearly every corner.

The heart of Red Bluff is still Main Street, a long, wide road with only two stoplights that lies on the edge of a downtown grid less than a mile square. The names of the streets running north and south are as all-American as a marching band: Washington, Jefferson, Madison, Monroe, Lincoln. And those running east and west ring as honest as wood: Cedar, Hickory, Walnut, Pine, Oak, and Elm. The Tehama County Courthouse presides over it all. Built in 1920, the impressive brick structure opens onto Washington Street, its front made appropriately solemn with massive columns and its entryway boasting trophies and ribbons from past rodeos, parades, and Little League championships.

A right turn on Oak leads away from the interstate to an older, quieter part of town, where shade trees have grown large and houses have settled deep into their shrubbery. It's a comfortable, quiet neighborhood, if not especially prosperous. Modest homes from the forties and fifties watch children pop wheelies on bicycles while local dogs sniff about for news.

A few of the homes are rented, as is 1140 Oak Street, a small stucco structure painted an unlikely pink and edged in a brick color that's almost red. The owners of the home, an elderly couple by the name of Leddy, live next door. They've seen a lot of tenants in the past thirty-odd years, but they recall that in 1976 and '77 they were renting 1140 Oak Street to Cameron and Janice Hooker.

Mrs. Leddy remembers them as "a nice couple." They paid the rent on time, were hardworking and quiet. Cameron struck them as the serious type. He piled the backyard high with young trees that he'd cut, then sold them in six- or seven-foot segments as fence posts. "He was all business, you might say," Mr. Leddy says.

After sixty years of marriage, the Leddys seem to agree on almost everything, and they agree that Cameron's thin young wife, Janice, was very nice. She sewed, crocheted, and used to come over and sit under the arbor to visit.

And the Leddys can't recall anything at all about the Hookers that they would call strange. "They were no trouble whatsoever," Mrs. Leddy recalls. "We liked them."

To neighbors and onlookers, Cameron and Janice Hooker seemed simply average, another young couple just starting out. At twenty-four, Cameron was tall and gangly. He worked as a millworker at Diamond International, a big lumber mill that at that time boasted of being Tehama County's largest employer. Janice, at nineteen, was still slim, despite having become a mother several months before. Both wore glasses, both had brown hair—hers wavy and long, his straight and shaggy.

They kept to themselves. They kept out of trouble. And none of their neighbors remember the slightest thing out of the ordinary, the smallest ripple of peculiarity about May 19, 1977.

There were probably dozens of reasons Colleen Stan shouldn't have been hitchhiking that day, but this was a time when hitchhikers were plenty and those reasons seemed less important. Thumbing rides on freeway on-ramps was almost a rite of passage for America's youth. Whether it was prudent or not was hardly a consideration. It was cheap. It was easy. And you never could tell what interesting people you might meet out there on the road.

Colleen left Eugene, Oregon, that morning at about eleven, when her roommates, Alice and Bob, drove her to the freeway. She stood at the side of the road under the gray Eugene sky looking virtually indistinguishable from any number of hitchhikers in a town nearly dominated by University of Oregon students. She wore a plaid wool Pendleton, jeans, and Earthshoes. She was medium height, medium build, and had thick, tawny hair so long that it brushed against the small of her back. And at twenty, her eyes still held a hint of naïveté.

Colleen's destination was Westwood, a small town in Northern California where her friend Linda lived. The occasion was Linda's birthday. This was Thursday. Colleen told Alice she'd be back on Saturday.

Interstate 5, the long ribbon on concrete that snakes all the way from the Canadian border to San Diego, would be her route.

She made good time. After just two rides, she was all the way down to Red Bluff, and it was just four o'clock. Here she would exit the freeway and head east, with another hundred miles to go.

A carload of guys offered her a ride, but she turned them down—too risky. Another car stopped, but the couple said they were only going a short distance, so she turned them down, too.

Then a blue Dodge Colt pulled over, and Colleen saw a young couple in front, the woman holding a baby in her arms. They looked about Colleen's age, and not very different from her roommates, Alice and Bob—not wealthy, but not hippies either. From the looks of their faded clothes, they probably didn't have much more than each other.

The man said they were headed toward Mineral, a giant step in the right direction, so Colleen tossed in her sleeping bag and backpack and climbed into the back seat.

Things started off badly. Colleen carried a jug of grape juice with her. She opened it to take a drink. As she raised it to her lips the driver accelerated, and purple juice spilled a stain down the front of her shirt.

But Colleen didn't take this as a bad omen. Nor did she pay particular heed to the odd wooden box sitting on the seat beside her. Nor did she notice the secret marital exchange that took place in the front seat as the little car sped out of town: The driver gave his wife a meaningful look; she frowned and shook her head, but said nothing.

When you drive east on Highway 36, the fringes of Red Bluff soon fall behind. The road climbs past pastures into hills of oak strewn with chunks of lava as it heads toward Mt. Lassen, a dormant volcano that heaved off its mountaintop in 1914, leaving the black spores of that spectacular disaster scattered across miles of terrain. At Dale's Station, the road banks right and climbs into the beginning of the pine country. To the right lies a magnificent canyon . . . but no matter how stunning the scenery, Colleen could not help but notice that the driver of the car kept glancing at her in the rearview mirror. It began to make her nervous.

A few miles up the road they stopped for gas, and Colleen took this opportunity to go to the restroom and change her blouse. Standing in the small, cool room, she had a strange feeling that she should escape, as if a voice were warning her: *Run! Get away!* She noticed the restroom's little window, and the voice insisted: *Crawl out the window! Run! You can get away!* But Colleen couldn't understand why she was having such crazy notions; she shook off the impulse to flee and went back to the car.

The wife had bought some candy bars, and as they continued toward Lassen National Forest, she shared these with their backseat passenger. There was chitchat, and soon the conversation turned to the subject of ice caves.

The driver was saying: "My brother said there were some ice caves up around here. Wouldn't that be something to see?" With another glance at Colleen in the rearview mirror, he asked, "You wouldn't care if we turned for a quick look, would ya?"

All Colleen wanted was to get to Westwood, but she told them she wouldn't mind a short detour.

There was some discussion in the front seat about where exactly the turn-off was, and soon they were off the highway, bumping down a dirt road, the afternoon sun flashing through the pine trees.

About a mile or so down the road they stopped. It was quiet, still, with the pine needles swaying only slightly in the breeze, a small stream bubbling nearby. They were completely alone, with only the mountain birds there to watch them.

The wife stepped from the car, carrying her baby over to the nearby stream. Then the driver climbed out, leaving Colleen momentarily alone in the back seat of their two-door Colt.

He came over to the passenger's side of the car, suddenly pulled the seat forward, jumped in, and put a knife to her throat.

"Put your hands above your head," he ordered.

Colleen froze, too frightened to move.

The man repeated the order, and she felt him press the blade harder against her skin. Its point pricked her throat, and she felt his hand shaking. Weakly, she lifted her arms above her head. She was shaking too.

A pair of handcuffs flashed across her vision. The man grabbed her hands, and swiftly locked them behind her back.

He had everything ready, and he moved quickly, with practiced motions. He pulled out a piece of cloth and tied it tightly over her eyes. "Are you going to do what I tell you to do?" he demanded. There was menace in his voice.

Colleen managed a feeble "Yes." Maybe if she went along with him he wouldn't hurt her, maybe she could somehow calm him down.

Next, she felt a strange leather strap encircling her head, tightened at her cheek until the strap beneath her chin made it impossible for her to open her jaw—a gag, of some sort. Then he grabbed her ankles, wrapping rope around them and tying an expert knot.

Now she was handcuffed, blindfolded, bound, and gagged. But he had more in store for her.

The peculiar wooden box that Colleen had noticed sitting on the seat beside her was this man's special creation. Its construction was deceptive, for though it was made of plywood and was only about the size of a hatbox, it was surprisingly heavy, weighing nearly twenty pounds. Dense insulation was sandwiched in between its double walls, and it was hinged with metal. He opened it now. The circular hole at the bottom split into semicircles on either side. The interior of the box was carpeted.

Forcing his hostage to lie down, he maneuvered her head into the box, fitting her neck into the sculpted hole. Then he closed it around her head with a snap.

It shut out all light. It muffled all sound. It pinched her neck, trapping her thick hair tightly against her nape, the stranglehold heightening her terror. The carpeted interior pressed against her face with a sickening closeness, and her breathing turned to gasps.

Colleen would come to know this horrific contraption as the head box.

The man covered Colleen with the sleeping bag she had so conveniently provided, and then he was done. He called to his wife, and she brought their infant daughter back to the car and got in. Then he started up the engine, turned the car back down the dirt road, and this average-looking family headed leisurely toward home, their human cargo secreted in the back seat.

The head box was suffocatingly hot, terrifyingly claustrophobic. And Colleen felt smothered beneath the sleeping bag. Her heart thudded in her ears, adrenaline shooting through her veins elevating her temperature. For a time, she felt the weight of the baby placed on top of her, but it cried and the mother took it back up front.

Now the car had turned back onto the pavement, and Colleen could feel it accelerate, rushing her toward some fearful destination. They wound downward, and she sensed they were backtracking, heading west now, back into the valley.

It seemed a long, hot eternity before Colleen could make out traffic noises, a few at first, then more, as if they were entering a town. She guessed it must be Red Bluff.

Suddenly the car stopped. Colleen could make out some conversation in the front seat; the woman was to go and get something. A car door opened, there was a slight shifting of weight, the door closed. Then they were moving again, driving short distances, turning, driving, and turning—aimlessly, as if they were circling the block. Then the car came to a stop again. The door opened, the woman climbed back in, and the car drove on. Odd.

They drove for a short time, the traffic lessening about them, and then the car came to a halt. To Colleen's relief, the sleeping bag was lifted off and the stifling head box unlatched. She could breathe again. They let her sit up, and she felt her skin start to cool, the sweat trickling down her back, her long hair sticking to her bare, damp arms. The blindfold and her other bonds stayed on, but she was immediately aware of the smell of food. It was hours since Colleen had eaten, but she felt no appetite. Her stomach was a knot.

The wife had fetched a fast-food meal, and now the couple sat in the front seat eating their greasy hamburgers and french fries. They were hungry, but they were also killing time, waiting for the sun to slip farther behind the mountains to the west.

It was dusk now, and the solitary car sat in a wide parking lot overlooking a fat expanse of the Sacramento River. Some ducks paddled downstream toward the diversion dam, birds chattered in the trees, and distant mechanical noises came from the low, gray buildings of the Diamond lumberyard across the river.

Colleen sat wondering where she might be and how she might get away, but the couple soon made her lie back down. The awful box was again snapped shut around her head, and the sleeping bag draped back over her. When they had finished their meal, they headed back into town.

It was after dark when the blue Dodge Colt pulled into the alley behind their house. The man climbed out, came around to the back seat, untied Colleen's ankles so she could walk, and took off the head box. Everything else—the blindfold, the gag, the handcuffs—stayed on. There was no danger of his hostage escaping.

Colleen was led out of the car, up some steps, and through a kitchen. Out of a narrow gap at the bottom of her blindfold, she glimpsed the base of a stove or refrigerator. Then she was guided through a narrow door and down a steep, short flight of stairs. The basement.

The woman didn't come down with them. Now Colleen was alone in the basement with her kidnapper.

"Stand up here," he ordered. Awkwardly, he maneuvered her up on top of something. As she stepped up, she saw that it was a green and white Coleman ice chest. He unlocked one wrist, then quickly draped the handcuffs across a pipe that ran along the ceiling and locked them again. Now her arms were suspended above her head. He proceeded to strip off her jeans, tossing them onto the floor. Colleen felt a wave of sick dread. This had to mean rape.

Suddenly, he snatched the handcuff from one wrist and locked the other to the pipe. She could feel that he was still shaking as he took off her shirt, one arm at a time.

Next, the handcuffs were replaced by wide, stiff leather bands, tightened around one wrist, then the other. These were then hooked to the ceiling, her arms stretched wide apart.

Colleen didn't understand what was happening.

At once, the support went out from beneath her. The world fell away, and there was a hot strain on her wrists, a wrenching of her shoulders. She wanted to cry out but couldn't—the leather strap trapped her jaw. Tears burned behind the blindfold. She thrashed the air like a frantic marionette, her naked legs striking out but meeting nothing, searching for something to raise herself up on. The hard leather cuffs cut into her wrists. She struggled, throwing her legs out again and again, churning the air.

Crack! Pain leapt across her back and wrapped around to her stomach. *Crack!* Another sharp line slapped around her torso. *Crack!* The whip struck again, and the man shouted at her to stop kicking and just relax. Colleen went limp, sobbing silently into her blindfold, and the whipping stopped.

She hung there, stunned and trembling with panic, trying to hold herself still, afraid that the whip would bite into her again. Hot, red welts rose on her back and stomach, like screams caught in her skin.

Now she could hear him moving about the basement. She tried to concentrate, to figure out what he was doing, but alarms were going off in her head. Taking deep breaths, she tried to calm herself. This couldn't be real. This had to be a nightmare.

Then, out of that slender gap at the bottom of her blind-fold, Colleen spied an open magazine. She cocked her head and tried to focus on it. It was opened to a photograph, and with a slap of recognition Colleen saw that it was a picture of a naked woman hanging in much the same position as she.

She couldn't quite grasp the significance of this, but it magnified her fear. There it was in black and white. This was no nightmare, this was reality.

In the back of her mind a small voice cried, *Why me? Oh God, why me?*

The chilling truth was that there was no one to save her. Her family in Southern California had no reason to think she'd left Eugene; her roommates in Eugene thought she was hitchhiking to Linda's and would be back in a few days. When would they realize she was missing? By then she might be dead.

The man's heavy steps came toward her and she held her breath, bracing herself for more pain. There was a dull scraping noise. The man grapped her ankles and something brushed against her toes. Just barely, on her tiptoes, she could stand, easing the weight off her wrists and shoulders.

Moaning deeply, Colleen didn't notice the man's footsteps on the stairs. He left the basement, fetched his wife, and brought her back down with him.

The small gap at the bottom of her blindfold afforded Colleen only a sliver of the scene below her. It was dimly lit, a single lightbulb casting a tentative spray of light about the room. The floor was concrete, and she could make out a low, wooden structure, something like a table.

Then she caught an unexpected glimpse of movement. Her captors. They seemed to be . . . taking off their clothes. She watched them lie down and embrace. Then, to her horror, she realized they were having sex—copulating almost at her feet, like hedonistic worshippers before some strange erotic icon.

She felt sick. This was too weird, too perverse.

When they had finished, she heard the woman's light steps on the stairs. The door shut solidly behind her. Now she was alone again with the man with the whip. She heard him approach. Perhaps he would let her down now.

Instead, the support was again yanked out from under her, and the pain shot down her arms, pulling at her underarms, across her back and ribs. She hung there for some time, sweating, her arms wide apart, naked but for the socks that he'd left on her feet.

The man watched her but she didn't kick this time, so he didn't whip her. After a satisfactory time, he pushed the ice chest back beneath her feet.

She could stand. The weight came off her wrists and shoulders with abrupt relief, but her body felt weak and rubbery.

Then the man unhooked her wrists from the beam and took her down. He steered her across a short distance, then forced her down into another of his strange contraptions. It was a box, roughly square, standing about three feet high. One end was open, and he maneuvered her into it face first, so that her bare back faced him. Grabbing her wrists, he lifted them and replaced the leather cuffs with chains. These were locked to the roof of the box.

She sensed the walls around her, as if she were being caged. Her position was cramped, with her arms awkwardly suspended above her and barely enough room to sit up. Then she felt the pressure on her jaw suddenly loosen and the leather gag come off. She begged him to please let her go, but her words were cut short as the awful head box was again maneuvered around her head. It snapped shut, closing tightly around her neck.

He had somehow affixed the heavy head box to the roof of the box. Its weight was supported, but she couldn't move her head. It was a petrifying sensation: sealed in darkness, each inhalation labored, no air, immobilized. The head box pinched her neck, choking her. She tried to yell into the box's thick lining, but her voice came back as a hoarse, strangled wail. She gasped, tried to swallow, the terror rising in her throat. The box held her in a deadly grip. She was suffocating! In a claustrophobic panic, she kicked the sides of the wooden crate that held her, pounding for her life with the only part of her body she could still move, kicking harder and harder.

Suddenly he was back. He grabbed her ankles, wrapped them with cord, then tied them to the side of the box so she wouldn't be able to kick. Then he was gone.

Colleen suffered in the basement for what seemed a very long time. Terrorized and in pain, she was still unable to accept the truth of her situation. She cried bitterly into the head box, her breathing now a tortured panting, sweat beginning to bead and run down her skin. From time to time she would yell, not knowing even if she could be heard. She thudded against the sides of the box with her feet, fighting as best she could against the cord wrapped around her ankles. She wasn't going to die without a struggle.

After some time he returned. His hands fumbled with the clasps of the head box, and in an instant it was open. She sucked the air into her lungs, but before she could speak he was shouting at her. "Why the hell are you making so much noise?"

"I can't breathe," she croaked. "Please, please let me out. Let my arms down. It hurts so much. I can't breathe."

But his only reply was to shut the head box back up again.

He left for a moment, found what he needed, and returned with something she couldn't identify. He fitted it around her chest and tightened it until the straps dug into her ribs. Now she could scarcely expand her chest; it was even harder to breathe.

And then something very odd. He put a prickly object between her bare legs. It felt similar to a hair curler, small and bristly. She didn't know it then, but it was an electrical gadget designed to shock her. To his great exasperation the device failed to work, so he shut the box up again and left her there.

As the husband and wife prepared for bed upstairs, Colleen Stan sat naked and gasping in a bizarre prison, the construction of a man with perverse obsessions and sinister habits. Her abduction had been carefully planned: the head box, the knife, the handcuffs, all the essentials of the kidnap had been placed in the car for the express purpose of capturing someone just such as she. When she had caught a ride out of Red Bluff with this wholesome-looking couple, she had fallen into his snare.

Now she was held captive in a box in their basement, her arms chained above her head, her legs tied, a spiny device between her legs, a constrictor cinched around her ribs, a blindfold around her eyes, and a sensory-deprivation box locked around her head. She could hear nothing but her thumping heart and her own tortured breathing. All night she thought she was going to suffocate. He left her boxed and bound and believing she was going to die.

Few prisoners have known a confinement more solitary, more frightening, more hopeless than the one Cameron Hooker was fashioning around his newfound slave.

2

It was a long night for Colleen. Intense discomfort and sheer fright kept her awake. A few times she was startled by her captor's hands unexpectedly against her bare back—she had thought she was alone, and suddenly he was there, touching her. Was he trying to scare her? Or was he just feeling to see if she was still warm and breathing?

For Cameron Hooker this night was surely thrilling almost beyond belief. No wonder he could hardly keep his hands off her; his fantasy had finally become reality. He had rehearsed it so many times in his mind. He'd built the head box; he'd prepared the blindfold and the knife and the handcuffs; he'd even readied the equipment in the basement. And he'd pulled it off flawlessly: She had succumbed with nary a struggle, not even a scream.

Now he had her totally within his conrol. And no one knew.

He'd waited a long time for this night. Nearly two years had gone by since he'd first discussed the subject with his wife. But the idea had been brewing inside him much, much longer.

Nothing in Cameron's upbringing would have predisposed him to unnatural or sadistic tendencies. He was raised within a traditional, warm and caring nuclear family—no child abuse, no divorce, no wife beating. He couldn't even remember any major battles between his parents.

In fact, nothing stands out about Cameron's childhood except impermanence.

Cameron was born in Alturas, California, on November 5, 1953, to a couple who had moved out from Arkansas in search of a better life. Harold and Lorena Hooker were simple folk, not highly skilled or well educated, and struggling to make ends meet. While Cameron was growing up they moved every two or three years, his father pursuing work in construction or in sawmills, his mother usually staying home to take care of him and his younger brother, Dexter. The boys' family life was secure, but they were constantly being uprooted: packing up, leaving school, and saying good-bye almost as soon as they'd made friends.

Cameron was generally quiet and kept to himself, though he was described as "a happy kid" in grammar school. He used to entertain the other children by pretending that he had a button in the middle of his back, and if anyone pressed it, he'd fall to the ground and play dead. It was a big hit during recess, especially with the giggling girls.

His sociable side seems to have taken a beating beginning about the time the Hooker family bought some property south of Red Bluff in 1969 and finally parked their mobile home at a permanent address. By now Cameron's hormones had begun their adolescent campaign: he'd hit those horrible, awkward teens.

Used to being the tallest kid in the class, he now shot up even more, ungainly and skinny. With his heavy, horn-rimmed glasses, toothy smile, and uncoordinated limbs, Cameron was spurned by the "in" crowd and relegated to what students at Red Bluff High School called the "quad squad"—those outcasts who tended to hang out in a particular area of the grounds.

He had no close friends. He joined no organizations or teams. He excelled at shop classes, learning about tools and machines and construction, but wasn't much of an athlete and barely passed his academic classes. He had lots of time alone, lots of time to think.

No one would have guessed that this bland, gawky kid had anything exceptional going on in his head. But Cameron Hooker apparently had fantasies. Wild ones. Fantasies in which he had absolute power over the frightened objects of his desire. It seems that, in his imagination, this awkward, spindly adolescent whom no one seemed to notice was powerful, commanding, virile—conjuring up visions of nude, bound women. Helpless. At his mercy. And when he discovered pornography, the magazines that he stashed away in secret places evidently fueled these fantasies with images of leather and handcuffs and whips.

When he graduated from high school in 1972, Cameron Hooker went to work at the local lumbermill, Diamond Lands Corporation. It was a manly occupation, working around large, powerful, deafening machinery, ear-splitting saws, and heavy, black chains. He grew sideburns and let his hair get shaggy.

To the handful of women at the mill, Cameron was still less than attractive—quiet, easily ignored, and from the outside, so unremarkable as to be almost invisible. But Cameron's secret daydreams of tying up and dominating women seem to have continued unabated. His mindless work apparently left him free to let his imagination run, to play back what he'd read in magazines, to concoct plans. He must have longed to realize them, to act out his fantasies; he just needed someone who would comply. . . .

A plain, shy fifteen-year-old was the answer.

In 1973, a mutual friend introduced Cameron to Janice, a naïve and insecure girl with frizzy brown hair, wire-rim glasses, and a personality less mature than her figure. Being so much younger than Cameron, she was also nonthreatening and pliant.

Still a wide-eyed ninth grader, Janice must have found the attentions of this strapping nineteen-year-old flattering beyond all expectation. Unlike the other boys she'd met, he was nice to her! She'd never been treated so well. The other boys walked all over her, but Cameron was gentlemanly, polite, and clearly a prize: well over six feet tall, congenial, with a big, warm smile. He even had a car.

They started dating—going out for drives, for burgers and fries, and to see horror movies like *The Exorcist*.

Perhaps they seemed an unlikely pair, but Cameron and Janice were similar in what they weren't: Neither was attractive, well-off, or popular. Neither had much apparent interest in sports, literature, or culture. And neither was originally from Red Bluff.

Janice's family had moved up from the San Jose area a few years earlier. They'd moved to a tiny house not very far from the Hookers', with an orchard and not much more. Like Cameron, Janice lived in a rural setting, and grew up in a family that did not put much emphasis on education and never had much money.

She was the youngest of four children, the baby of the family. She doesn't remember her parents as warm or demonstrative. Her father, a blue-collar worker who worked long hours, wasn't around much. Neither was her mother, whom she describes as a strict and reproachful woman. Janice was left to be raised, mostly, by her older sister, Lisa.

Lisa looked out for her and taught her how to sew, but Janice says she also harbored feelings of jealousy and resentment toward her older sister. She felt Lisa was always the favorite, soaking up the attention for which Jan constantly thirsted.

Jan had epilepsy as a child and somehow connected her illness with her parents' indifference. She thought her father believed that people who had epilepsy were possessed by demons, and so he kept his distance. Whatever the cause, Jan recalls feeling rejected and disapproved of at an early age and says she was often told she was stupid but rarely told she was loved.

Janice's submissive side emerged early on. Unattractive and insecure, her first infatuations with boys were marked by a fear of rejection: "No matter how good or rotten a guy was to me, I just kind of latched on to him."

So a few months into her relationship with Cameron, when he proposed something peculiar, her reservations were quickly dispelled. In Janice's own estimation, she was the "kind of person who just gave in so somebody would love me."

He wanted to hang her up, suspend her by the wrists from a tree without her clothes on. He told her his other girlfriends had let him do this, that lots of people did it. Not wanting to lose him, Janice went along.

He took her into the nearby mountains, strapped her into his handmade leather cuffs, and hung her up.

Jan was scared. It hurt: the leather cuffs cutting into her wrists, the pain shooting down her arms and back. But Cameron was so affectionate when he took her down—holding her, hugging her, and so obviously happy—that it was easier for her to agree the next time.

These excursions into the woods became regular events. Two or three times a month, he'd take Janice out to Tehama County's vast woodlands to experiment. And though Janice was still little more than a child, her first sexual experiences involved a practice not many people know much about: bondage.

Cameron tied her up, staked her out on the ground, or hung her from trees. It frightened her but she endured it, waiting for it to be over because Cameron was always so sweet and tender to her afterward. It seemed worth the temporary pain. Soon he brought out the whips and beat her—not hard enough to leave permanent marks, he was careful of that, only welts. And when she'd beg to be let down, he'd let her down.

Sadism wasn't a familiar word to Janice, nor was *masochism*. She didn't think Cameron would *really* hurt her, and he seemed to know what he was doing, so when he wanted to tie her up and dunk her in the creek, she agreed.

It was a singularly harrowing experience, a brush with death by drowning that Janice would never forget. Still, she was too afraid to tell her aloof and aging parents, too embarrassed and ashamed to tell anyone else what was going on. The sex, the whippings, the photographs he took of her—she knew they weren't right. Who knew what her parents would do if they found out? Probably punish her. Or worse, make her stop seeing the boyfriend who, except for this idiosyncratic side, was the nicest guy she'd ever met.

Jan's emotions were jumbled. While disturbing, Cameron's appetite for bondage seemed less important because he was always so loving toward her afterward. She couldn't risk losing this relationship; it offered security, and no matter what the problems (which she didn't fully understand),

Cameron gave her the attention she was getting nowhere else.

And in some ways Cameron was good for her. He took her places she'd never been, and even taught her to water-ski and snow ski. Still just a young and idealistic girl, she romanticized the relationship, trying to ignore his bad points by concentrating on the good—his politeness, his easy-going manner, his sense of humor.

During a year and a half of dating, Janice decided she was in love.

But did Cameron love her? She thought she needed some kind of commitment from him. When she worked up the courage, Jan lied that she was pregnant and exacted a promise of marriage.

Janice's sister had had to wait until age eighteen to marry; their parents weren't thrilled about Jan getting married at such a young age, but they thought the world of Cameron, so at sixteen, Janice was given permission to wed. Instead of a big ceremony, she was given five hundred dollars for a wedding present. (In the back of her mind, Jan said later, she wondered why the rules should be different for her and her sister, and she suspected that maybe her parents just wanted to get rid of her.)

Cameron and Janice were wed on January 18, 1975, in Reno, Nevada. The young bride and groom said their vows, seemingly full of love and hope for the future—yet it was hardly a promising union, founded, as it was, on deceit.

And in fact, the two didn't have much of a future to look forward to. Janice, not quite seventeen, dropped out of high school. And though Cameron had noted for his senior class yearbook that he desired a career in construction, that would remain but a hobby. He continued to work as a laborer at the local mill.

They didn't have much money, but then Cameron and Jan didn't have high expectations. They made do, moving into a cheap row of duplexes—boxy structures with little character and a shared cement alley for a front yard.

Outwardly, Cameron and Janice Hooker were just another hopeful young couple starting a new life together. No one knew what went on behind closed doors: The sadistic experiments continued, becoming even more severe. Sometimes, Cameron choked Jan until she passed out. Not long into their marriage, when Janice and Cameron had a fight, he got so mad he put a knife to her throat and asked her if she wanted to die. Another time, Cameron showed her a scene in one of his underground newspapers, a horrific crucifixion, and told her that if he ever killed her, that's how he would do it. It was becoming harder for Janice to ignore the possibility that her husband might actually kill her.

The first couple of years of marriage, she tried to fulfill her husband's strange fantasies by being ever more submissive to his demands. But when Cameron produced an Army surplus gas mask, its eyes and air-holes taped over, she balked. The gas mask terrified her, and Cameron had to gag her to keep her from screaming when he fitted it over her head.

Cameron's experiments seemed to be getting more violent, more bizarre. Though she was afraid to actually stand up to him and refuse, Jan was no longer so keen on participating. It was too painful.

Perhaps Janice's fearfulness made her a less exciting partner, or maybe Cameron was simply growing bored with her. More likely, one person was no longer enough to satisfy his cravings. In any case, Cameron began discussing a fantasy that he'd had for a long time: He wanted to bring a third person into the home, another woman who would submit to his sado-masochistic experiments, "a girl who couldn't say no."

He told her that this third person would take part in his more demanding practices. It would be easier on Janice, he said, if she would just go along.

And, finally, she had.

The underground papers Cameron read always had lots of listings in the back; maybe they could run an ad. Of course, most of the ads were from people in the San Francisco Bay Area. And it might be expensive—running an ad, bringing someone up. The woman might want to be paid. That was a problem. And it would only be temporary.

While Cameron fussed about the logistics of finding and keeping another woman, Janice worried that this third person would be a threat to their marriage. Despite his darker habits, Jan still felt that she loved Cameron; she'd grown so dependent on him, she could hardly imagine being without him. So, while she was relieved by the idea of Cameron focusing the more painful acts—especially the hangings—on someone else, she was insistent that there should be no sexual intercourse between her husband and this other woman. They were man and wife, and as she saw it, true intimacy should be reserved solely to them.

It's not clear exactly when or how, but ultimately Cameron and Janice reached an understanding. It was a tradeoff. He could kidnap someone if she could have someone as well. She wanted a baby.

By now they'd found a more suitable address: 1140 Oak Street. It was a small two-bedroom house with yards front and back, hardwood floors, a nice dining room, and a basement.

The basement was tiny, but it would do. With boards from the Diamond lumberyard, Cameron constructed a wide table—a platform, really—that he dubbed the rack. He affixed eye-hooks at each corner so the leather cuffs he'd made could be easily attached when he wanted to stake out Janice. He put additional hooks in a beam in the ceiling, for hanging. And then he built the head box.

It was an ingenious contraption, built strong and heavy—surprisingly heavy, with those big metal hinges and its dual walls. He had Janice come down to test it, and sure enough, the neck hole was the right size and it closed as it should.

But not everything went according to plan. Though Cameron's preparations were ample and his plans well thought out, finding the right person wasn't so easy. Janice got pregnant and had her baby, a girl, in the fall of 1976, but Cameron still hadn't managed to accomplish his end of the deal. He had all the equipment ready in the car, had even stalked a few women, snapping photos with his telephoto lens, but none of them had panned out. Though he'd come within a fraction of realizing his single, driving ambition, something always went wrong.

But on May 19, 1977, Cameron Hooker's luck changed. At the end of his shift at Diamond, he came home from work as usual at about four o'clock. He picked up his wife and baby, and they went for a drive. They drove around for half an hour or so, and then he saw her.

Standing at the side of Antelope Boulevard, Colleen Stan wouldn't have struck most people as distinctive. She was an average size and wore the casual attire of young people everywhere. Looking closely, one might notice her soft features and crystalline blue eyes, but from the perspective of a speeding car, she was just a young female hitchhiker.

He stopped and offered her a ride. Colleen surveyed the man, his wife, and their infant daughter, and decided they seemed innocuous enough.

The next morning Cameron Hooker came downstairs and took Colleen out of the box. He walked his exhausted captive across the basement and laid her down on the rack. He now locked the chains that were still around her wrists to the hooks at the rack's top corners and tied her ankles to the ones at the bottom. Then he left her there, with the head box still on, for the rest of the day.

That evening, Janice and Cameron finally brought down Colleen's first meal. Cameron let her up from the rack and removed the head box, but the blindfold stayed on. Her dinner was a bowl of potatoes au gratin and a glass of water. Sitting on the edge of the rack, she was allowed to feed herself, the chains dangling from her wrists as she blindly scooped up the food.

After she'd finished her meal, Colleen was permitted to use a bedpan, which Cameron later emptied upstairs. Then the chains on her wrists were replaced with the leather cuffs, and Cameron hung her for a while. Later, he put the head box back on, chained her down on the rack, and left her to the darkness. . . .

Colleen remembers her second meal very well. It was a hot day, the heat exacerbated by the stuffy head box, and she had been lying on the rack, sweating. It had been another twenty-four hours since her last meal, and her captor apparently expected her to be hungry. He brought her down a glass of water and a plate with two large egg salad sandwiches and let her up so she could eat.

But heat and anxiety had taken her appetite away. She ate half of a sandwich, drank all the water, and told him she was full.

"You should be grateful I brought this to you," he scolded. He told her she was wasting good food and demanded that she finish it.

Colleen replied that she *was* grateful, but she was just full.

Now he was furious. He slapped the leather cuffs on her wrists, hung her from the beam, then set about teaching her a lesson: He whipped her until she passed out. When she came to, she was standing on the ice chest, still hanging from the ceiling. She felt faint, and her knees gave out from under her, but rather than take her down, Cameron pulled the ice chest out from under her again and beat her some more.

Finally Cameron took her down. He set her back on the rack, placed the egg salad sandwiches in front of her and said, *"Now* do you want to finish this?"

The last thing Colleen wanted to do was eat. Her back was on fire and she felt weak, but she was afraid of what Cameron might do if she refused, so she forced down the rest of the sandwiches. Then he snapped the head box back on, locked her again on the rack, and left.

Thus Colleen was initiated into what would become routine: one meal a day, extreme isolation, torturous restraints, and unexpected brutality. Time was no longer defined by the hands of a clock, but by the hands that turned the keys and unclasped the locks of her confinement. She teetered between hope and dread, yearning for those hands to release her bonds, yet fearing the pain those same hands could bring. She existed in a black, grim limbo. Helpless.

Even so, Cameron Hooker realized that keeping her chained to the rack was not the safest arrangement. True, she was secured in a cement basement with its two high windows covered and its single entrance locked, but it was just conceivable that she could alert neighbors or visitors by somehow making lots of noise. And if anyone entered, she was in plain view. No, the rack would not suffice for the long term.

3

While Colleen sweated on the rack in Hooker's basement, her roommate up in Oregon was growing concerned. Colleen had told Alice Walsh that she would be back in Eugene on Saturday, May 21. When Colleen failed to appear, Alice guessed that she might have continued down the length of California to visit her mother in Riverside. On Monday, May 23, Alice called Colleen's mother to see if Colleen was there.

Their conversation left them both worried.

Though Alice remembered that Colleen had intended to visit Linda Smith in Westwood, she had no way to get in touch with her—Linda didn't have a phone. On Tuesday, Alice called the Westwood police. They checked with Linda, who told them she hadn't seen Colleen for some time, and they reported this back to Alice.

By Wednesday Alice knew it was time to contact the Eugene Police Department. A missing person report was filled out, a description given:

Stan, Colleen Jean. DOB: 12-31-56. White female. 5'6", 135 lbs. Long, light brown hair; blue eyes; freckles. Last seen wearing gray T-shirt, blue jeans, plaid jacket, brown shoes; has sleeping bag, sweater, and purse.

Like so many missing person bulletins, this one elicited no response. It was filed and forgotten.

Colleen had simply vanished.

There was no evidence to assume that Colleen had been kidnapped and no evidence linked her disappearance to any particular locale between Eugene and Westwood. Cameron Hooker had left no clue that could be traced back to him.

On the surface, life at 1140 Oak Street went on as usual. Janice focused her attention on the baby, trying her best to ignore what was going on literally beneath her feet. Only rarely did she venture down into the basement. She felt an unreasonable fear of Colleen, and the first time she went down to check on their captive, whom she could hear moaning and making noise, she took the shotgun with her, just to be on the safe side.

Meanwhile, Cameron carried on with his working-day routine at the lumberyard. And no one paid much heed when he loaded some heavy particle board into his pickup. A lot of the employees took home a little lumber.

While all else seemed to proceed as usual, Colleen was on the brink of a change—not a major change, but her world had shrunk to such mean conditions that any alteration loomed large.

She endured long stretches of total immobility. Naked. Her head enclosed in the head box. Gagged, once again, and always blindfolded. A maddening stillness enveloped her, a blanket of isolation that her senses examined for the slightest fraying or variation. Finding none, her mind wandered.

How could she escape? She examined the possibilities. Her only chance would be when she was let up to eat, but then what? She couldn't overpower the man, he was much larger and stronger. Perhaps her best chance was in persuading him to let her go. He must be sick. If she could somehow understand him and help him, maybe he would set her free . . .

The hours stretched on. Tired of puzzling over a seemingly impossible escape, Colleen dozed and daydreamed, her thoughts drifting through an imaginary future of splendid things she would do when set free, then turning to recollections of friends, of family, of times that were rapidly slipping into the distant and irretrievable past.

Colleen's childhood virtually began with her parents' divorce. She was just three, the eldest of a trio of daughters, when Jack and Evelyn Martin split up. But the usual disruption that follows divorce was muted; neither of Colleen's parents moved away after the break-up. Though Colleen was mostly raised by her mother, a sociable, chatty woman, she managed to stay close to her father, a quiet man who was an only marginally successful contractor.

(Both her parents eventually remarried, and Colleen and her two sisters, Janice and Bonnie Sue, ended up with two half-sisters and a half-brother.)

At the very least, Colleen grew up with a sense of place: Riverside, the site of California's first navel orange tree, was always home.

In most respects Colleen's seems to have been a pleasant and unremarkable upbringing in sunny, smoggy Southern California. She played with her younger sisters, made average progress in school, and at some point developed a penchant for poetry. It was typical of Colleen to write and design cards, or make gifts for people as an expression of her love. She had a creative, warm, dreamy side.

While some high school students were tending their grade point averages with an eye toward higher education, Colleen seemingly lost interest in academics. It wasn't in the cards for her to go on to college, and unfortunately she would acquire her education in that proverbial school of hard knocks.

At sixteen she dropped out of high school and married twenty-two-year-old Tom Stan.

Not much was known about Stan, a young man from out of town whom Colleen had met a few months earlier. Colleen's father gave her permission to marry, and she and Tom were wed in Carson City, Nevada, on December 12, 1973. Colleen was just a few days shy of seventeen.

She moved with her new husband to his home state of Ohio, but they evidently started having problems as soon as they set up house. The marriage dissolved, and within a year Colleen had returned, brokenhearted and alone, to Riverside.

Back on her home turf, Colleen had the good sense to go back and pass the high school equivalency exam, but she apparently entered a restless period; nothing seems to have held her attention for long. She evidently held a smattering of jobs, moved around Riverside a bit, and had boyfriends off and on. Then she made friends with a couple from Oregon—Alice Walsh and her boyfriend, Bob.

Colleen seems to have embraced Alice, Bob, and their two-year-old son, Tomack, almost as an adopted family, as if she were searching for a place to belong. Apparently discontent with Riverside and inspired by her new friends, she moved with them up to Eugene.

They found a place together, but jobs were harder to come by, and even with the help of welfare it was difficult to make ends meet. During her few months in Oregon, Colleen earned what little cash she could by collecting and selling moss.

So, at twenty, Colleen Stan was living on the fringe, a long way from the romantic married life she must have envisioned at seventeen. Apparently having little direction or focus, she'd been blown across borders by the winds of fate. But if she wasn't an especially dynamic or ambitious person, Colleen Stan was certainly a caring friend, loving daughter, and devoted sister—the kind of child who didn't forget to send cards, who wrote and called home often, and who, one spring day, tried to hitchhike to Westwood to wish a dear friend a happy birthday. . . .

Whatever hopes and regrets occupied her thoughts as she lay spread-eagled on the rack in Cameron Hooker's basement, Colleen's mind returned, always, to prayer. Hers hadn't been a strongly religious upbringing, and this was a very long way from the comfortable pews of her childhood church, but now prayers poured through her.

She prayed for freedom. She prayed for the wisdom to understand her captor. Whoever he was. She prayed that she would be rescued, that she could escape. She prayed for survival.

She prayed in utter blackness, mortality hovering nearby, with only God to hear. Perhaps only those who have prayed in the face of death—the sick, the dying, the deeply bereaved —can understand the fervor of the prayers emitting from that hot, claustrophobic head box.

Her long periods of sensory deprivation were broken only in the evenings, usually at about eight o'clock, when the Hookers had finished dinner. Cameron and sometimes Janice would come down with leftovers. For a brief period, Colleen would be freed from the head box and let up from the rack. She must have felt tremendous relief just to be able to change her position, to breathe some relatively fresh air (though the basement was actually rather musty), and to focus her eyes on the tiny segment of the world she could see out of the gap between the bridge of her nose and the bottom of her blindfold. As much as nourishment, that single meal was refreshment to a mouth that tasted only a gag during the day.

Her drink was always water. And she used the bedpan with the blindfold in place, without privacy. Afterwards, Cameron would frequently hang her up and whip her. This became her bleak routine.

But one particular afternoon Colleen broke this pattern. She felt her bowels churn, and she knew she wouldn't be able to wait until the bedpan was brought down that night. To avoid the humiliation of soiling herself, she tried to attract the attention of the man or the woman, whoever was upstairs, by making as much noise as she could. She hollered past her gag, into the head box's carpeted interior, kicked, and rattled her chains.

Too late, she realized her mistake. The man rushed downstairs, unlocked her chains and wrapped the hated leather cuffs around her wrists. She cringed, knowing she was going to be hung again. Cameron cursed her for making so much noise—no excuses. He hooked the leather cuffs to the beam, kicked the ice chest out from beneath her feet, and then whipped her to unconsciousness.

She learned not to make noise, but to lie quietly on the rack until her captors decided to let her up. It was better to soil herself than get whipped.

But soon Colleen's long stretches of solitude were shattered by the sounds of Cameron Hooker industriously pursuing his next project. He came downstairs in the evenings and began moving things about, sawing and hammering. He had brought down the particle board he'd gotten at Diamond, and now he was building something.

It was a big project. Working for a while every day, it took Cameron some time to complete. And though he was working within inches of Colleen, who lay uncomfortably on the rack beside him, he spoke scarcely at all.

Even at meals her captor gave her little opportunity to learn who he was or why he was keeping her here. He reacted to her attempts at conversation with anger. And when she repeatedly asked him when he would let her go, his reply was always the same: "Pretty soon."

It took Cameron Hooker about ten days to complete his construction. It was heavy and solid and built to last. It stood about three feet tall and six and a half feet long and had a lid that opened at the top. It took up about as much space as a freezer, but was double-walled, so the interior was smaller, more confined, like a coffin.

Colleen was put into the box without comment. One small consolation was that Hooker removed the head box and the gag, but she was still blindfolded, still naked, as she'd been since her abduction. He made her step over the side to get in, then lie down. He had already put her sleeping bag on the floor of the box, so while it was hard, it was slightly padded.

Now Hooker brought out the long chain. He put it around her neck and locked the wrist chains to it before pulling it down to her ankles and securing them. As one final insult, he put wax earplugs in her ears. Then he shut the box and locked her inside. Even with the earplugs, she could hear the latches close and the padlock click shut.

Chained and blindfolded inside a locked box—elaborate as a Houdini trick. But surrounding her was not an expectant audience, just the indifferent cement of the basement walls. And there wasn't the slightest hope that Colleen could escape from within that double-walled box. She was entombed. And no matter how desperately she might pray, this was where Colleen Stan was going to stay.

4

Father's Day fell exactly three weeks after the day that Alice Walsh had contacted the Eugene police about Colleen's disappearance. In Riverside, Colleen's father, Jack Martin, worried when no word came from his eldest daughter. Colleen almost always remembered birthdays and other occasions with a card or a call.

As Colleen's absence stretched to more than a month, hopes of her turning up were growing dim. Jack Martin called Colleen's mother, and though they'd been divorced over eighteen years, suggested they drive the more than one thousand miles to Eugene to collect their missing daughter's things. They made the drive over a weekend, and on Saturday, June 25, they contacted the Eugene police. The police could tell them nothing new, so they had no choice but to turn around and solemnly head back to Southern California with Colleen's boxed belongings. These would be stored in some dark and quiet place, in mute and unrecognized irony.

As they drove north toward Oregon and then south back to Riverside, Colleen's parents could never have imagined that as they sped past Red Bluff on Interstate 5, they passed within about a mile of where their daughter was being held. Nor could they have imagined, in their worst fears, the conditions under which Colleen was being kept. But if they feared their daughter was dead, they weren't far wrong.

Colleen lay motionless, in the dark. It had been more than five weeks now since she had bathed, brushed her teeth, or washed her hair. She'd stopped menstruating.

She existed on the barest necessities: food and water.

Colleen learned to mark the flow of time by the simplest measures. If she was cool, it was morning. (Hearing one particularly loud car drive by every day affirmed this.) The box gradually warmed, the day's heat penetrating into the basement while her body warmed the box from inside. By afternoon, the heat at its zenith, her sweat soaked into the sleeping bag. The temperature slowly eased until about eight P.M., when Hooker would come downstairs and let her out, allowing the hot air within the box to escape. When she was put back in, it would have cooled, and the temperature would continue to drop until morning. Then the cycle began again.

Cameron had installed a "blower," a makeshift device that was really nothing more than an old hair dryer on a no-heat setting, to circulate air through two small airholes drilled in the side of the box. This may have kept the inside of the box from becoming even more stifling, but it did nothing to alter the temperature, and Colleen, meanwhile, had to listen to the motor's constant whine.

Cameron Hooker was figuring this all out as he went along. When it became obvious that Colleen's weight was plunging, he decided to keep track of it. He'd bring down the scale, put it on the floor of the box and have her stand on it, noting the figures on a piece of paper. One day, she caught sight of the paper: 113 pounds.

The man's wife generally stayed away. Once in a while, thinking only she and Cameron were in the basement, Colleen would be startled during her meal to hear Jan's voice come from the stairs. And one hot afternoon Janice had surprised Colleen with a glass of lemonade, letting Colleen sit up in the box to drink it. But the woman remained more or less invisible, a specter hovering in the background, a disembodied voice that floated in at unexpected moments.

Colleen was sometimes locked down on the rack, but more often hung, usually by both arms and always naked and blindfolded. She was frequently whipped. On occasion she knew her captor was taking photographs of her: She heard the click of the camera, saw the flash of the lights.

No matter what else the man did to her, the pain of simply hanging was awful. The leather cuffs bit deeply into her wrists, cutting her skin, hurting those sensitive nerves that run into the body's most important tools, the hands. But that was only one focal point; the pain pulled down her arms into her back, across her ribs, knotting under her arms. Sometimes she momentarily escaped the pain by blacking out, but when she came to, it was as if it had been saved up, and it hit with excruciating force.

Cameron Hooker was well aware that hanging someone by the hands is not only painful but dangerous. The cuffs act as a tourniquet, cutting off the circulation. If one is hung by the wrists more than twenty or thirty minutes, the tissue starts to die and gangrene sets in, requiring amputation or eventually causing death. So Hooker was careful not to hang his victim for too long; a corpse would be terribly inconvenient.

Three months elapsed, and Cameron Hooker finally had to admit that he needed to give his captive a bath. She was filthy. She smelled bad. She looked awful.

So one August evening, after the baby had been put to bed, Cameron got Colleen out of the box and brought her upstairs. He walked her through the kitchen, through the dining room, and around to the bathroom, where he filled the tub.

He tied her hands behind her back. He taped over the blindfold with duct tape, taped her mouth. And he tied her legs to a broomstick. Then he put her face down in the water.

He held her down, even though her struggles were ineffectual. She couldn't raise herself up because the broomstick, lodged across the tub's rim, kept her from pulling her knees up under her. He held her head under until she couldn't hold her breath anymore. When the bubbles ceased and she started sucking in water, Hooker pulled her up by the hair, then dunked her again.

As he dunked her over and over, he took the opportunity to focus his camera, which he'd already loaded with film and had on hand, and take some pictures. Submerged and helpless, Colleen must have seemed an interesting subject; he took several shots, dunking her at least two dozen times before finally stopping.

When she was finally allowed to sit up and catch her breath, she sucked in air with painful gasps. Her lungs ached strangely.

Now Cameron enlisted Janice's aid for the nasty business of doing something about Colleen's hair. It was tangled, matted and filthy, and the tape left a sticky residue in it. Regular hair conditioner had only a negligible effect, so Janice tried putting vegetable oil on it. She still couldn't comb the knots out, so she gave up and got the scissors, snipping out one tangle and then another, and finally cutting off about five inches.

After her bath, Colleen's blindfold was tightened. Then she was led back downstairs and put in the box, her lungs still aching.

If the ordeal had left her cleaner, it had also underscored the terrifying control her captor had over her. He was all-powerful. She existed completely at his whim. And now he had given her life: He hadn't killed her.

5

So complete was Colleen's isolation from the world above her that she didn't even notice when the wife left late that summer.

Janice didn't know what else to do. The sick drama unfolding in the basement left her terrified at the thought of being found out, and guilt dogged her steps as she went about her daily chores. She tried not to think about it, but she felt so sorry for Colleen that she could scarcely put together a plate of sandwiches for her without feeling waves of shame and remorse. Yet her feelings were confused. Along with the despair came pangs of jealousy and resentment.

Despite her misgivings, Janice hadn't the courage to completely sever her ties with Cameron. (Hadn't he told her that if she ever left him, he would track her down and come after her?) So, to put some distance between herself and the situation at home, she retreated to the home of the older sister on whom she'd been so dependent as a child.

Jan found a job with Exatron, an electronics firm in the Silicon Valley. Though she commuted home to Red Bluff on the weekends, she stayed with her sister during the week and had ample opportunity to let slip some hint of what was going on at 1140 Oak Street. She didn't. She'd learned long ago to deal with frightening and unsavory truths by simply blocking them out. And she was good at keeping secrets.

So was Cameron. Despite all the time and energy he put into his private obsessions, he kept them hidden, compartmentalized from the rest of his life by doors and locks and silence. He made whips and hid them. He stocked up on hard-core pornography and squirreled it away.

None of the hundreds of slides and photographs he took of Janice and Colleen, for example, were sent out to be developed; he did all the work at home, in his own makeshift darkroom in the basement. He'd even built his own enlarger —nothing fancy, but functional. Sometimes he'd develop film while Colleen was sitting on the rack, eating with her plate in her lap; she could hear him shut off the lights and see the red glow out of the edge of her blindfold. Yet for all any outsiders knew, Cameron Hooker was just a harmless shutterbug, snapping photos at family gatherings.

Meanwhile, within the secret box in his basement, Colleen Stan was all too intimate with Hooker's private interests. As the days crawled by, the list of sadistic fantasies he acted out on her lengthened. Once, while he had her hanging by the wrists, he held a heat lamp next to her skin, watching her writhe in pain as it burned. Another time, he touched her with live electrical wires. He hung her upside-down and bound her in strange ways. He made her orally copulate him. He strangled her. She was little more than his guinea pig, and he subjected her to just about anything he could imagine and devise, short of technically breaking his promise of fidelity.

Hooker remained a mystery to Colleen. She could make no sense of how he treated her; sometimes she was tortured as punishment, sometimes it was apparently just entertainment. And sometimes he was unexpectedly kind to her, like one morning when he brought down some pancakes for her; she ate twice that day. And once or twice he brought down some toast. Yet there seemed to be no connection between her behavior and these benevolent gestures.

She examined his words for some key to his psyche, but he spoke little and she stayed bewildered. Whenever she asked when he would let her go, he still replied: "Pretty soon." It was maddening. Months had passed already.

She despaired . . . and finally stopped asking.

Eventually, Colleen managed a small victory: She learned her captor's name. She thought she'd heard the woman calling him Cameron, and now she had it absolutely confirmed.

One evening when she was out of the box, spying out the tiny slice of light at the bottom of her blindfold, he'd turned his back to her at just such an angle that she could see "Cameron" engraved on the back of his belt. So, he had a name. And when she heard him call his wife Jan, so did she.

Learning the names of her captors was the first news she'd had in months. Locked in that double-walled wooden box, she lay suspended in an informational vacuum. It shut out all light and deadened all sound so that Colleen's world was perpetually dark and silent—as if she'd been struck blind and deaf.

Just as she hadn't known that Janice had left, Colleen didn't know that after a few lonely months of commuting home on weekends, of missing the husband she believed she loved, and of getting over the shock of having a captive in the basement, Janice had had enough of that long, hot drive up Interstate 5, and had moved back home.

By now the seasons were changing, and this was news Colleen could discern even from within the box. The amber hills around Red Bluff, which the summer had parched to within a spark of spontaneous combustion, were dampened by the first rains of autumn. And as the temperatures fell outside, Colleen, still naked and chained within the box, felt the change. When the mornings turned cold she finally had to ask for something to wear, and Cameron gave her the Pendleton shirt that she'd had with her when she was kidnapped.

The weather wasn't all that was changing. In November, six months into her captivity, Colleen was about to be put to work.

Cameron Hooker's first experiment with making his captive useful required some elaborate rigging on his part. The head box Colleen had been kidnapped with was actually one of two head boxes Hooker had built. The other was larger and so heavy that it would be difficult for Colleen to wear while standing.

But now Hooker wanted her to wear this second, heavier contraption, and he wanted her to wear it while she was doing a job for him. So, with a system of ropes and pulleys rigged to the ceiling, Hooker managed to counterweight the box with a gallon jug of water so that it was usable. With the jug swinging in the air, he placed the cumbersome box on Colleen's head. Her instructions were to sand a redwood burl that Hooker had brought downstairs. Sightless, the weight of the bulky box only partially offset by the jug of water, she did the work clumsily, by touch. After such a long period of inactivity the work was physically exhausting, but over several days she managed to complete the job.

Now Hooker busied himself with a new project, more construction within a basement already crowded with his strange assemblages. He designed it to fit beneath the staircase, and so it was triangular in shape and small. It had a door, a ceiling, and even a light—similar to an oddly shaped closet. He gave it a concrete floor to add stability and carpeted the walls for sound-proofing. He dubbed this new little room "the workshop."

Hooker got Colleen out of the box and put her inside it, unshackled but still blindfolded. He left a large sack of walnuts at her feet, and once the door was bolted shut, instructed her to remove the blindfold and shell the nuts.

For the first time since the kidnap—six full months—the blindfold came off and Colleen could see. Something so simple. Yet after half a year of near-blindness, simply looking about with unobscured vision was surely close to phenomenal. Everything was so *bright*.

The workshop wasn't much bigger than the box, but at least it was vertical. And not only could she see, she had some freedom of movement. There was even a chair!

She examined this place—what had he called it?—and realized she was completely enclosed within a tiny area beneath the stairs, locked in with the walnuts and a bare lightbulb. She had heard him slide a board across the door, but now tested it, pushing as hard as she could. It didn't budge.

With nothing else to do she settled down to work—cracking the nuts, neatly separating the meats from the shells, eating some of them—working through the night as she'd been told.

In the morning before going to work, Hooker came down to get her out. He told her to put the blindfold back on before he opened the door (looking at his face was still forbidden).

Then he chained her again and put her back in the box.

With an alternate place for keeping his captive. Hooker established a new routine. Colleen still spent all day locked in the box, but at night, after she'd been let out to sit on the rack and eat her meal, and sometimes hung from the beam or staked out on the rack, she was usually locked inside the workshop. She often worked all night on some project that either Cameron or Janice gave her to do, frequently macrame or crochet.

Though this new arrangement was more trouble and a bit riskier, it was already paying off. The Hookers loaded up the fruits of Colleen's labor and sold them at a big flea market down in San Jose. It wasn't a lot of money, but it helped.

And so the secret circumstances in the basement of 1140 Oak Street underwent a significant shift. It's unclear whether the Hookers fully appreciated the ramifications of putting Colleen to work for them. More than just giving her something to do with her hands, it changed Colleen's status within the household. Now she was more than a kidnap victim, a captive, an object of abuse. Now, quite clearly, Colleen Stan had become their slave.

PART TWO

The Chorus of Disbelief

November 19–December 6, 1984

When you are held captive, people somehow expect you to spit in your captor's face and get killed.

Patty Hearst

6

It's not a through street, the approach to Diamond Lands Corporation south of Red Bluff. The road is heavily trafficked by big trucks carrying lumber in and out and by the many pickups of Diamond's employees. It winds past huge piles of sawdust, mountainous stacks of logs, signs exhorting safety, and finally ends at dusty parking lots. Workers climb out of their vehicles, put on their hard hats, and disappear into cavernous buildings, where the roar of heavy equipment makes protective earmuffs mandatory and talking absurd.

Peeling the bark off huge logs, carving them into boards and then drying them in massive kilns demands strong equipment and lots of power. Carbide-tipped saws are changed for sharpening every four hours, and Diamond runs up more than two million dollars a year in electricity bills. Doing roughly forty-five million dollars in business every year, turning out half a million feet of lumber a day, Diamond Lands Corporation is just about Red Bluff's largest employer. Everyone calls it, simply, Diamond.

Cameron Hooker worked in this complex of buildings, including the adjacent pulp plant that Diamond sold off in 1982, a total of twelve years. For the last few years, Hooker's job was to make sure six massive conveyors—deep trenches which carried useless wood to be chopped up for fiber in the "chipper"—were running freely. Most of the time it wasn't a demanding job; he just had to keep moving, checking one conveyor and then another. But if one got jammed, perhaps by a large board sticking up, it was critical that he immediately climb down and wrench the obstruction free. Overall, it was a low-skill job, but Hooker showed no inclination to take on more responsibility. He had the reputation of being a clock watcher, and as soon as his shift was over, he was out the door.

The single road exiting the compound happens to wind past the building that houses the *Red Bluff Daily News*. In all the years he wound to and from work past that newspaper office, Cameron Hooker surely never thought he would be the object of so much speculation within its walls.

On November 19, 1984, the day after Hooker's arrest, Police Chief John Faulkner released the first scraps of information to the press. Declining to give full details, he disclosed only the essentials: that Cameron Hooker had been booked for kidnapping, rape, sodomy, and assorted other charges. A short article, headlined "Police Arrest Suspect in Kidnap-Sex Crimes," was the first glimmer of a story that would prove to be the *Daily News*'s biggest scoop ever, not only dominating the local paper's front page many times through the year but drawing media attention from around the world.

By the next day, more details had emerged, and a picture of Cameron Hooker accompanied the front-page article: "Police: Sex Victim Held 7 Years." The article described the events preceding Hooker's arrest: the kidnap, various crimes, and, most astonishingly, the box. It explained that an "unidentified 27-year-old woman," who had been working recently as a motel maid, had been held captive "for seven years as a sex slave."

With sensational elements like sex slavery, a seven-year captivity, and a box beneath the master's waterbed, Red Bluff promptly found itself the focus of unprecedented media attention. In wire service offices, radio and television stations, and big-city newsrooms, editors consulted maps and dispatched reporters to the scene of the crime.

Newspeople rushed into town seeking to fill column-inches or allotted time slots, searching for fresh angles. They queried law enforcement officers, questioned the district attorney's office, and pestered neighbors—who became so exasperated with sightseers and the press that one finally put up a Private Road sign to try to deter them. The *Red Bluff Daily News* even ran a story complaining that "reporters, photographers and newscasters have swarmed into town, taken it by the throat and shaken it for every possible last bit of information."

Somewhere along the line, this peculiar story was tagged first The Girl in the Box Case and then The Sex Slave Case. In no time it was making headlines across the country, through Europe, to Tokyo, and back.

Meanwhile, the story broke around the local people with an unintelligible clatter. It was inconceivable that a man and his wife could kidnap a woman and secretly hold her captive for more than seven years, especially in a town as small and a community as tightly interwoven as Red Bluff's. None of it made sense. Here was a woman who had been going to work and returning home every day; how could it be that she was held against her will? Why didn't she just run away? And who could believe that a full-grown woman could be kept for years in a coffin-size box?

"You'd think that if something like that happened to someone they would have stuttered a lot or would have been malnourished, but she was very outgoing. She always had rosy cheeks," Doris Miron, Colleen's former employer at the King's Lodge told the *San Francisco Chronicle.*

Mr. and Mrs. Leddy, the little old couple who'd rented 1140 Oak Street to the Hookers years earlier, politely answered reporters' questions but still felt the whole wild story couldn't possibly be true. "I don't understand this," Mrs. Leddy said. "She had freedom—shopping and all that." Reflecting on her former tenant, Mrs. Leddy said of Cameron: "Quiet as he was and everything, it's hard to believe he'd do those things."

That seemed to be the consensus among most of Hooker's more recent neighbors as well. One neighbor told local reporters, "I knew the girl and I knew Cameron, and they were so normal. If you'd line up ten men you knew in a row for something like this, Cameron would be the last one you'd pick."

Neighbors described Hooker as "nice," "courteous," "quiet," "friendly," and "a really nice guy," but no one, it seemed, could claim to know him well. He was called "good-tempered" and "easy to get along with," but his very mildness seemed to be what characterized him most. He kept his distance, as if he didn't want to attract attention to himself.

But at night, yes, there was quite a bit of activity over at the Hooker place—lights on at all hours, noises.

"At night you could hear his electric saw going in his shed," a neighbor said. "He was always busy doing something."

Another neighbor remembered sitting on his porch in the dark, watching Hooker carry buckets of dirt out of the shed and then dumping them on a mound, over and over again.

No one recalled any incidents of abuse or perversion, not the slightest hint of anything sinister in connection with the lone, single-wide trailer at the end of the short dirt road where the Hookers lived. The family seemed not to have much money, but there's nothing dishonorable about being a bit shaggy, and they weren't much different from other families in the area.

Neighbors remembered the woman they knew as "Kay" taking the Hooker girls for walks, riding past on her bike, and jogging around the neighborhood. To most, she'd seemed sweet, friendly, and apparently free to come and go at will.

"Everything seemed normal to us," one neighbor told an out-of-town reporter. "She seemed real friendly. She would slow down, wave, and smile. We didn't pick up on anything wrong."

Cameron Hooker's coworkers at Diamond responded to the news of his arrest with almost universal skepticism. During the twelve years he'd worked there, Hooker had proven himself a dependable worker—mechanically inclined, clever, and even having some artistic talent, with those carvings and sculptures he was always working on. Although some of the women who worked at Diamond regarded this tall, gangly fellow as "a nerd," Hooker was generally well liked.[1]

Moreover, he'd never given the smallest indication of anything awry at home. He rarely talked of his family life, hardly ever brought up sex, and in complete contradiction to stereotypical visions of burly, brutal rapists, Hooker was generally mild, quiet, and good-humored. The rumor even began to spread that Jan and this other woman were in cahoots together—maybe they were lesbians—and they'd cooked up the whole story just to fix him.

The townspeople read the newspaper accounts and wondered.

But to one local family, the press coverage was more than just startling, it was painful. For more than a decade, Harold and Lorena Hooker had quietly owned a twenty-acre ranch off of Highway 99, south of Red Bluff, near the town of Gerber. Now the peace of these wide open spaces was shattered, and their elder son was being held on $500,000 bail. Mrs. Hooker, a tall, dignified woman with sad eyes, declined to talk to reporters except to state that the media had "been having a field day with this."

---

1. Hooker's locker at work was broken into shortly after his arrest. There are conflicting opinions about the significance of this. No one admits to having done it, and it's impossible to know what was taken.

The police, who were at first unaware of a locker at Diamond, wouldn't get around to searching it for more than a month. They assume that a friend or friends of Hooker's removed incriminating items. "It just goes to show how well liked Hooker was," Lt. Jerry Brown believes.

Others say this was simple curiosity on the part of Hooker's coworkers—they wanted to see what he had—but nothing was taken.

One Diamond worker, who asked not to be identified, reported that a couple of "nosy guys" broke into Hooker's locker, removed some items, and threw them into "the chipper"—a piece of machinery that "looks like a vegematic" and shreds wood up "like wooden potato chips" to make fiber for paper. He didn't know what items were destroyed but speculated that the motivation was to protect Hooker or themselves.

In any case, when the police finally got around to getting a search warrant for the locker, they found some negatives, a bag of clay, and some soft-porn molds, but nothing of profound interest.

Mr. Hooker, looking gaunt and worn, told reporters, "We're almost sick over the situation."

However, he took the time to try to defend his boy. "We thought we had the greatest son in the world," he said. "He was a good, easy kid to raise, no trouble at all. He never, ever let his temper get away with him."

The Hookers found it impossible to believe that "Kay" had been kept against her will. She'd come over with Jan and Cameron a number of times, and they'd seen no evidence that she'd been kept by force—nothing strange, no bruises, no scars, not the slightest indication that she was anything but a babysitter. It seemed to them that she got along well with the girls, with their son and daughter-in-law, and that she was free to come and go as she pleased.

Asked about his daughter-in-law, Janice, whose allegations had led to Cameron's arrest, Mr. Hooker said, "She won't say anything that makes sense. She's really upset."

Now, Mr. Hooker worried, "it seems like the publicity's got him guilty before they even get him to trial."

Some of the loveliest buildings in the area are located in the heart of Red Bluff. These handsome old Victorians bespeak a more elegant past—when the railroad and the river were the main arteries of transportation, long before Interstate 5 would pull commerce to the other side of the river, spawning graceless housing developments and shopping centers surrounded by asphalt.

There's little time or money today for the craftsmanship that went into these old Victorians, and few can even afford to heat their spacious, high-ceilinged rooms. Many are becoming shops and law offices—like the large and impressive office of Rolland Papendick, on the corner of Washington and Hickory Streets.

Papendick, like his office, commands respect. Tall, good-looking, and almost inevitably dressed in a suit—not so common in this rural area—Papendick looks the part of the prosperous, capable attorney. He can be charming and smooth, but he's not all refinement and solemnity. There's an athletic quality to him, a youthfulness that goes beyond simply having a full head of dark hair going into middle age.

His quick movements reveal a restrained energy that sometimes makes him seem about to spring out of his chair—less like an attorney than a basketball player waiting to be called into the game.

But perhaps it's more tension than athleticism that fuels Papendick's energy, for it's surely not clean living that has left Mr. Papendick so apparently fit: He smokes, he drinks, and a brooding temper lurks behind those snappy blue eyes. In court or out, his words can be curt, abrasive, and sarcastic. He's not a man you'd want to cross, and he's definitely someone you'd want on your side.

Shortly after Cameron's arrest, his younger brother, Dexter, hailed Mr. Papendick on a street corner and asked how much he charged as a retainer for a criminal case. Papendick mentioned a figure, and Dexter had the check waiting on his desk that afternoon.

"Then I found out what I'd gotten myself into," Papendick recalls.

Papendick spoke with the Hooker family at length. After learning some background and the charges against Cameron, he was inclined to accept the case, but he told them that the final decision was ultimately up to the actual client. "First," he said, "I'll have to talk to Cameron."

But before Papendick even had a chance to approach Cameron Hooker, he was visited by Hooker's wife.

Perhaps the only way to understand Janice Hooker's actions during this period is to imagine her on an emotional see-saw. She had turned Cameron in, but now she was shaken by the resulting commotion. The father of her children was in jail, she felt guilty for putting him there, and when he phoned her making various requests, she did her best to comply.

Janice also talked with her in-laws. Perhaps as a way of deflecting responsibility for Cameron's arrest away from herself, she said some rather astonishing things including that she knew "for a fact that Colleen wasn't raped." Mr. and Mrs. Hooker suggested she tell this to Papendick.

And so, to Papendick's surprise, he found Janice standing in his office saying she could "destroy Colleen's story" and indicating that she wanted to talk about the case.

From the start, it was clear to Papendick that if he accepted this case, Janice Hooker would be testifying for the prosecution. He took mental notes of what she said but cautiously advised her that, since he was probably going to be representing Cameron, she would need to seek separate counsel. Then he referred this woman, whom he found "very, very, very emotionally distraught and confused," to Ron McIver, another respected criminal attorney in the area.

Shortly thereafter, Rolland Papendick seated himself across from Cameron Hooker in the attorney visiting room at the county jail, a pane of glass separating them across a shared table. A slot at the bottom of the glass allows the attorney to pass papers back and forth to the prisoner, but other than this, there can be no physical contact between the two.

When Hooker was brought in, clad in his blue inmate's uniform, Papendick appraised the lanky, six-foot-four-inch fellow, introduced himself, and started asking questions. . . .

Papendick came away from this first meeting with the opinion that his new client was "totally and completely honest." What impressed him most was that when he asked, "How did you meet Colleen Stan?" Cameron unhesitatingly replied, "I kidnapped her."

7

Most crimes are over in a matter of moments—a trigger pulled, blood spilled, the law broken in a snap—but here was a succession of crimes spanning more than seven years, a pattern of abuse that had become a way of life. And as soon as Deputy District Attorney Christine McGuire heard about the "sex slave" case, she knew it belonged to her.

She'd been on an out-of-town trip when the case broke. Her first day back in the office, she heard all about it—weird evidence like a "stretcher" and a "head box" and something akin to a coffin. This was the wildest case ever to hit Tehama County, and the details only strengthened McGuire's conviction that of all the attorneys in the office, she ought to be the one to prosecute Cameron Hooker. She was the office "sexpert," the specialist on prosecuting sex offenses, and Hooker was due to be charged with at least a dozen felony sex crimes.

The problem was that no one else in the office seemed to be making what she thought was an obvious connection.

She'd come into the office early that morning, half expecting the Hooker file to be on her desk. But not only was the file absent, by mid-morning no one had even consulted her about the case. Offended, she sat hunched over a stack of papers at her desk, her dark hair shrouding her face, a cup of coffee in hand. She and the coffee were both steaming.

Voices were discussing the case just outside her door. She put down her pen and listened.

"I can give you a report on what the victim had to say. I

interviewed Colleen Stan last week." The voice was familiar: Detective Al Shamblin.

"Fine. Bring that by, and let's go over everything we've got against Hooker." McGuire recognized the other voice as Assistant District Attorney Ed King.

So, she thought, King was getting the Hooker case.

Dammit, she'd paid her dues. She'd been prosecuting sex crimes for four years, practically since the first day she'd walked in the door. Everyone was delighted to have her handle those messy interviews with rape and child molest victims, but now, when a really big case comes along, it was passed along to someone higher up.

How many times since she'd come to work as the only female attorney in the office—in fact, in the whole county— had she come up against that feeling of being passed over and shut out?

When she'd accepted the job in 1980, McGuire knew it wasn't going to be easy being the only woman lawyer in a county so red-neck, so dominated by cattlemen, that the Tehama County emblem was the head of a steer. But at twenty-eight, she'd been excited by the prospect of trying felony cases—feasible in a small DA's office, whereas in a big-city office she would have spent years working her way through infractions and misdemeanor cases. Here, she was trying felonies her first year.

Not long after she was hired, McGuire learned that, because she was a woman, many of her peers thought she'd been employed for reasons other than her professional skills. Indignant, she just dug in and worked harder.

McGuire might have come in a little green, but she won cases. After encountering her in court, her colleagues began to get the message that she was not to be underestimated because of her size or her sex; she was feminine and petite, but not fragile.

But in the process of sharpening her prosecutorial skills, McGuire also managed to alienate a few people. While obliterating that first impression of being "tiny" and "delicate," McGuire tended to come across as pushy, overly serious, and combative. She didn't mean to be that way, but that's how her crossed arms and compressed lips were interpreted.

She'd even had jurors come up to her after trials (which she'd won) to advise her to smile more.

McGuire didn't see herself as especially somber, and she was puzzled when people told her to "lighten up." That unsmiling manner was just her style.

"I don't joke around in court," she said. "Some attorneys do that, but I think it undermines the jury's confidence in you—not to mention the victim's—if you're seen laughing it up with the defense counsel and the judge. In chambers or outside of the courtroom, I'm as easy-going as anyone else, but I am serious in court. I guess that's why people keep calling me 'intense.'"

McGuire's background probably accounts for much of that intensity. Her Irish-Catholic upbringing didn't leave much room for coddling. The second girl in a family of three daughters and one son, McGuire grew up in a working-class suburb of Cleveland. At an early age she learned to be ultraresponsible, very serious, and self-reliant.

Realizing that she was bright but no genius, she threw herself into her studies and, out of sheer tenacity, graduated from high school at sixteen. Then she went to work.

Holding down a full-time job as a secretary, she put herself through night school and, in 1972, became the first person in her family to finish college, even managing to graduate cum laude.

Though she hadn't been shy about setting unexpectedly high educational goals, Christine hadn't completely abandoned the conventions of home and family. Just out of college, she married handsome Steven Takacs, a chemical engineer whom she'd known for about three years. They were wed in a small outdoor ceremony on a hot summer day in August 1972.

McGuire's desire for a warm and secure homelife, however, was due to clash with her desire for a career. She and her husband moved to Southern California, where she put so much into speeding through Southwestern University Law School in two years rather than three that her marriage died from neglect. In 1978, Christine and Steven were divorced—a fate to which no good Catholic girl is easily reconciled, but particularly upsetting for Christine, who was the first in her family to get divorced.

Still reeling from her failed marriage, Christine spent one lonesome year in private practice in Orange County before becoming disenchanted with the flash and fast-lane frivolity of sprawling Southern California. Yearning to do something socially responsible and personally fulfilling, she tried a stint with VISTA, working with Nevada Indian Legal Services.

At the end of her commitment, she started putting resumes in the mail, landing an interview with Tehama County District Attorney Bill Scott and then a job in Red Bluff—a "hick town," in her estimation, but not a bad place to learn the fine art of prosecution.

She'd come to Red Bluff recognizing that, being a rural area, it wouldn't be as progressive as L.A. But some of the attitudes she encountered among police officers and her colleagues made her stop and swallow. She was offended by their insensitivity toward victims of sex crimes, especially their "didn't-she-enjoy-it?" attitudes about rape.

It seemed that either no one wanted to handle these cases, or no one took them seriously, because a lot of them were being plea bargained away—meaning that rapists, child molesters, and wife beaters were back on the streets in a relatively short time. McGuire raised a stink about it, the cases started ending up on her desk, and more or less by default, she became the office specialist on the prosecution of sex crimes.

And she got convictions. By the end of 1984, her conviction rate was running at 90 percent.

So why hadn't she been given the Hooker case?

By the end of the day she was privately fuming. She went home to her six-month-old daughter, Nicole, and relieved Rose, the grandmotherly nanny. Still angry, she fed the baby while mentally reviewing all the reasons she should be the one to try Cameron Hooker.

When her husband got home, she could finally keep it in no longer. She broke the unspoken rule of not discussing work at home.

Her husband, James Lang, was the District Attorney. They'd been dating in 1982 when he ran against her boss,

Bill Scott, for Tehama County DA. He won, they married, and now she found herself in the frequently awkward position of working for her husband.

Except for their profession, James Lang and Christine McGuire seemed an unlikely pair. Her manner was quick, his was methodical. Her voice was keen, with a distinct Midwestern twang, his was deep and resonant. She was just a few years out of law school; he'd spent 20 years as a cop, some years as a judge, and was about 30 years her senior.

But in their conservative politics and law-and-order ethics, Lang and McGuire stood as matched as bookends. They were a career-oriented couple. In fact, their relationship had sprung from Christine's deep respect for Jim's professionalism.

McGuire had noticed Lang's deftness in the courtroom soon after arriving in Tehama County in 1980. She had marveled at his ability to take a case apart from several different perspectives, admired his sharp legal mind, his easy rapport with the jury, his skillful presentations in the courtroom. He tried a case "with such effortlessness," she said, "he could have been shopping for groceries."

Her first years in Red Bluff, McGuire had often sought out his advice, and in some senses, he'd become her mentor. But once they married, they determined not to mix their professional and private lives. Christine basically agreed with this, but sometimes felt exasperated by Jim's secretiveness. From his point of view, he was being protective of her by insulating her from conflicts with the Board of Supervisors or judges or whomever, but she felt shut out and jealous of his easy camaraderie with the others in the office. At work, they maintained an uneasy distance.

So McGuire had kept her desire to try Hooker bottled up, resisting the urge to approach District Attorney Lang on the subject, believing that, eventually, he would come to her. But by nightfall she was so thoroughly convinced the case was rightfully hers that when Jim came home she let him know she was angry at not having been assigned it.

"Why did you give the sex slave case to King? I'm supposed to be handing the sex cases, Jim. Why shouldn't I be the one to prosecute Hooker?"

Lang, who didn't feel *anyone* had been assigned the case yet, didn't see what she was so perturbed about. "The only reason he's been looking into it is that he tries the homicides and we've been trying to connect Hooker with a 187 charge. But since there isn't enough evidence for a murder charge, we'll have to go with the Stan case."

He gave her a level gaze and added, with characteristic gruffness, "If you think you can handle it, by god, handle it!"

Reviewing the evidence and plowing through stacks of police reports, McGuire tried to parcel this wild amalgamation of information into the legal segments that make a case. The circumstances were so bizarre and the time-span so phenomenal that it was difficult to digest.

It didn't make sense that Colleen Stan claimed to have been held against her will, yet had ample opportunity to flee. When she finally went home in August of 1984, she hadn't even contacted the police! But the most glaring flaw in this case, the incident that made McGuire cringe, was that inexplicable trip to Riverside in March of 1981. How could she possibly explain that to a jury? For that matter, how could she explain it to herself?

She sighed with frustration. They had big statute of limitations problems, particularly in terms of the kidnap. It had taken such a long time for these crimes to come to light that Hooker could get away with many of them even if he confessed.

Burdened with a full case load, her regular office duties, and a colicky baby at home, McGuire scarcely had time to prepare for the preliminary hearing, set for little more than a week away. The preliminary hearing would determine exactly what Hooker could be charged with. The judge would hear testimony, then arguments from the prosecution and the defense, and decide whether there was enough evidence to bring Hooker to trial. But before she could present evidence against Hooker, McGuire had to familiarize herself with seven years of events, and if she overlooked something during the prelim, there would be no second chance to bring it in later.

Her task was complicated by the fact that she had only barebones summaries, not transcripts, of police interviews with Janice and Colleen that had transpired over several hours. But the good news was that one of her favorite detectives, Al Shamblin, had conducted the interviews.

In McGuire's estimation, Shamblin was one of the most reliable investigative officers on the force. Though you couldn't tell it from his slow manner, his lame grammar, or his shaggy-dog looks, Shamblin was no dummy. He got all the details, and he knew how to investigate a case. McGuire and Shamblin had teamed up on a number of cases, and she knew from experience that she could count on him to get his facts straight.

Knowing how dependable Shamblin was, McGuire expected that he would have answers to most of her questions about the crimes Hooker had allegedly committed. What she hadn't expected was the bombshell of evidence that literally fell into his lap.

It was a slide, not unlike the hundreds of slides that police had confiscated from Hooker's mobile home. But rather than being neatly marked, boxed, and stashed, this one had been hidden and forgotten, tucked between the pages of one of Hooker's sketchbooks. By chance, Shamblin had picked up the sketchbook and thumbed through it, and the slide had dropped out.

When he showed it to McGuire, she held it up to the light, squinted, and explained, "Al, we've got our first big break!"

According to Janice Hooker, she and Cameron had destroyed a barrelful of potential evidence, including one particular sheet of paper, the slavery contract. But while Hooker had made sure the original had gone up in smoke, he'd apparently forgotten that, ever the photographer, he'd preserved the contract on celluloid.

McGuire's first meeting with Janice Hooker came on the heels of this exciting discovery, on the afternoon of Tuesday, November 27. The meeting was ostensibly to prepare Janice for the potentially unnerving experience of testifying at the preliminary hearing. But besides reviewing common-sense points such as speaking clearly and not guessing at answers, this preparatory interview allowed the prosecutor to get a feel for her witness—what type of character she was, how she might respond on the stand.

At first meeting, McGuire decided that as a principal witness Janice Hooker left a lot to be desired. Jan entered the coffee room at the Red Bluff Police Department (RBPD) wearing a rumpled sweatshirt and blue jeans that were too small for her stout figure. She peered out from beneath her long, frizzy hair with a wary expression, making it immediately clear that she was uncomfortable.

Detective Shamblin greeted Janice and introduced Deputy DA McGuire, who smiled and tried to put Janice at ease, but the two women seemed to have nothing in common and zero rapport. The atmosphere was strained until McGuire asked the names of Janice's daughters and told her about her own baby girl. Soon they were sharing photographs of their children, mother to mother.

The interview got under way, McGuire leaving most of the questioning to Shamblin. "Let's start at the beginning," he said, and Janice talked for the next five hours, starting with the events of May 19, 1977.

She was much more coherent than the first time Shamblin had interviewed her, but her answers often came slowly, after much consideration, and she frequently claimed memory lapses. She seemed evasive, as if she were still unconvinced that the immunity she'd been granted would protect her from prosecution. Once or twice, she asked that the tape recorder be turned off so she could discuss something without being recorded.

She did better when asked to ID the evidence—the box, the head box, the whips, assorted photographs and magazines—but was visibly shaken to learn that they'd found the slavery contract. And when they asked Jan to ID slides of herself, projecting them against a screen in the back room, she was distressed by the thought of complete strangers viewing these in the courtroom.

(The prospect was disturbing to McGuire as well. The photographs were graphic depictions of Janice being hung, stretched, and bound in various ways, and she wondered what effect they might have on a jury. If the jury were offended, these photos could backfire, damaging Jan's credibility as a witness and undermining her testimony.)

During the interview, McGuire watched Janice closely. She couldn't help but notice that Jan had the worn and weathered hands of a much older woman and that, from behind her wire-rim glasses, her eyes spoke of pain. This was a woman who had been through a lot. But Janice Hooker was also an accomplice, worried about protecting herself, and McGuire's legal instincts told her to be watchful for lies and contradictions.

The interview finally ended, and once Janice had gone, Shamblin and McGuire compared notes. Overall, Janice was doing well—her story was consistent, she wasn't contradicting herself—but the prosecutor still had misgivings.

"She seems a little shaky, doesn't she? I hope she doesn't balk at the last minute. If I have to do the prelim without her it's going to seem like a vendetta—Colleen against Cameron."

And there was an even more fundamental reason for getting Janice to testify. If McGuire could get her on the stand at the preliminary hearing, Mrs. Hooker would be waiving her marital privilege not to testify against her husband, a privilege that once waived is waived forever under California law.

They'd learned from Janice that Cameron had planned to capture more slaves, that he had stalked women, taking photos of them with his telephoto lens. This was the impetus behind a search that proved pivotal to the case.

Ed King had hastily obtained the first search warrant at the time of Hooker's arrest, and that had yielded the head box, the stretcher, and various bondage articles. Now McGuire obtained another search warrant—the second of what would ultimately be a total of five. Call her compulsive, but McGuire's thoroughness would pay off.

Detective Shamblin and Lieutenant Brown went back to the Hooker residence and seized Hooker's photographic equipment—a handmade enlarger, a slide rack with candid slides of women, a camera, and lenses. Also, on the bottom of a bedroom drawer, they found two undeveloped rolls of film.

Back at RBPD they took a closer look at these forgotten rolls and learned that this type of film had been discontinued in 1975. The film was so old that it would have to be sent away for special processing by the FBI in Washington, D.C.

The day before the preliminary hearing, Colleen Stan and her father drove up from Riverside together.

McGuire's first impression was that the victim of the sex slave case didn't look very slavelike, nor even much like a victim. Juries, McGuire knew, tended to judge people from the outside, and this woman who claimed to have been imprisoned and deprived looked normal, neat, well-fed, and pretty.

Worse, McGuire had a feeling Defense Attorney Papendick was going to try to portray Colleen as "the other woman." Unfortunately, she looked the part. Though a year older than Janice, she looked much younger and vastly more attractive. In fact, McGuire thought she looked too sexy and cheaply dressed in her tight-fitting top, tight pastel jeans, and stiletto heels.

There wasn't time to do as in-depth an interview as they had with Janice Hooker. McGuire outlined the areas she would cover with Colleen on the stand but, beyond advising her to answer truthfully, didn't touch on the substance of Colleen's testimony—that would be coaching, strictly outside the rules. She gave the standard explanation of court proceedings, a few pointers on how to conduct herself on the stand, and let her know what to expect.

"Don't be surprised if the defense attorney seems hostile, but don't get flustered. Just answer his questions as clearly as possible. I'll object if the questioning is improper," McGuire told her.

Colleen sat very still, amicable and apparently alert yet with a strangely vacant look behind those pretty blue eyes, like a doll on a shelf. Colleen seemed shy, a bit apprehensive, and unnaturally passive. There seemed not an ounce of vengeance in her, which was peculiar in McGuire's experience with victims.

The interview was over in a couple of hours, and then Colleen had an appointment for a physical examination to see if her physical condition corroborated her story.

As she bid good-bye, McGuire remembered to suggest that Colleen wear a dress in court tomorrow.

Once they'd gone, McGuire turned to Shamblin and said, "You told me to expect her to be quiet, but she and her father were both so docile, they're like sheep!"

"Kinda spooky, isn't it?" Shamblin agreed.

"Well, maybe they were just tired after that long drive up from Riverside. But I sure hope she's more animated tomorrow."

Who could believe a victim who was so dispassionate about the crimes committed against her? She'd expected outrage, tears, and instead she'd gotten something vexingly close to apathy.

Moreover, she was amazed to learn that this woman who had allegedly endured years of almost unheard-of deprivation and abuse was now living such an outwardly ordinary life. Wouldn't you expect she'd have fallen apart? But Colleen seemed to have quickly adjusted to the outside world. She was living with her father and his wife, holding down a full-time job, going to church, and meeting new people. She commuted daily to her job at a hospital where she was doing what she'd learned to do so well over the past several years: She cleaned. It seemed that Colleen was putting her life in the most mundane and normal configuration she could muster.

Not until much later would the prosecutor understand that while she was attempting to probe beneath the surface of those seven years, Colleen was doing her best to bury them.

Rolland Papendick had presented a motion to bar the press from the preliminary hearing, but attorneys representing major newspapers flew up from Sacramento to file counter arguments. Soon it seemed that every newsperson who could figure out how was filing a supporting brief before Judge Dennis E. Murray.

At thirty-four, Murray was young for a judge. He ran a

conservative courtroom, legally straight and narrow, but he had a sympathetic nature and was concerned about protecting the witnesses, who would be offering very personal and emotional testimony in this case. He denied Papendick's motion to exclude the press, but when the media requested permission to film the proceedings, the baby-faced judge said he hoped to control "the circus atmosphere" and denied this request as well.

Freedom of the press had prevailed, and when Deputy DA McGuire entered the courtroom the morning of December 5, she was stunned to find it filled—camerapersons and newspeople occupying every seat and lining the walls. Standing room only.

This just never happened in Red Bluff.

She was nervous. The baby had kept her up part of the night, and she'd tossed and turned the rest. She was acutely aware of gaps in law enforcement's knowledge of this case, and during the night the gaps had grown into huge chasms. She had the feeling that anything could happen.

There was rampant skepticism about the case. Lt. Jerry Brown had told her that he'd heard nothing but dubious remarks from the media after the press conference, and it seemed that she and the police were the only ones who believed in the charges against Hooker.

But the purpose of a preliminary hearing is to determine whether there is enough evidence to bring the defendant to trial, not to convert disbelievers, and the judge would be the one to decide whether to try Cameron Hooker.

Several issues had to be discussed in chambers before the preliminary hearing began, but at least all was in order and the two attorneys entered the courtroom and took their seats.

Hooker, wearing a flannel shirt, gray cords, and a two-tone blue ski jacket, was brought over from the jail to take his seat next to Papendick at the defense table. He flashed a brave smile at his parents, younger brother, and sister-in-law, who sat in the spectators' seats behind him. With his round face and wire-rim spectacles, he looked more iike a boyish country accountant than a sadistic criminal.

At the table for the prosecution, Officer Shamblin sat jiggling his leg nervously while Deputy DA McGuire shifted papers and fidgeted. Janice's attorney, Ron McIver, took a seat in the empty jury box.

It was after ten-thirty by the time order was called and the proceedings began.

The Court: People of the State of California versus Cameron M. Hooker. This is the time and place for the preliminary hearing in Case No. 13961. Are the People ready to proceed?

Ms. McGuire: Yes, Your Honor, we are.

The Court: Mr. Papendick, is the Defendant ready?

Mr. Papendick: Yes, we're ready, Your Honor.

The Court: Ms. McGuire, you may call your first witness.

Ms. McGuire: Call Janice Hooker.

Janice Hooker was brought in, and everyone scrutinized her as she was sworn in. Wearing, again, jeans and a sweatshirt, her long, wavy hair partially obscuring her round face, she doubtless disappointed those expecting leather and chains. There was nothing at all racy about her. She looked like some overweight shopper you'd see pushing a cart at a discount store.

McGuire started almost immediately with the kidnap, and within a few minutes Janice had set the tone for the rest of the day. Frequently wiping a nervous hand across her face, avoiding her husband's eyes, she responded after long, empty pauses—or sometimes not at all. She often offered nothing more than, "I can't remember," or "I don't know." And she spoke so softly that more than once the judge had to ask her to speak up.

For McGuire, "it was like pulling teeth." She finally resorted to leading questions, which only provoked objections from the defense and admonitions from the bench.

After long and tedious questioning, the prosecutor elicited a recounting of the kidnap and the first several months of captivity, having Mrs. Hooker identify the knife, the head box, a whip, and the Bible. But when she came to the slavery contract, Janice became even less responsive. She replied in hushed monosyllables and claimed to know very little about the contract or how it came to be signed.

Though she tried to appear calm, the diminutive prosecutor was furious. During the course of her direct examination she had to refresh Janice's recollection twice, and Jan's unwillingness to talk at least doubled the time it took to present the case. With so many lengthy pauses and dead-end questions, the day dragged by.

On the surface the prelim was proceeding at a numbingly slow pace, but McGuire felt an underlying sense of urgency. Slogging through Jan's testimony, she feared the case against Hooker was coming out as unconvincing and fragmentary. Somehow, she needed to shake Jan up.

During recesses McGuire went back to the jury room and tried to bolster some kind of allegiance with Jan, hoping to break down her resistance.

"I know this is taking a lot of courage on your part, Janice. I know it's not easy to testify against your husband. But it's very important that you be clear in your answers and tell the court exactly what you told the police."

"Okay," Jan answered dully. "I'll be careful, think more about my answers before I say them."

McGuire gnashed her teeth. Did Janice really think she was being cooperative? Or was this just her way of frustrating the prosecutor? McGuire couldn't tell, and she didn't want to risk a confrontation. It was bad enough that Janice was being so mulish; it would be worse to have her hostile.

Janice Hooker's attorney, Ron McIver, a man so warm-hearted it's hard to believe he's a lawyer, sympathized with the difficulty his colleague was having with his client. He came back to the jury room and tried to lend McGuire support, joining in the pep talks: "We know you're nervous, Janice. You're doing fine."

Privately, he told McGuire that Jan had been vacillating up to the very last minute. The night before, he said, he thought she was going to back down.

That was the bright side: Bad as she was, at least Janice was on the stand.

But whatever the two attorneys said, it seemed to have no

effect on the torpid Mrs. Hooker. Her testimony resumed at the same wearisome pace.

When Papendick began his cross-examination, Jan was more responsive. Her monosyllabic responses became complete, if short, sentences. It was if she were testifying for the defense rather than for the prosecution.

Still, her memory lapses continued, and Mr. Papendick finally zeroed in on the reason.

"Are you under any medication today?"

"Yes, I am."

"What medication have you taken?"

"Xanax, Desyrel."

Janice had been taking these two drugs—Xanax, a "mood elevator" or antianxiety drug, said to stop spontaneous and situational panic attacks, and Desyrel, an antidepressant—since September. Because appearing in court put her under additional stress, she'd decided to take a double dosage, which explained her excruciating slowness. But Papendick used this information to attack Jan's credibility.

"Do you think it affects your ability to remember things?"

"Yes."

"In what way?"

"It makes me not be able to think quite as clear."

"Does it cause you any problem in understanding and answering questions?"

"At times."

Then Papendick got Jan to admit that she had lied that she was pregnant to get Cameron to marry her, implying that lying came easily to her. He also established that Colleen had worked—unsupervised and unrestrained—as a housekeeper and a babysitter. Also he repeatedly underscored the fact that Colleen had held down an outside job.

But perhaps the most damaging and shocking admission was that Janice and Colleen had gone to bars to drink and meet men. The next day, this would lead the story in the *Red Bluff Daily News* ("Wife Testifies Hooker Let Women Visit Bars"), fueling the already vociferous skepticism being voiced in the community.

Reflecting on the day's testimony and Mrs. Hooker's "unstable" condition, Lt. Jerry Brown shook his head and said, "Poor Christine. She had a heck of a day."

Janice's testimony began the second morning as a virtual repeat of day one. She was a bit less sedated but still reluctant to answer questions. McGuire only hoped they could get through Janice's testimony quickly so she could get Colleen on the stand.

But that was too much to hope for, and some of Janice's responses under cross-examination nearly sent Christine into a panic.

Papendick asked: "While you lived on Oak Street, did Cameron and Colleen leave the house together alone?"

"Yes," Jan replied.

"How often?"

"Every weekend."

"And how long were they gone?"

"All day."

"They went out and cut posts, didn't they?"

"Yes."

"When Colleen left the house, was she restrained, bound, gagged in any way?"

"No."

At the next break, McGuire rushed back to the jury room where Colleen was waiting and confronted her with this new information.

"But that's not true," Colleen protested. "I never left the Oak Street house. Jan's wrong: she's lying."

With that, McGuire hurried to the office where Jan was kept and confronted her with Colleen's denial.

Janice looked puzzled. "Well, I could be mistaken," she said.

That didn't help. Now the prosecutor had a major inconsistency to worry about and she didn't know whom to believe.

Throughout the morning, Papendick painted Colleen Stan's captivity in pastel shades and got Janice to make more damaging revelations. Moreover, he portrayed Janice Hooker as a jealous woman, desperate to get Colleen Stan out of the house and away from her husband.

"Did you believe, in 1984, that Colleen loved Cameron?"
"Yes."

"And isn't it a fact that the reason you went to the police
is because you feared that Colleen and Cameron would get
back together?"

"No."

"Did you tell Cameron that?"

"Tell Cameron what?"

"That you feared that if Colleen came back to Northern
California that she and Cameron would see each other?"

"Yes."

McGuire crossed her arms with irritation. This hearing
wasn't going at all as she'd expected. Papendick was turning
it into a disaster for the prosecution, and she'd had just
about enough of Mrs. Hooker's surprises. She only hoped
that Colleen would be a better witness.

Shortly before eleven, both attorneys completed their
questions of Janice Hooker and Deputy DA McGuire called
Colleen Stan.

Reporters craned to take in this mysterious "sex slave" as
she entered the room and approached the stand, noting the
enormous difference between this young woman and Mrs.
Hooker. Janice was heavy and untidy; Colleen, while a bit
plump, was attractive and neat. (McGuire inwardly cringed
at the spike heels and slinky dress she wore, thinking they
made Colleen look "flashy" and gave credence to Papendick's version of the story.)

Looking pale and nervous, her wispy, light brown hair
falling past her shoulders, Colleen Stan took the stand and
was sworn in. Again, the prosecutor began her questions
with May 19, 1977—the kidnapping.

After Janice's monosyllabic responses, Colleen seemed almost loquacious, though she spoke softly and in brief sentences. She recounted the events of the day that began with a
hitchhiking excursion and ended in the basement of the
Hookers' house. But as Colleen answered questions about
the knife, the head box, the whipping, and the rack, Christine couldn't help but be struck again by her flat and unemotional tone.

On nearly every point, Colleen's testimony mirrored

Janice's exactly. But not always. Christine noted with interest that the two had divergent versions of one small but provocative episode. Janice had testified that she had come downstairs the second day of Colleen's captivity and covered her with a blanket, but Jan's recollection clashed with Colleen's.

"Do you recall whether or not, one time, Janice Hooker came down and had a conversation with you approximately the second day on the rack?"

"Yes."

"And what was that conversation?"

"She asked me if I knew where I was, and I said, yes, that I was in Red Bluff, and she said, no, I wasn't in Red Bluff. And she asked me, if she let me go, what would I do, and I told her I would go to the police and tell them I was kidnapped. And she told me I was stupid, and she shut the box back up and went away."

McGuire wasn't sure who to believe on this point, but she made a mental note that Janice Hooker may have been trying to portray herself in an unrealistically favorable light.

At the lunch break, Al brought in sacks of fast food for Colleen and her father so that they could eat in private. Christine meanwhile went to the frozen yogurt shop to indulge her notorious addiction, an almost daily pilgrimage.

At two P.M. the court reconvened, and the prosecutor's questioning continued. She focused on the issues of domination and subjugation and on the rapes and other crimes that Hooker would be charged with if the case went to trial. Through it all, Christine was surprised by Colleen's openness. Some of what she described was quite graphic. And some of it was almost painful to listen to.

The questioning of Colleen Stan moved much more quickly than had that of Janice Hooker, for Colleen was alert, if not terribly emotive. Soon McGuire sat down and turned her witness over to Papendick for cross-examination.

Again, the defense attorney brought out some startling testimony that didn't seem to fit, making McGuire wonder again just what had happened and who these strange people were.

"Did you tell Cameron, in 1981, you loved him?"

"I don't know if it was in 1981. I did tell him one time I loved him."

"When was the first time you told him you loved him?"

"I don't know."

"How many times did you tell him you loved him?"

"I don't know."

"More than once a week?"

"No."

"More than once a month?"

"No, I don't think so."

"Did he tell you he loved you?"

"When?"

"While he lived on Pershing."

"Yes."

McGuire sat quietly at the prosecution's table, stunned and bewildered. In light of the physical evidence and previous testimony, this whole, wild tale seemed full of contradictions.

Behind her, the press was furiously scratching out notes. While the alleged "sex slave" sat impassively on the stand, speaking in her flat, soft voice, they scribbled what would, at day's end, turn into shocking and puzzling news. This story seemed to have everything—from pornography to the Bible, from waterbeds to whips. It made little sense, but great copy.

By late afternoon both the prosecutor and the defense attorney had finally come to the end of their questions.

Now it was up to the judge.

Judge Murray took a recess to review his notes and survey the small sampling of physical evidence. McGuire waited tensely, mentally reviewing what had transpired over the past two days.

In a few minutes the judge resumed the bench. Christine held her breath and listened.

Judge Murray ruled that Cameron Hooker would have to face charges of kidnapping, rape, sodomy, oral copulation, and rape with a foreign object. Calling the case "extremely serious, and, to put it mildly, bizarre" and declaring that, if the charges were true, Hooker "would certainly be a danger to the community," the judge maintained bail at half a million dollars.

Papendick was appalled; McGuire was ecstatic. Still running on nervous energy, she bid a warm farewell to the enigmatic Colleen Stan and her dutiful father, then went out to face the reporters.

The first day, unused to being in the eye of the media, she'd dodged questions and shied away from the cameras. But today, realizing these people were just doing their jobs, she stopped outside the courthouse and fielded questions.

Finally, with all the loose ends wrapped up, the adrenaline spent, and tiredness setting in, she headed off into the early December darkness. As Christine McGuire turned toward home it began to sink in that the preliminary hearing was over, the trial was on, and the biggest and strangest job of her career was just beginning.

— PART THREE ———————

"K"

Winter 1977–Spring 1979

. . . I feel a responsibility towards him that I don't really understand. I so often hate him, I think I ought forever to hate him. Yet I don't always. My pity wins, and I do want to help him.

It's because I never see anyone else. He becomes the norm. I forget to compare.

Miranda, *The Collector,* by John Fowles

8

Winter blew across Northern California with a wet, gray chill. Storms stripped leaves off the old oaks in the hills, leaving them rattling their bare tree-bones. The Sacramento River turned slate gray and pushed heavily against its muddy banks. Short, cold days and long stretches of rain conspired to dampen spirits and sow depression.

But one more downpour and the hills began to blush green beneath their yellowed summer coats. And then Christmas approached.

Good cheer rang through the air like Salvation Army bells, and fat Santas popped up everywhere. Yuletide aromas wafted from kitchens as families celebrated homecomings with splendid food, songs, presents, and all the special trappings of Christmas. And Janice and Cameron Hooker, like most people, spent Christmas with their families. They exchanged neatly wrapped packages that were soon torn open with excited cries and thanks. They shared sumptuous meals and good-humored banter and never let on that anything was amiss at 1140 Oak Street.

Meanwhile, Colleen spent another dark, cheerless day locked up in the basement. It's depressing to spend Christmas alone, and Colleen's could hardly have been more solitary. But to compound her loneliness, her birthday came with the holiday season, so this time of year had always been doubly special.

This year's birthday should have been an extravagantly celebrated event, but on December 31, New Year's Eve, Colleen spent a sad, lonely birthday in the box. She turned twenty-one.

The holidays did yield one surprise. Cameron gave Colleen a blue terrycloth nightgown. It was long and warm. She'd been complaining about being cold in the workshop during the night; now she had something to wear.

Soon it would be eight months since that spring day when Colleen Stan had unfortunately climbed into Cameron Hooker's car to sit in the back seat next to that head box. No one can accurately say what those long months had done to her mental state. The human psyche is a malleable thing —it bends. And it can break. A few hours of simple isolation and sensory deprivation would be an ordeal; a day or two would be cruel; *months* is macabre, brutal beyond imagining. But more than an extreme solitary confinement, more than a living death in a box the size of a coffin, Colleen had suffered a netherworld of terror and pain. She had been subjected to recurrent whippings and hangings, as well as incidents of strangulation, dunking, burning, electrocution, and sexual molestation.

Now, after months of continual humiliation and abuse, whatever tenuous grasp on reality Colleen had left was about to be replaced by an elaborate and terrifying fiction.

Cameron Hooker had a vast collection of pornography, ranging from *Playboy* to hard-core S/M (sadomasochistic) and B&D (bondage and discipline) publications. Some of it impressed him so much that he felt compelled to take photographs of the photographs in the magazines. In any case, the magazines that he retrieved from the pulp plant at work and that he bought at various adult bookstores were more than simply entertainment—they were inspiration.

Cameron especially enjoyed one underground newspaper, *Inside News,* which he bought regularly. But however interesting its articles usually were, the January 1, 1978, edition was riveting. He looked at page six, and an idea hit him so hard it must have nearly made his ears ring. He read it over and over again, and then he showed it to Janice.

"They Sell Themselves Body and Soul When They Sign THE SLAVERY CONTRACT," it was headlined, and not only did it detail the supposed hot trade in female flesh in the United States, it had a sample of the slavery contract. Could they get Colleen to believe this? Apparently, the possibility was exhilarating.

Hooker had to somehow duplicate the slavery contract, but this proved difficult. He tried photocopies, but they only looked like photocopies, and he wanted something that looked authentic. He tried lifting the print off the page, but that ruined the newspaper. He bought more copies. A convincing counterfeit was going to require some work and even a little cash, but, well, this was an investment.

Finally, Cameron rented a typewriter and had Janice type the slavery contract. For the space designated "Master," he instructed her to use an alias, Michael Powers, instead of his real name, on the line marked "Witness," to use Janet Powers for herself. Then, with some stencils he had bought just for this purpose, he carefully reproduced the calligraphy at the top. And for a final touch he put a seal at the bottom of the page, an "S" with a cross through it. When it was done, he had an exemplary piece of work.

On the evening of January 25, 1978, Cameron Hooker came downstairs into the basement with high expectations. He opened the door of the workshop. Colleen was inside, without the blindfold and unrestrained, sitting in a chair.

For the first time since May, she saw the face of her abductor. It was a large face, with blunt features, wire-rim glasses framing sleepy-looking eyes, sideburns bracketing broad cheeks, and full lips that pursed in irritation. This face loomed over her. He seemed extraordinarily tall.

He gave her a clipboard with paper and pen and told her to practice writing her name. She didn't understand why he wanted her to do this, but did as she was told. Then he handed her a newspaper article and told her to read it.

Colleen had read nothing in 251 days. Now she was confronted with a story about the buying and selling of women. She tried to focus on the words, trying to understand. . . .

With mounting horror, she read that "the S/M rage" had created a demand beyond common prostitution and had given rise to a new, more depraved trade. Even in the United States, it said, women are forced to sign contracts totally relinquishing control over their lives, their bodies, their souls. Sold into slavery, these women have no rights and no recourse; their owners can do with them whatever they wish. An underground brotherhood of slave traders, as large and well-oiled as the Mafia, not only controls this traffic in young flesh, but also enforced order, hunting down and punishing runaways.

By the time she reached the article's end, Colleen was thoroughly shaken. That such evil commerce could exist in America was hard to accept, but here it was in print. And didn't the picture of the woman, naked and bound, look all too much like what she'd suffered uncountable times? Hadn't she been snatched from her ordinary life and suddenly deposited in a hell far removed from what she'd once believed to be the realm of possibility? Was it so difficult to believe that what had happened to her could happen to anyone?

Cameron interrupted her thoughts. "They know you're here," he said. Colleen was confused. Who? Did he mean the police? A quick beat of hope passed through her.

But Cameron explained that it was *the Company* who knew she was there. The Company: the organization described in the article, a network of slave traders who turned captive women into profit. And now that the Company knew he held Colleen Stan prisoner in his basement, he would have to register her.

Janice was standing next to him. A sheet of paper in hand, a knee brace and bandage on her leg. Cameron took the paper and handed it to Colleen, telling her that the Company would take her away unless she signed it. Alarmed, Colleen saw that she was holding a contract exactly like the one in the article, a slavery contract, with "This Indenture" written in heavy black ink across the top. Clasping the official-looking document, she tried to comprehend its arcane and legalistic language. It read:

THIS INDENTURE, Made the 25th day of January in the year of Our Lord One Thousand Nine Hundred and Seventy-Eight, BETWEEN Colleen Stan, hereafter known as Slave; AND Michael Powers, hereafter known as Master; WITNESSETH:

That Slave, for and in consideration and in humble appreciation of such care and attention as Master may choose to afford her, has given, granted, aliened, enfeoffed and conveyed, and by these Presents does give, grant, enfeoff and convey unto Master:

ALL of Slave's body, and each and every part thereof without reservation, every bit of her will as to all matters and things, and the entirety of her Soul,

TOGETHER with, all and singular, every privilege, advantage and appurtenance to the same belonging or in anywise appertaining;

ALSO all the estate, right, title, property, claims, ego and id of Slave in, of and to the same and in, of and to every part and parcel thereof;

TO HAVE AND TO HOLD, all and singular, the above-described body, will, Soul and premises, with all appurtenances thereof, unto Master and any of His assigns forever.

AND the said Slave does covenant, promise and agree:

1. She shall immediately, diligently and enthusiastically comply with and submit her full being to any and all directions or desires of Master or His assigns which He or They may express by word, signal, action or any other means.

2. She shall at all times afford Master absolute respect, shall address Him only as "Sir" or "Master," shall station herself in a physical position subordinate to His whenever possible, and shall speak to or otherwise distract Him only when granted His permission.

3. She shall constantly maintain her female body parts in such circumstances as will demonstrate and ensure that they are fully open to Him. In particular, she shall never cross her legs in His presence, shall wear no undergarments at any time, and shall cover no part of her body with apparel or material of any description except when the act of doing so and design of the item are expressly approved by Him.

4. She shall preserve her female body parts for the ex-

clusive use of Him and His assigns, which use shall be the
sole source of her pleasures, and she shall engage in no
self-gratification nor any physical contact with any others.

AND Slave does hereby irrevocably declare and ac-
knowledge her everlasting unconditional dedication to
serving Master to His full satisfaction; AND she asham-
edly confesses that prior indulgence of her untempered
conduct by others may have permitted her to become af-
flicted with inferior habits that may prove unsatisfactory
to Master, from which imperfections she implores Master
to free her by retraining with corporal punishment or any
other means which He, in His unquestionable wisdom,
deems effective toward directing her to her sole ambition
and life-destiny of perfectly fulfilling His every desire of
her.

IN WITNESS WHEREOF, Slave has hereunto set her
hand, and Master has designed to Seal these Presents by
permanently affixing His Collar about her neck, on the
date first above written.

This is the work of the devil, Colleen thought. She felt
overwhelmed, unable to move. But he was standing there,
waiting for her to sign. . . .

As Cameron waited, he watched the devastating effect the
contract was having on Colleen, gratified to see that she was
crying, even shivering with fear: She believed it.

Finally, she managed to ask, "What if I don't sign it?"

"If you don't, I'll sign it for you and make you wish you
had."

This threat sunk in, and then she asked, "Well, who is
Michael Powers?" She knew, she said, that his name was
Cameron.

"I'm known by two names," he answered coolly. "That's
my Company name."

One word was unfamiliar, "enfeoffed," but when she
asked what it meant, Cameron couldn't tell her. Instead, he
warned her to hurry up and sign the contract. She was keeping the Company messenger waiting upstairs.

Still reeling, Colleen had one final statement of defiance

before she signed herself into slavery. He might hold her hostage in his basement, he might force her to sign the contract, and he might even have control of her body, but "you can never have my soul," she told him.

He was willing to concede this small point. He said, "I know, that's God's." But he continued to wait expectantly for her to sign.

In tears and trembling, she disguised her signature; with a wavering hand she inked her name on the line designated "Forever Slave." As a witness, Janice signed "Janet Powers."

The groundwork had been laid. Cameron had convinced Colleen the Company was real, and now it was just a question of strengthening that belief. He told her the Company required that she wear a slave collar as identification, and of course he had prepared one: a tight-fitting collar made of a stretchy, gold metallic material that joined with a gold leaf. He fastened it around her neck and she felt it constrict and itch against her skin.

It was costing him fifteen hundred dollars to register her with the Company, he said. Now that she was signed in, he would be able to let her out to do things for him because the Company would back him up. They would provide security —watching the house, monitoring the phones. And if she ever tried to run away, they would catch her and torture her so mercilessly that she would be lucky if she survived. In graphic detail, he described how runaways were punished by having their hands nailed to a beam from which they were left to hang for days.

Intensifying Colleen's horror, Cameron launched into a story about Jan. She had also been a slave, he said, but she'd tried to escape. She was hitchhiking to freedom when a policeman spotted her and picked her up. She thought she was safe, but the policeman was actually a member of the Company and knew she was a runaway. He took her back to her owners, who nailed her up by the hands as punishment. She hung for about three days, then went into convulsions and had to be taken down. But her punishment wasn't over—she was put on a rack and her legs were twisted, permanently damaging her knees and hips.

(Colleen had noticed the brace and bandage on Janice's leg. Janice *did* have knee problems; she'd just gotten out of the hospital after knee surgery. But that wasn't part of the story Cameron told his slave.)

After that, he continued, Jan had to go back to work for her owners. They ran a place in L.A. called Rent-a-Dungeon, a den of prostitution for members of the Company where any member could pay a fee, pick a girl, and take her to a dungeon where he could torture her however he liked. If he accidentally killed the girl, he would have to pay a fine of $10,000 or more.

On a visit to this particular establishment, Cameron had noticed Jan, who was just fifteen. After her escape attempt she was made to wear a cross, an indication that she had been marked for death. Cameron felt sorry for her. To save her life, he bought her and married her. Since then, he said, he'd had surgery done on her hands to remove the scars left by the nails.

It was melodramatic stuff, but Hooker told it with conviction and Colleen bought it all.

Over the next days and weeks Cameron embellished his stories about slaves and the Company, polishing details and wiping out any skepticism that might be lurking in Colleen's subconscious.

He even gave her a slave name. After a lot of thought, he'd decided on "K," he said. Just the letter. He'd considered "D" and "B" but decided they were too common, so from now on his slave would be known simply as K.

Colleen was all too susceptible to this sudden onslaught of detail. Having endured an almost unfathomable stretch of sensory deprivation, her brain was starved for information. And now the man who had total control over her life, whose power bordered on omnipotence, was finally explaining how the whole puzzle fit together.

She must have felt dazed by the awful illumination of it. All the horrors clicked into place—how such a terrible fate could befall her, how this evil man could possibly get away with what he was doing. There was an entire underground organization, almost a cult of men who preyed on young women like herself. The Company. There was a frightening logic to it all, and at last she had a way of comprehending how she could be held hostage to this nightmare.

9

Now it was clear-cut and in black and white. She was a slave. He was the master. And that relationship was as fixed as the seal on the slavery contract.

She was no longer Colleen Stan, but simply K. A servant. Property. A skinny, sad twenty-one-year-old with long dirty hair and a slave collar around her neck.

Having signed the slavery contract, she must strictly obey its dictates. She must always address Cameron as "Sir" or "Master," and always address Jan as "Ma'am." She must never look her master in the face. She must never cross her legs or wear underwear. She must kneel before her master to ask a question, and must ask permission before doing anything.

If she tried to contact her family, Hooker warned, the Company would retaliate with five days of crucifixion for her, and death for any family member she contacted.

With those rules established, K was allowed to come up out of the basement.

At night, with the draperies drawn and no company expected, K was brought upstairs to work. They gave orders, and unless she didn't understand, she obeyed without comment. She wasn't allowed to talk except to ask instructions. (Cameron mined the idea of any contact between the two women with fear; he told K that if Jan were displeased, she would kill her.)

K's chores were simple, mostly cooking, washing dishes, and cleaning up—drudgery, but nonetheless an improvement over the timeless claustrophobia of the basement. And now K was afforded a few small amenities, such as limited access to the bathroom, though she had to kneel and ask permission first.

To discipline her more strictly, Cameron contrived the "attention drill." Whenever he shouted "Attention!" K had to strip off her clothes, stand on her tiptoes, and reach her hands up to the top of the arched doorway between the living room and dining room. She must stand there, tensed and naked except for the slave collar, until he told her she could relax. He wanted to impress on her that the slavery contract wasn't just a sheet of paper, that it represented a whole new way of life: total subjugation.

Though her world had more than doubled in size, it was still limited to small spaces of cement and linoleum and wood. The stairs became familiar, but she was continually locked in cramped enclosures, in darkness and in silence. Her environment hadn't changed greatly, but the climate of her thoughts had been disrupted, her identity profoundly altered, her perception of reality twisted. Now her waking hours were menaced by an unknown and sinister presence: the Company.

A couple of weeks after she'd signed the contract, Cameron came down into the basement and let her out for her plate of leftovers, as usual. Then he casually remarked, "Oh, I got this from the Company today." He handed K a typed card, nothing fancy, sealed in plastic. A registration card. Short and businesslike, it simply acknowledged receipt of fifteen hundred dollars for the registration of Colleen Stan as the slave of Michael Powers. K looked at it and gave it back to him; he put it back on top of the workshop, where she supposed it was kept.

The card had taken little time to prepare, and this minor incident took only moments, but it was effective. The image of the card took root in K's subconscious—another proof of the Company, another link in the chain of lies that Cameron so steadily fashioned. Link after link, he invented details about the Company, welding it all with truth.

In K's mind the Company loomed as a large, efficient secret network. They had bugged the house. They were monitoring the phone. Like Big Brother in Orwell's *1984,* the Company hovered always in the background, an imperceptible but constant threat. Its members could be men anywhere, its victims were women who never let down their guards even for a moment. K feared the Company even more than the master at whose hands she'd suffered so much pain.

Hooker played on this fear. He told her that he and his brother had been raised around the slave-trading business, that he'd earned extra cash by tracking down runaways, building up his Company account. His father and brother were no longer active within the Company, but he warned that if they knew he had a slave they might want to "borrow" her for "parties."

He told her, too, the story of a runaway who'd made a grave mistake: She'd written an article about her ordeal. It took three months for the Company to track her down. By then, they'd devised a special punishment.

First, they pulled off her fingers, one at a time. Then her toes. A member who was a surgeon was called in to remove her arms and legs—without an anesthetic. Still alive, she had her tongue cut out and her hearing destroyed. They blinded her with a soldering gun. Yet she lived. Finally, they hung her from her braided hair on a hook next to her master's bed.

And so K learned there were worse things than being a slave to Cameron Hooker—especially if she ran away and told anyone about the Company. Cameron made sure she understood that.

The Hookers were astonishingly successful at concealing the peculiar circumstances of their household from intruders. But they failed to perceive that the real danger to their weird status quo came not from outsiders, but from within.

Janice—scared, intimidated, and barely twenty years old —found the whole situation unnerving. She apparently felt lost, overwhelmed, but Cameron was her husband, the father of her child, shouldn't she do what he told her? If she loved her husband, that was the most important thing, wasn't it?

The problem was that with this new woman around the house, Janice felt doubtful of Cameron's love for her. And so she decided to test him.

The agreement had been that there would be no sex between Cameron and his slave. This was still technically true —and Jan believed it—but she was worried. So early one morning, while she and her husband were still in bed, she asked him a question to see what his response would be. She asked if he wanted to bring K upstairs and have sex with her.

She soon regretted asking.

Cameron went down to the basement, got K out of the box, and brought her upstairs—naked, afraid, and with no idea what was about to happen. He put the leather cuffs on her wrists, secured the blindfold around her head with tape, and gagged her. Then he placed her on the bed and proceeded to stake her out, tying her wrists to eyehooks in the headboard, tying her feet to the bottom corners of the bed. K didn't even realize that Jan was in the room until the couple got on the bed with her.

Cameron lay between the two women, kissing and touching both of them. Then he mounted K.

This was too much for Janice. She got up, rushed crying to the bathroom, and got sick. K could hear her retching while Cameron raped her.

Jan put on her clothes and was starting to leave when Cameron got up and stopped her. He calmed her down, talked her out of leaving, and put K back in the box in the basement.

It was a brief episode, but it marked a shift, a further tilting of the relationships in that already bizarre household. Cameron had crossed over a line, broken a mental barrier. K had fallen to another level of degradation. And Janice, whose illness may have been caused as much by morning sickness as by the scene unfolding in her bedroom, had her faith in her husband shaken.

No immediate consequences arose, and life went on much as before. But there was no going back.

* * *

One morning, rather than putting K back in the box,
Cameron left her to sleep in the workshop. This was strange
in itself, but then there was some sporadic commotion upstairs and an unusual racket—a pounding and clatter—in
the basement.

K was kept in the workshop for about forty-eight hours.
The second night she wasn't even let out to eat. Dinner time
came and went, her stomach rumbled, but nothing was
brought down. Eventually she forgot she was hungry.

It was much later, about 3:00 A.M., when Hooker finally
let her out. He handcuffed and blindfolded her, led her upstairs, through the kitchen, and out the back door. For the
first time in nearly a year, K was out of the house.

Jan was already waiting in the pickup with baby Cathy.
Cameron hurried K over to Jan's side, maneuvered her into
the cab, and had her sit with her head down in Jan's lap so
that she couldn't be seen.

The doors were shut, the engine started, and the pickup
drove out of the alley and back onto the street. With this
same cast of characters, with K handcuffed and blindfolded
and the pickup heading out Oak Street, it was almost the
kidnap in reverse.

The streets were nearly deserted as they sped south on
Main Street and out old Highway 99.

It was a short trip, about five miles, then the pickup
turned down a bumpy road, gravel crunching briefly beneath the tires before it came to a halt. K was taken out of
the cab into the cool night air, then led up some steps, in a
door, and to the right. Here her blindfold and handcuffs
were removed.

She was in a bedroom. Before her stood a large waterbed,
its headboard and sides upholstered in black, the whole
frame raised on a high, wooden pedestal. Cameron gestured
toward a hole at its base, an entrance to a space beneath the
bed, and said, "This is where you're going to be staying."

10

The Hookers had bought an acre of land out beyond the city limits in a sparsely populated stretch of neglected property, some of it pasture, some of it just there, all of it now turned to emerald and dotted with spring wildflowers. Their yellow and brown single-wide trailer stood apart, as they wanted, at the very end of a dirt-and-gravel lane just off Pershing Road. They had a few neighbors, but no immediate ones. And not far behind them, to the west, ran Interstate 5, the distant freeway noise competing in the air with the constant calling and chatter of birds.

It was a good move for them, rural but not too remote, with the big sky overhead and lots of room for a garden. And it was *theirs;* they wouldn't have to worry about bothersome landlords popping in to remind them to mow the lawn or water the roses. They were glad for their new privacy and glad to leave the little house on Oak Street. That place had worried them, with the Leddys living just next door and the house perched so close to sidewalk traffic. And so they'd decided on a safer, more secluded residence.

Moving had been a chore, but Cameron had thrown himself into it with characteristic vigor. He'd built the waterbed himself, including the elaborate pedestal. He figured there was no place to keep a slave out at the trailer except under the bed. So he'd measured and sawed, keeping K locked in the workshop while he cut the box down and shortened it to fit neatly into the waterbed's plywood base. Then he loaded the whole thing into the pickup, drove over to the trailer and assembled it. It had to be ready when they moved K.

The first she knew of the new box was when he told her to get in. She had to enter from the end of the bed, crawling in on her hands and knees. Once she was inside, Cameron placed a board across the opening the bolted it shut. This he covered with a panel that he'd cut specially. It fit tightly into place, disguising the opening. Finally, he pushed some steps up against the foot of the bed. Anyone entering the room couldn't help but notice this large, impressive waterbed, with its black vinyl edging; no one would guess a human being was imprisoned underneath.

K found this box not so different from the one she'd already spent so many months in, though it was smaller, more confining, even more coffinlike. And it smelled of sawdust from its recent alteration. The green plastic bedpan was there, and she found her sleeping bag spread across the floor, but the "blower" or hair dryer that had been set up outside the box on Oak Street was now inside the box with her, just inches from her head. A couple of air-holes had been cut in the bottom of the box, and K soon discovered that she could look out and see a tiny spot of the world outside—not much, but enough to tell if it was day or night. And when people walked through the mobile home the floor vibrated, signaling her of traffic she couldn't see.

Other than these small changes, she was encased in the same soporific blackness, the same endless night. And though the address had changed, K's routine hadn't. She was still let out for just an hour or so a day, in the evenings, to eat, brush her teeth, use the bathroom, clean out the bedpan, and help with chores. About every two weeks she was allowed to shower and wash her hair.

Usually Janice prepared her meal—still leftovers or sandwiches or something simple—which Cameron brought to her. She ate in the bathroom and sometimes worked on macrame projects there, staying out of the box for longer periods. In a sense, the bathroom had replaced the workshop that Cameron had disassembled. (He hadn't left much evidence of K's captivity at the Oak Street house, even going back to sweep out the basement to make sure the next tenants would find nothing unusual. But the cement base of the workshop was too heavy to carry upstairs; it had to stay behind—an inscrutable triangular object that may have invited questions, but offered no answers.)

As the Hookers and their slave settled into their new quarters, May 19, 1978, came and went, quietly marking the passing of a year since Colleen Stan's abduction. Then the hot summer months took hold, and day after day the temperature in Red Bluff zoomed past 100 degrees . . . 105 . . . 110 . . . 115. The mobile home broiled beneath the sizzling California sky. A swamp cooler chilled the air in the kitchen and living room where little Cathy and Janice, now noticeably pregnant, spent most of their time, but the bedroom door stayed shut. No cool air relieved the heat in the room where K lay locked in her stuffy, tiny space. She was left to swelter in a box turned to an oven.

On Cameron's day off he would take K out of the box and put her to work in the yard—filling in ditches, cleaning pipes, hoeing weeds. Before getting K out of the box he always had Jan find something for her to wear; she had long ago abandoned the long nightgown as too hot, and he certainly couldn't have her working out in the yard without clothes.

K didn't mind the hard work; at least she was out of the box. But one day Cameron took her out behind the trailer and gave her a job that terrified her. He handed her a shovel and told her to dig a hole, the dimensions of which were ominously rectangular. He offered no explanation, and as she scooped up the dirt, shovelful after shovelful, she couldn't shake the horrifying notion that she was digging her own grave.

But when the hole was finished K was not assaulted with bullets or poison. Rather, to her great relief, she was told to bury a large, heavy plank—a railroad tie. The significance of this escaped her, but Cameron apparently knew what he was doing, for he laid a cement foundation just where it had been buried. And then he started construction.

They needed some sort of outbuilding for storage, and Hooker could use some extra space for his hobbies, so, ever-industrious, he set about building a shed in the backyard. It wasn't a large shed—nowhere near the size of a garage, not even as roomy as that little basement on Oak Street—but it was big enough. And when it was done, Cameron decided to try it out.

He came up with some old clothes for K, got her dressed for the walk outside, and took her out to his latest construction. Once inside, he ordered her to get undressed again, then hung her up by the wrists. That familiar, mean pain shot down her arms and across her back.

Since the move she'd spent most of her time in the box and was no longer used to being hung; the pain hit with fresh intensity. She struggled and thrashed the air with her legs.

Cameron was provoked, but it wasn't until the next week that he gave vent to his anger.

He got K out of the box as he had before and took her out to the shed. Jan was with him this time. He gagged K and then put a cloth over her eyes, taping it about her head. He put the leather cuffs on her wrists, stood her on a bucket, and hooked the cuffs to the rafters. To inhibit her movement, he tied her ankles to a stick, and then kicked the bucket out from under her.

In pain, K swung her legs and made plaintive noises in her throat. Cameron scolded her, warning her to still. "If you'd done it right the first time, you wouldn't have to go through all this," he said. But she continued to fling her legs about, searching for something to lift her weight and ease the strain on her arms.

Then, by the worst luck, she accidentally kicked Jan in the stomach. Cameron was furious that his misbehaving slave had kicked his pregnant wife. She would pay for this. He bolted from the shed and rushed to the house.

Since she was blindfolded, K scarcely realized what she'd done, but she knew she was in trouble.

Cameron returned with a whip. He ordered her to "just hang there and behave!" and lashed at her with the whip. The leather whisked through the air and bit into her, wrapping around her like a snake, leaving a trail of hot, red welts.

K tried to block out the pain and be still. In time, the whipping finally stopped. She hung there, sweating, trying to will herself to be calm, but the unrelenting pain down her arms and sides seemed unbearable. Almost involuntarily, she started kicking her legs again, trying to find something to brace herself on.

Cameron saw this as blatant disobedience. To stop her from kicking, he grabbed her legs and tied them to something heavy—an engine, K thought. Still, she struggled and groaned, her pain only provoking more anger. Cameron decided his unruly slave needed more severe punishment and again he rushed out of the shed to the trailer.

K sensed that Jan remained in the shed with her, though her pregnant mistress said nothing.

In a moment he returned. The door opened and shut. And she heard the first match strike.

K could see a tiny fraction out of the bottom of the blindfold, and she saw the flame as it came close to her breast, watching as it seared her skin. At first she wailed in pain. But then, as he kept burning her, telling her to shut up, striking match after match, burning one breast and then the other, it was almost as if someone else was being burnt. She distanced herself from it, watching the flames flicker next to her nipples, feeling nothing. She didn't even flinch.

It was a subtle act of courage, even of defiance.

At some point K had decided she wouldn't cry in front of Cameron Hooker. He could hang her up, whip her, torture her, but she would withhold her tears. Only when she was alone would she finally weep. In the box. In private. Whatever sadistic pleasure Hooker derived from hurting her, he wouldn't get the satisfaction of seeing her cry. In that, if nothing else, she had complete control.

The slave collar around K's neck tarnished, turning her neck green, and began to deteriorate. According to Hooker, the Company required that every slave wear a collar for identification, so late in the summer he replaced the old collar with something new.

As usual, he offered no explanation of what he was doing. He first put aluminum foil around her neck. Curious. Then he encircled her neck with a thin rod of stainless steel. When he soldered the ends of the steel rod together to make a ring, it became clear that the purpose of the foil was to deflect heat.

K found this collar looser than the first, more comfortable. And Cameron also found it satisfactory: It was permanent.

Whether soldering steel, building sheds, fashioning head boxes or laying cement, Cameron Hooker proved himself a remarkably handy, self-reliant, and motivated man. There were few jobs around the house he wasn't equal to, and some of the things he single-handedly managed were downright amazing.

Not the least of these accomplishments took place on September 4, 1978. Hooker could work wonders with castoff lumber and a few tools; now he would prove adroit with softer materials.

For his own reasons, Hooker didn't put much faith in hospitals, and he didn't want his second child born in one. He told Janice he was afraid someone might switch babies on them. Whether this was a true paranoia or simply a rationale for secret concerns, he made a persuasive argument and convinced his wife that the baby should be born at home. A doctor could be called in case of emergency, the hospital wasn't all that far away, and there was no reason to expect a problem birth. Cameron was fully prepared to deliver their second child himself.

The due date approached and Jan grew larger, enduring the last, heavy weeks of pregnancy in Red Bluff's infamous summer heat. Then, finally, she was in labor.

As her contractions came closer together, Cameron scrubbed up and got some things ready. Then he came and stood in attendance at the side of the bed. His wife panted and pushed, the baby's head crowned, and Cameron welcomed into the world a beautiful baby girl.

The whole while—from the start of labor, through the delivery, even past the cutting of the umbilical cord—K lay just inches below the bed, listening in awe to the unseen miracle of birth.

11

Summer slid into autumn, and from the floor at her elbow to the ceiling at her fingertips, K remained encased in a blackness so dense her hand was invisible just inches from her face. Her routine rolled slowly forward, the long spells of darkness broken only when the panel was pried away and the board unbolted from the foot of the bed. Then she would scoot out into the light to accept work or nourishment or abuse, whatever was dispensed.

For Cameron, the changing seasons signaled the opportunity to engage in a little private enterprise. Rains quenched the dusty ground, the fire danger abated, and the cutting season began. With a permit, he could go into Diamond's timberlands and scavenge lumber, cutting up cedar and oak to sell as fence posts or firewood. Though Hooker was no stranger to hard work, this year he would have his slave's assistance.

Up in the mountains, they set to work, looking for lumber allowed by the permit. Then they measured, cut, and split the trees into posts, bursting the pristine mountain stillness with the nasty growl of the chain saw or the clean staccato of the splitting maul. They labored and sweated, their breaths hanging in the wintry air, and soon the wood was broken into logs that they carried over to the truck, piled into the bed, and hauled home.

For K, it was a treat just to be out in the fresh air, despite her sore muscles and the branches that scratched and tore at her clothes. And for Cameron, with his slave working obediently at his side, this was what he would later call a "perfect" time.

But the Hooker household was on the eve of yet another change.

With gasoline prices soaring, high inflation, and five mouths to feed now, money was tight, so after some discussion it was decided that Janice would look for a job. At twenty-one, Jan didn't have many marketable skills, but she landed a job at Foster's Freeze, a little fast-food place on Main Street.

Jan started work on April 21, 1979, dispensing milkshakes, cones, hamburgers, and sandwiches to lounging teenagers and harried families on tight budgets. The pay was low, but it was better than nothing, and the hours worked out well. While Cameron worked, she could stay home with the kids. When he got off at four, they'd have a brief overlap, and then she'd start work at five, working through the dinner hours until eight or, during the long summer nights, as late as midnight.

Once Jan had gone, Cameron opened the secret panel at the foot of the bed, got K out and brought her into the living room, where she would kneel and ask her master's bidding. Sometimes Jan would have prepared dinner before she left, but as a rule he had K cook dinner. While he and little Cathy ate, K fed and cared for the baby, only sitting down to eat when Cameron gave her permission. Sometimes she was allowed to sit at the table, sometimes told to sit on the floor.

Since K was in the box when Jan left for work and again when she came home, Jan had only a faint idea of what went on while she was gone. Though Cameron told her that he had K cook dinner, it was Jan's understanding that Cameron took care of the girls, and he said nothing to disabuse her of this notion. Still, he saw no reason to burp the baby, change diapers, and wipe up spilled baby food when he had his slave there to do it.

During Jan's employment, K was regularly let out of the box for longer periods. She and Cameron were alone together more often, but Hooker didn't talk to her much. When he did, it was usually about the Company.

His threats and stories continued. More neighbors were moving into the area now, and he told her that some of them were involved with the Company. She believed him. And when she asked about possibly seeing her parents, he told her the Company wouldn't allow it, that no slave had ever been allowed to visit their families after signing the slavery contract and that she should forget her past and her family.

Steeped in Hooker's lies, K remained servile and compliant during her three or four hours of limited nocturnal freedom. She was a good slave. She showered when Cameron gave his permission. She did macrame projects as Jan instructed. She continued to address them as Sir and Ma'am.

During the summer, K's only clothing was a couple of pairs of shorts and two tank tops that the Hookers had provided, but (as stipulated in the contract) no underwear.

Hooker underscored his control over her with more drills. He started taking her out for exercise, making her run. In the evenings, after Jan had left for work, he loaded up his daughters and his slave and drove out east of town to Hogsback Road, a long, winding dirt road that stretches east, all the way to Lassen National Forest. The first part of Hogsback Road is paved, but they proceeded to a more remote area, past open pasture and neglected signs that local boys had used for target practice, signs declaring "Range Cattle," and "This Road Is Not Maintained Beyond This Point. Proceed At Your Own Risk."

With no one around to observe, Cameron stopped the car, told K to get out, and ordered her to run down the road. She took off at a trot, Cameron driving the car slowly alongside. On the first occasion that he did this, K was quickly winded and wanted to stop, but when she slowed he leaned out the window and barked, "You better not stop or I'll beat the hell out of you!" She kept jogging. When he thought she'd run far enough, he topped off the exercise session by ordering her to strip off her clothes and swim laps in a pond just off the side of the road.

This was just the first incident; Hooker took her out for runs on Hogsback Road several times.

As the calendar peeled off month after month and K's captivity stretched past its second anniversary into its third year, Cameron tackled the problem of pursuing his interests within the cramped confines of the trailer. His hobby of construction came in handy.

The ceiling of the living room, Hooker found, was too weak to support the weight of a hanging woman. He tried to hang Jan, but to his great annoyance the screws pulled out. So Cameron set to work building a sturdy, rectangular structure which he dubbed the frame.

It stood about six feet or more off the ground, with hooks at the top so that the leather cuffs could be easily affixed. The structure wasn't completely stable, so when set up in the living room, it was supported by a rope that wrapped around the top of the frame and through a hook in the ceiling. And it was bulky and awkward, so Hooker had to keep it outside, next to the woodpile.

In the fall of 1979, as a punishment for failing to follow directions on a macrame project, K was strapped to the frame and shocked with electrical wires. She was shocked several times before Hooker was finally satisfied that she'd learned her lesson. More than traumatizing her, more than sending current ripping through her nerves, the electric shocks scorched her skin. Within hours, blisters erupted at the four points where the wires had touched, and though the marks on her breasts eventually faded, her thighs were permanently scarred.[1]

This was punishment, but other incidents were clearly meant simply for Cameron Hooker's entertainment.

The day that K was introduced to the "stretcher," for instance, Cameron took her out of the box, put leather cuffs on her wrists and ominously announced: "I'm not doing this to punish you. I'm doing this because I enjoy it."

The stretcher was a construction of almost medieval design: two heavy boards nailed in a T-shape, with a winch affixed to the bottom and hooks at each end of the cross. He put K down on it, securing the cuffs to the hooks at the top,

---

1. Hooker later told her these scars were sufficient identification for the Company. He then put both hands on the stainless steel slave collar and broke it from around her neck.

locking her ankles to the chain that wrapped around the winch.

When she was securely fastened, he started turning the winch, tightening the chain. It clicked metallically, stretching her tighter and tighter. When it reached a certain tension, he used a steel bar to keep the winch from unwinding, then felt the tautness of her body before tightening the chain some more.

The cuffs sliced into the tender skin of her wrists, cutting off her circulation. Her whole body ached, and the constant pull on her diaphragm made it difficult to breathe. She panted in quick, short breaths, her hands, wrists, ribs, legs and ankles screaming a message of pain.

But this wasn't entertainment enough for Cameron Hooker. He put his hands around her neck and strangled her, choking her until she blacked out. Then he eased his grip, waited until she started to come to, and squeezed her throat again.

When K flickered back into consciousness she was seized with terror. She didn't realize he'd relaxed his hold long enough to let her breathe, but only knew that he was choking her, strangling her, and she was facing death.

Finally he relaxed his grip and she gasped for air. He told her to beg for mercy. She tried to croak out some words, but it was difficult to speak. Hooker chided her for begging so poorly.

At some point he'd taken off his clothes; that K was in so much pain excited him. Now, before she even had a chance to recover from being strangled, he forced her to give him oral sex.

K's entire ordeal on the stretcher lasted about an hour—sixty minutes of suffocation and pain. At one point Cameron put so much tension on her that one of the metal hooks broke and her arm snapped free. Furious, he unlocked her from the stretcher and hung her again on the frame.

But this was just her initiation. Another day, Hooker locked her down on the stretcher and raped her. And once he stretched her so intensely and for such a long period that he cut off the circulation in her hands. When he let her up she couldn't move them.

Seeing this, he knew he'd gone too far. He rushed her into
the bathroom and put her hands under hot running water,
trying to get the circulation going again. Slowly, she
regained control of her hands and fingers, but he'd stretched
her so severely that her sides and back continued to ache.
For a week it hurt so much to lie on her sides that it made
her cry, so she had to lie flat on her back in the box.

Hooker used the frame, the stretcher, and other devices
on both his wife and his slave, but K never saw Jan hung or
whipped. She was always kept out of the way until Hooker
wanted to include her. Jan, on the other hand, saw K hung,
whipped, and abused, though only a portion of the times this
took place.

Cameron was meanwhile clever enough to maintain the
pretense that he had no sexual involvement with K. He
often got her out of the box when Jan and the kids had gone
shopping or visiting relatives. If they came back early, he
made them wait outside while he hustled K back into the
box and got rid of the bondage and torture equipment. Jan
accepted this as in keeping with their agreement and chose
to believe that Cameron limited his exploits with K to hanging, whipping, and bondage. In fact, Cameron Hooker subjected his slave to many kinds of sexual abuse, including
rape and sodomy.

Jan's blindness to the sexual nature of K's captivity seems
astonishing in light of Cameron's initiation of sexual contact
between the two women.

One afternoon he took K out of the box and had her sit on
the floor. He handed her a bottle of cheap wine and told her
to drink. Dissatisfied with her dainty sips, he tipped the
bottle up and made her guzzle it. Then he declared that as
an obedience test the Company wanted her to have oral sex
with Jan, whom he tied to the bed.

When K was put back in the box she was ill. And while
she vomited into her bedpan, she could hear the Hookers
having sex above her.

With K now being let out of the box more frequently,
there was more danger of her being discovered. Janice's parents stopped by at least once a week, and Dexter, Cameron's

brother, came by fairly often as well. So Cameron and Jan were careful about when they let her out. If they had unexpected visitors, their watchdog would bark so they had time to rush K back into the box before letting their guests inside. Usually.

One day they had gotten her out of the box to do chores, and she was down on her hands and knees in that blue terrycloth nightgown, scrubbing the floor of the hallway. Suddenly, without knocking, Cameron's father opened the front door.

Instantly, Cameron swept K off into the bedroom, and while Jan kept up a conversation with his father, he quickly found some clothes for her to put on. He hurried K back into the living room in a ridiculous, ill-fitting outfit of checks and plaids, and introduced her to his father as "Kay," a friend who had come over to help them out around the house. Then he announced that he'd better be taking "Kay" home and propelled her out the door.

Outside, he rushed her over to the shed, locked her inside, hurried over to his pickup, got in, and drove off. He drove around to kill ten or fifteen minutes, then casually returned to his wife and father at the trailer.

It had been a close call, but Mr. Hooker neither raised awkward questions nor seemed the least suspicious. After he left, Cameron retrieved K from the shed and put her back in the box. Life in the brown and yellow mobile home off Pershing Road went on pretty much undisturbed.

PART FOUR

Dangerous Precedents

December 7, 1984–January 1985

People saw in me weaknesses in themselves that they were afraid of—like fears that they could be broken down. It's hard for people to face that.

Patty Hearst

12

Conventional wisdom among many local lawyers had it that Christine McGuire was in way over her head. With only a few years' experience as a DA, McGuire was still considered a neophyte, and the Hooker case promised to be extremely complex. Moreover, her opponent, Rolland Papendick, was older, more experienced, and had a sterling reputation.

McGuire wasn't aware of her colleagues' presentiments, but she was fully conscious of Papendick's high standing in the legal community. One of her peers once commented with obvious admiration that "Papendick is always way ahead of the rest of us. He's doing things we've never even thought of."

Before going into private practice, Papendick had worked in the district attorney's office in neighboring Shasta County, where he'd not only mastered prosecution but had established a reputation for superior professional acumen. Now, working on the side of the defense, he wasn't intimidated by district attorneys and could often anticipate their moves.

But this wasn't McGuire's first face-off with Papendick. During past trials she'd found him resourceful, adroit, and shrewd. He'd outmaneuvered her at times, but she had yet to lose a case to him.

Faced with a difficult case and a skilled opponent, McGuire's strategy was, as always, simply to work harder.

With the preliminary hearing just days behind her, she was already planning for the trial, sitting at the kitchen table with papers spread about as if she were studying for a law school exam. She sifted through the facts gleaned from the preliminary hearing, reviewed lists of evidence, and had a gut feeling she needed more.

The box, by itself, was fairly convincing evidence. But it was difficult to imagine anyone actually staying in it, sleeping in it, living in it, and hard to picture it set within a pedestal beneath a waterbed. The idea was too outlandish. McGuire didn't want a jury of twelve unknown men and women having to strain to imagine the scene; she wanted them to see it, to climb into the box and lie in it. If they had questions about whether it was *possible* to keep a woman in a box beneath a bed, let them try it out for themselves.

She decided on another search warrant; she wanted that bed.

It was a Friday night, and officers Al Shamblin and Mack McCall may have begrudged the prosecutor her interruption of their personal lives, but they obliged her request: The officers went back to the Hookers' trailer, let the water out of the mattress, unbolted the frame, and brought the whole bulky set-up to police headquarters to be logged in as evidence.

As the investigation advanced, parts of Colleen's and Jan's stories received outside corroboration. But while police continued with interviews and the footwork of building a case, McGuire struggled with legal foundations and technicalities. What she found was discouraging.

With so many crimes occurring over such a long period of time, the Hooker case had major statute of limitations problems. And in searching for legal precedents, McGuire found nothing comparable. Kidnapping, enslavement, prolonged captivity, and sado-masochism—Colleen Stan had endured a singularly brutal ordeal. There was simply no precedent for it.

But while the duration and combination of crimes was highly unusual, taken singly, they weren't so rare. McGuire therefore rolled up her sleeves and researched the crimes one at a time.

First, the kidnapping. From the start, she'd been wrestling with the problem that the statute of limitations for kidnapping is only three years. Since Colleen's kidnap had occurred in 1977 and Hooker hadn't been charged until 1984, the three-year statute had lapsed. On the face of it, Hooker could not not be convicted on that count.

But when filing the Information,[1] some distant recollection had rumbled in the back of McGuire's mind, making her think she could get the kidnap charge to stick. Now something clicked into place, and that persistent rumbling suddenly came out as one clear word: Parnell.

She pulled out the Annotated California Penal Code, and flipped through its pages until she found *Parnell* v. *Superior Court,* a precedent-setting case in which the defendant was charged with kidnapping, false imprisonment, and miscellaneous sex offenses. The facts of the case were as follows:

On December 4, 1972, a seven-year-old boy, Steven, was abducted by two men as he was walking home from school in Merced, California. The men, Kenneth Parnell and Ervin Murphy, held the boy in a cabin for a short time, Parnell telling the child that he'd gone to court to obtain custody of him. He changed the boy's hair color, gave Steven sleeping pills when he would be left unattended and after three weeks left Murphy behind, taking the child with him to Santa Rosa, California.

Over the next several years, Parnell and the boy moved from town to town, Steven attending school as Dennis Parnell. Parnell committed sodomy on the boy and involved him in acts of oral copulation. Beyond threats of spankings, however, there was little actual physical restraint or punishment.

Seven years passed. Though it was mandatory that Steven obtain Parnell's permission before leaving his presence, the boy was frequently unsupervised and apparently free to come and go. He rode bicycles, stayed overnight at the homes of friends, and went on school outings. In high school, he joined the football team and participated in out-of-town games.

On February 14, 1980, Steven came home to find that

---

1. The legal term for the actual charges brought against the defendant based on the evidence presented at the preliminary hearing.

Parnell had abducted another boy, a five-year-old by the name of Timmy. Two weeks later, while Parnell was at work, the two boys hitchhiked from Parnell's cabin in Manchester to the nearby town of Ukiah, where Steven led Timmy to the door of the police station and instructed the younger boy on how to turn himself in. When Steven turned to go, Timmy got frightened and ran after him, attracting the attention of the police, who then stopped and questioned both of them. Though it took some coaxing, Steven finally disclosed that he, too, had been abducted.[2]

Ordinarily, prosecution for the kidnapping of Steven would have been barred because no complaint had been filed within the three-year statute of limitations. But when Parnell was tried in 1981, the court held for the first time that the defendant could be prosecuted for kidnapping even though the statute of limitations had elapsed because the victim was held by the threat of force, and that as long as such detention continues, the crime of kidnapping continues.

Here it was, the sole precedent for continuous kidnapping. If McGuire could prove that the kidnapping was continuous, she could counter a defense based on the statue of limitations argument.

But while the Parnell case helped, it differed factually from the Hooker case. In both the Parnell and the Hooker cases, the victim had been held for seven years, but the Parnell case involved a minor—a seven-year-old. Parnell was able to continue the kidnap, the court found, by exercising his "parental authority," an argument that McGuire certainly couldn't use in Colleen Stan's case.

From Papendick's line of questioning at the preliminary hearing, it was already clear that he planned to base his defense on the issue of consent. Colleen stayed, he contended, because she'd fallen in love with her captor. And if Colleen had consented to stay, not only would the statute of limitations have elapsed on the kidnap charge, but the rape charges would be nullified as well.

---

2. Cal. App. 3d, *Parnell* v. *Superior Court,* 119 Cal. App. 3d, 392 at 173.

What was it, then, that made Colleen stay?

Janice Hooker had already offered her own distinctly un-conventional explanation: brainwashing. Police had aired the brainwashing theory to the press shortly before the pre-liminary hearing, and a handful of articles appeared linking this case to mind control.

But McGuire instantly rejected this argument as ridicu-lously melodramatic and legally unsupportable. It was diffi-cult enough for defense attorneys to claim that clients were not guilty due to insanity, but basing a prosecution on so unlikely an argument as brainwashing seemed absolutely foolhardy. As far as she knew, it had never even been at-tempted. And while the prosecutor could accept that Col-leen had stayed with the Hooker's out of fear, she found it implausible that anyone as coherent and apparently normal as Colleen Stan could have been subjected to mind control.

A startling story was published in a Chico newspaper on December 20, the same day that Hooker was arraigned on eighteen felony counts. Headlined "Hooker Being Probed in Another Abduction," the article was the first public disclo-sure that Cameron Hooker was suspected of having kid-napped and murdered Marie Elizabeth Spannhake, an eigh-teen-year-old Chico woman, in 1976.

Sergeant Earl Summers, Chief of the Chico Police Detec-tive Unit, told reporters that Janice Hooker had given police a detailed account of the five-foot-five-inch, 110-pound woman's abduction, murder, and burial.

But in Red Bluff, forty miles northwest of Chico, the story was quickly hushed up. Police Lieutenant Jerry Brown re-fused all comment on the Spannhake case. And when Police Chief John Faulkner was asked about the alleged murder, his answer was guarded: "The only comment we will make is that we are conducting an investigation to ascertain if Hooker had any involvement in the disappearance of Miss Spannhake."

Despite law enforcement's attempt to keep the investiga-tion under wraps, other newspapers quickly picked up the story. And as the news spread that Hooker was suspected of murder, his defense attorney noticed a change in the tenor of public opinion.

Since Hooker's arrest in November, Rolland Papendick had received calls from irate friends, relatives, and coworkers who wished to testify on Cameron's behalf. But after the Chico story the tenor of the calls changed. Now Papendick noted that instead of saying "No Way!" people began to ask, "Do you think he really did all that?"

It was time, Papendick decided, to seriously consider a change of venue.

On January 4, Deputy DA McGuire interviewed an amicable, heavily made-up blonde by the name of Connie Fleming, who offered new insights into Janice Hooker's character. Janice had asked Connie for advice a few days before she contacted the police. Fleming, a receptionist whom Janice had met by chance at a doctor's office, revealed that Janice had come to her with serious personal questions about strength, initiative, guilt, and fear.

Connie painted Janice as a deeply troubled woman, whose struggle with her conscience finally compelled her to go to the police. This was news to McGuire. After dealing with Jan as an extremely uncooperative witness, she felt little sympathy for Mrs. Hooker. Now she began to understand more of her complexity.

According to Fleming, Jan was close to a nervous breakdown when she finally contacted police. Jan had told her that fear was "taking over her body." When Fleming asked what she was afraid of, Janice was at first reluctant to say but finally admitted that it was her husband. She stated that he was evil, then related some of the shocking details of their relationship.

Janice also told Fleming about the kidnapping. Jan said that Colleen had fought Cameron for a long time, but she'd been severely punished, and Cameron had scared her with stories of "the Company." Eventually, Jan had told her, "Colleen was brainwashed."

Brainwashed. The word came up again and again. But what did "brainwash" really mean?

After Fleming left, McGuire flipped through her dictionary and found: "The systematic alteration of personal convictions, beliefs, habits, and attitudes by means of intensive, coercive indoctrination."[3]

She sighed. Though she knew Colleen Stan had been subjected to extremes of mental domination, she continued to feel that introducing brainwashing into her legal argument would only hurt her case. It was an almost untried issue, with virtually no legal precedent except one major and controversial trial: *United States* v. *Hearst,* 412 F.Supp. 889 (1976).

In February of 1974, nineteen-year-old Patricia Hearst was forceably kidnapped and, like Colleen, subjected to isolation, humiliation, and terror. Bound and blindfolded, Hearst was locked inside a closet and kept totally dependent on her captors. They made her eat with the blindfold still in place, controlled her bodily functions and hygiene, and sexually abused her. After about eight weeks, Patty's captors let her out of the closet, took off her blindfold, and incorporated her into the Symbionese Liberation Army. Like Colleen, who was given the slave name K, Patty Hearst was given a new name, Tania.

Comparisons between Patty Hearst and Colleen Stan were obvious—the press had already drawn parallels—and in truth, McGuire felt that Colleen and Patty had much in common. But Colleen had been subjected to much more severe treatment and for a much longer period of time. Patty Hearst spent about eight weeks in a closet; Colleen spent years in a box. Patty was allowed to bathe once a week; Colleen went for three months without a bath, then was nearly drowned and bathed infrequently thereafter. Both were threatened with death, but Colleen encountered that threat in a far more painful, real way, being repeatedly whipped, hung, strangled, burned, even electrocuted.

But to a legal mind, the crux of the matter was not the kidnapping or the extent of suffering, but the fact that in February of 1976, just two years after her abduction, Patty Hearst found herself on trial for a bank robbery she partici-

---

3. *The Reader's Digest Great Encyclopedic Dictionary,* 1977, Reader's Digest Association Far East Ltd.

pated in while under the control of the SLA. Her defense was that she had been brainwashed, or "coerced." The court even allowed an expert to testify on this point, since it lay beyond the common experience of most jurors.

Nonetheless, Patricia Campbell Hearst was found guilty of armed robbery and of using a firearm to commit a felony. She was sentenced to seven years in prison.

This was a lesson that Deputy DA McGuire couldn't afford to ignore. Brainwashing was not easily proved, even by the best attorneys. Being conservative in her legal approach, she didn't want to try to set precedents to risk comparisons between Colleen Stan and Patricia Hearst.

In Colleen's best interest, McGuire was inclined to shy away from any argument so untried and reckless as brainwashing.

PART FIVE

Homecoming

Late 1979–March 1981

Sometimes I feel that being your slave has made me more of a woman. But then there are other times when I feel it has made me less of a woman. You know how to make me feel good about myself. And I love you so much for it. I only wish that my dreams could be fulfilled with you. Because I feel a strong love and need to be with you. I'll always serve you with singleness of heart.

K

13

K's captivity spanned such a long period that single days became lost in the flood of months and seasons. Her days varied little from day to day, and simple repetition caused days and events to blur and run together. Certain occasions, especially birthdays and holidays, served as measures by which to gauge the ebb and flow of her enslavement, but even these got lost and confused in the monotonous, unrelenting push of time.

Late in 1979, for instance, Janice asked K what she would like for a gift. K thought it was to be a Christmas gift; Jan recalls that it was for K's birthday, December 31, when K would turn twenty-three. In any case, K didn't ask for anything at first, but after some thought got up the nerve to tell Jan she would like a Bible. Cameron and Jan bought one for her. It doesn't really matter whether they intended it as a birthday present or as a Christmas gift, because K received nothing on either of these occasions.

The Hookers didn't present their slave with the Bible until January 11, and this date is certain, for the front of the Holy Book was ceremoniously dated and signed. Cameron and Jan signed their real names, and Jan wrote in that the Bible belonged to "Kay Powers," using Colleen Stan's full slave name.

Now K had inspiration fueling the prayers that wove through her waking hours. Whenever she had the chance, she read the Bible in the light of the back bathroom. She read it hungrily, absorbing what she could to sustain her through the deprivation that was her daily routine. And when it came time to climb back into the box, God went with her into that blackness beneath the bed. She knew it.

About this time, K's enslavement began a slow but dramatic evolution. She entered a period of relative liberty, a time that she would loosely refer to as "the year out."

The texture of her captivity changed. She was gradually let out for longer periods and given more responsibilities with less supervision. She was allowed to work outdoors in the Hookers' vegetable garden, which she found such a joy that she often started at the break of day, working outdoors in the fresh air with an almost maniacal zeal. Meanwhile, babysitting became totally K's province, and she committed herself to the little girls' care with singleminded devotion. In time, she was even permitted to go into town, to shop, to meet and talk to people—things she hadn't experienced for three years, things that Colleen Stan used to do, but K had never done.

K had gradually come to accept that it was her lot in life to be a slave. And she tried to be a good one—even Cameron could see that. During the course of her captivity she had proved again and again that she was hardworking, subservient, and—most important—that she could be trusted not to do anything foolish.

But as a precaution Cameron continually emphasized the threat of the Company. His lies grew and twisted like wellwatered weeds, and K harvested them as truth. He often attributed her treatment to Company orders. The punishments, the drills, the bizarre tortures and sex acts weren't his idea, but the policy of cold and distant leaders.

He told her, for example, that since she was being let out of the box the Company needed further identification. Having removed the second slave collar, he now said the scars on her upper thighs wouldn't be sufficient. So, after piercing it himself with an ordinary needle, Hooker inserted a gold earring through her right labia.

One of K's first excursions out of the mobile home came early in 1980. The Hookers got her out of the box, told her to shower, and fixed her up with some of Jan's clothes, a new hairdo, and a bit of makeup. To her amazement, she was told she was going to go out dancing with Janice.

Jan and K went out on the town while Cameron stayed home with the girls. It was Jan's idea: She drove, she paid for everything; K simply went along—with Cameron's approval.

At a local bar called The New Orleans, they drank beer, danced, and even met a couple of men, who invited them to Sambo's for coffee afterward. From there, they accompanied the men to an apartment. Jan and her date went together into his bedroom; K and the other fellow stayed in the living room, talking very little, until the two came out. Then Jan took K back home and put her in the box.

At twenty-two, after five years of an increasingly rocky marriage, Jan probably did this as a way of both eliciting jealousy from Cameron and of combatting her own jealousy toward K. But try as she might, she wouldn't be able to provoke the same jealous rumbling within Cameron that she felt within herself. He just wasn't made that way. He cared so little that he even gave Jan permission to date other men.

For a couple of months, Jan continued to date the guy she met at the bar that night, with Cameron's knowledge but with no apparent jealousy. The affair was short-lived. Jan had another brief interlude, but that affair also died quickly and quietly.

Her discontent and frustration evidently continued unabated.

Jan lost her job at Foster's Freeze in January, and money was tight again at the Hooker residence, but Cameron hit on a plan to make some extra cash: He decided to put K to work.

The big excursion fell on Easter weekend. As shops around town did a brisk business in chocolate bunnies and fancy baskets, Cameron got K out of the box and told her they were going to Reno. He didn't say why.

It was well after dark when they finally pulled onto Reno's neon-lit streets, and though it was already late, Cameron promptly put K to work. He'd met another slaveowner, he told her, who had bragged about how much money his slave had made panhandling at a concert. Cameron had bet that *his* slave could do better, and so K for about four hours found herself walking up and down the sidewalk, asking strangers for spare change. She didn't get much, but all the money, of course, went to Cameron.

They slept that night in the pickup, parked in the MGM Grand parking lot. The next morning, after an inexpensive breakfast, he put her to work along the main strip again. Later, he took her over to the Civic Center, where the Jehovah's Witnesses were having a convention, and she stood outside and panhandled for some time. This was a more generous crowd.

In all, K stood out in the cold asking for money for about six hours that day, with Cameron watching, most of the time, from within the heated pickup. At the end of the day, she gave all the money to Cameron, and they finally headed back to Red Bluff, with Cameron stopping on the way home to buy an Easter Lily for Janice.

The panhandling didn't prove especially lucrative, but after their excursion to Reno Cameron possessed the exhilarating knowledge that K would do her best to follow his orders not only at home, with the threat of the whip nearby, but unaccompanied and in public. She hated begging for money—she even complained to him about it—but she did as she was told.

In total, Cameron Hooker had K panhandle for him on four occasions: that one time in Reno, once in Red Bluff at the Raley's supermarket parking lot, where she asked for spare change until a man from Raley's told her to leave; and twice in the nearby town of Redding, one day at both Payless Drug Store and McDonald's, and another day at the Mt. Shasta Mall.

It's true that while she was out mingling with the crowds, K could have tried to run away, pleaded for help, or told somebody that she was being held captive. But from her point of view that was worse than useless, it was dangerous. No matter where she went, the Company would track her down, capture her, torture her, probably kill her. And if she went home—the only place she wanted to go—she would only be putting her family in jeopardy. She couldn't risk it.

* * *

More people had moved into the neighborhood now, and
when they wandered over to the mobile home at the end of
the lane for a friendly chat, the young woman laboring in
the Hookers' garden required some introduction. She was
"Kay," the neighbors were told, their live-in babysitter and
housekeeper.

K wasn't overly friendly with the neighbors. Cameron
had warned her not to speak to anyone, Jan included, unless
spoken to. She could answer questions and respond politely,
but wasn't to volunteer conversation. And when others were
around she should forgo the usual rules of kneeling to ask
permission and of calling Janice "Ma'am" and Cameron
"Sir" or "Master." Their master/slave relationship, in short,
was to remain invisible to outsiders.

And it did. None of the neighbors thought too long or
hard about the ménage à trois in their vicinity. The Hooker
family seemed fairly ordinary, and "Kay" was pleasant
enough, if a bit shy. The only hint of anything odd was
"Kay's" poverty. Day after day, she was out working in the
garden or walking the kids or mowing the lawn in the same
old clothes.

About two hundred feet to the east lived Dorothy and Al
Coppa, the Hookers' closest neighbors. They had moved
into their single-wide trailer shortly after the Hookers.
Though they didn't know Jan and Cameron particularly
well, they maintained a warm neighborliness—lending tools
and assistance, chatting about weather and soil—but to a
couple as secretive as the Hookers, their outgoingness could
easily be mistaken for intrusion.

Al first glimpsed K working around the Hookers' property shortly after they moved in, but wasn't introduced to
her until many months later. He was told that Cameron and
Jan had picked up "Kay" while she was hitchhiking and
were giving her a place to stay. It sounded temporary, yet
she stayed and stayed.

Over the months, he and his wife, Dorothy, a matronly
woman with graying hair and a soft voice, took a liking to
the Hookers' live-in babysitter and housekeeper. "Kay"
seemed sweet, likable, and hardworking, though a bit on the

quiet side and notably waifish. (Seeing that "Kay" had few clothes, they once passed on a pair of Al's jeans, saying that he'd gotten too fat to wear them.)

Sometimes the Hookers' two little girls would wander over to visit, and when K came to retrieve them, Dorothy would take the opportunity to talk with her for a few minutes (though K was always careful about what she said—gardening, the children, and religion were safe topics). For a while, Dorothy tried to get "Kay" to come to church with her, but "Kay" seemed oddly hesitant to go and reluctant even to discuss it.

With K's new freedom she was even allowed to go jogging, unsupervised and on a regular basis, though she had to ask permission each time, of course, and Cameron delineated the route she should take. He even timed her, so he knew it took fifteen minutes for her to jog the mile-long course.

K usually ran in the evening, while the Hookers were eating dinner. She jogged down the dirt road and turned right at the end of the lane, savoring the fresh air and the company of the Hookers' little dog, Misty, who trotted along beside her. More than just a healthy work-out, this was private time, a brief interlude of independence, a respite from the demands the Hookers put on her, and something she did just for herself. For a few minutes, she felt free.

But to keep the specter of the Company ever-present, Cameron told K that neighborhood members would be watching. And one evening she had this confirmed.

Cameron had told her that he was planning to go to a Company meeting in Sacramento on Sunday. It happened that as she jogged past the home of one of the neighbors, Mr. George, he was standing outside talking to his father, who also lived nearby, and she overheard them mention plans to go to Sacramento the next day, too.

Pure coincidence, but this chance encounter reinforced K's belief that members of the Company were actually in the neighborhood spying on her. She was sure now that Mr. George and his father were involved with the Company. She imagined that Mr. George looked down on her because she was a slave, and when his dog chased after her as she jogged by, she believed he had sicced it on her.

One day Al Coppa hailed K as she was jogging past. She stopped, and it turned out that Al just wanted to chat. He couldn't have known how distressing this idle conversation was to K, who was acutely aware that Cameron was timing her. She'd never been late before, and she was afraid of what might happen if she was. Though she was anxious to get back, she didn't want to be rude to Al, so she spoke with him a few minutes before hurrying back to the trailer.

She came in fifteen minutes late. Both Jan and Cameron were furious. They said they'd just put in a call to someone in the Company to chase her down and implied gruesome consequences if she'd been caught. "It's lucky that you got back in when you did," they told her.

She didn't get to go jogging much after that.

Jan's summer return to the job market precipitated a major turn in K's captivity. Jan's new job at the Pac-Out, a fast-food place in Redding, required that she be away from home during the day, when Cameron was working, so in the mornings Jan and Cameron rode to work together, leaving K at home to babysit the girls. For the first time, K was now out of the box with neither Jan nor Cameron there to supervise.

She did not run screaming to the neighbors. She did not call the police. She did nothing that might provoke the ire of the Company. Rather, K did her chores, minded the children, and did as she was told. She was not a troublemaker.

Around this time Cameron initiated an important change in K's sleeping quarters: instead of being locked in the box every night, she slept on a sleeping bag on the floor of the back bathroom. Most of the time she was chained to the toilet.

Grim as it sounds, the five-foot chain around her neck at least allowed her to stand and move around. After more than three years of sleeping and waking encased within a space smaller than a closet, unable even to sit up and having to use the bedpan in a prone position, being shut up inside the tiny bathroom of a mobile home came as a dramatic relief.

While in some ways K's conditions improved, the physical and sexual abuse became a regular occurrence. K was raped repeatedly: while hung on the frame, tied to the stretcher, hanging in the shed, or bound in other ways. But Cameron was always careful about shielding his daughters from this; he waited until Jan and the girls were out shopping or visiting someone before he got out his bondage and torture equipment.

Though the girls were still very young and the Hookers tried to protect them from the unsavory side of K's role, raising them with a slave around the house was sometimes problematic.

One morning Cathy got up before her parents. Knowing that K was in the bathroom, she opened the door and asked her to fix her some cereal.

"I'm sorry, honey, I can't," K told her.

At age three, Cathy couldn't understand the chain around K's neck, or why K, who usually made her breakfast, wouldn't come to the kitchen to do so. She asked again.

"Well, maybe if you go ask your daddy, he'll let K make your breakfast," she finally suggested.

That's what Cathy did, and she got her breakfast. But Cameron wasn't happy about what K had said to his daughter or that Cathy had seen her chained to the toilet. From then on, K was to lock the bathroom door from the inside in case one of the girls tried to get in.

Working at the Pac-Out meant that Jan was having to commute about thirty miles to Redding and back every day. After a couple of months, she quit and found a new job in Red Bluff with a small electronics firm called JLA. Jan worked "prepping" parts, or cutting out parts to fit onto assembly boards.

JLA was then doing such a brisk business that they were having trouble keeping up with demand. Hearing opportunity knocking, Jan got her boss's permission to bring work home. When Cameron came by to pick her up in the evening, they would load the small machine that cut the parts into the car and would bring it with them. K would do the work that night, and then Jan returned the next morning with both the machine and the newly cut parts.

This arrangement worked out well at first, but Jan's boss disliked paying time-and-a-half for the extra work. He suggested that she fill in another job application so the work could be paid at a straight time wage. Jan brought home an application and Cameron told K to fill it out with her maiden name, Colleen Martin. JLA was soon issuing checks to her, which she signed over to the Hookers so they could deposit the money into their checking account.

During this time of unparalleled freedom, K resumed asking to see her family, and Hooker took a softer position, perhaps because he was now so confident of his control. On three occasions he allowed her to write to her sister, though she had to limit the contents to vague and mundane matters. She told her sister that she was living with a family, taking care of the kids, and learning to can fruit (she even enclosed some recipes). But, of course, she wasn't allowed to give a return address.

Cameron checked the letters carefully, making her rewrite some sections before he posted them from a nearby town.

Still, these unanswerable letters did little to allay her yearning to see or hear from her family, and she kept pestering Cameron for the chance to contact them. Now, for the first time, he relented and let her phone home.

He took her and his daughters to a pay phone in Chico, a small college town about forty miles southeast of Red Bluff. With many admonitions about what she could and couldn't say, he let K call.

As Cameron stood next to her, she dialed her father's number and listened to it ring. Her younger sister, Bonnie, answered. It had been so many years since she'd heard from Colleen that she didn't recognize her voice. "Who is this?" she asked.

The strange voice replied, "It's your sister, Colleen."

A brief and emotional conversation ensued. Colleen told her sister she was all right and learned that everyone was well except one aunt, who had cancer. And though she'd known at the time of the kidnap that her stepmother was expecting, K learned for the first time that in September of 1977 she'd given birth to a baby girl, Leslie. Now Leslie was nearly three.

Practicing the restraint she'd learned over years as Hooker's slave, K tearfully divulged only as much as Cameron would permit. But Bonnie, also in tears, peppered her sister with questions. "Where are you?" she asked.

Colleen was evasive, saying only that she was "up north." And when her sister asked why she hadn't written more often, Colleen simply didn't answer.

Too soon, Cameron told her to hang up, but this fleeting contact with her sister was as precious as any gift her master could have given her. She was deeply grateful that she'd finally been allowed to call home.

In fact, K now found many reasons to be thankful. Besides being given permission to contact her family, she was out of the box and afforded numerous small freedoms. These, coupled with her growing acceptance of her slave status, affected K in ways she didn't fully understand. During "the year out"—despite the victimization and brutalization, despite the continued hangings and abuse, despite the fact that Cameron raped her so frequently that when he told her to shower, she knew what was coming and started shaking as she washed—K started expressing love for her captor.

No hearts or flowers or valentines, this was certainly love outside the common realm and a long way from most pop-forty love songs, but K told Cameron that she loved him.

Telling him this seemed to soften the edge of mistreatment. He showed a bit more leniency and granted small concessions, though she was still quite clearly the slave and he the master.

This must have come as a sublime affirmation for Cameron. The books and articles were right! All women really wanted was to be dominated, and this proved it. His vocabulary of love was one of pain and subjugation and absolute obedience; K loved and respected him because he was powerful. Now he had achieved the ultimate relationship, one of absolute domination and submission.

Difficult as it is to imagine, Cameron Hooker also pro-

fessed love for his slave. He shared with her his secret fantasies for the future. The whole family would move to the
Lake Tahoe area, he said, where she would have her own
private cabin. At one point he told her that the gold ring in
her labia, more than just identification for the Company,
was a symbolic wedding ring. Someday, he said, she would
be his slave wife, and they would have children together.

Meanwhile, the relationship between Janice and K teetered on the brink of hostility. K's perception of Jan was
filtered through Cameron's stories; K was afraid of her. And
since he had told her not to talk to Jan, their contact was
mostly limited to giving and taking orders. Their lives
moved in parallel, but they rarely connected, and they coexisted uneasily, sporadically bickering over household matters.

Jan had mixed feelings toward this other woman in the
house: She was both jealous of and sorry for her. If K put on
makeup or cooked something special for dinner, Jan perceived it as an attempt to garner favor with her husband, so
while she felt guilty about keeping a slave, she also felt
threatened. She nagged Cameron to let her go.

Only the faintest glimmer of the ongoing tension at the
Hooker residence became visible to outsiders: One day K
was so upset by something Jan had said that she risked
alarming the Company by doing something she was not supposed to do.

K had apparently developed an attachment to the kind
and motherly Mrs. Coppa and on this day paid her the ultimate compliment of seeking her out for consolation. No one
was home except the kids, and they were napping. She decided she could slip away for just a minute. To Dorothy
Coppa's surprise, K showed up at her door in tears.

Upset as she was, K wouldn't say what was wrong except
that it had something to do with Jan. This was as much as
she dared risk; her fear of the Company prohibited her from
saying more.

Mrs. Coppa hugged her, offering what comfort she could,
and K's tears gradually abated. Since Jan seemed to be the
problem, Dorothy proposed that if K wanted to move out,

she could stay with some friends of hers. But K quietly demurred. Finally, Mrs. Coppa suggested they pray.

And so they knelt, this gentle, graying woman and the younger one—a secret slave—to offer up their separate prayers. A small comfort. And perhaps the closest K had ever come to telling anyone her sad and very strange story.

The Christmas season of 1980 was unlike any that K experienced while the Hookers' captive. Not since 1976 had she felt the special warmth of holiday preparations. In some ways, this was the pinnacle of her "year out." It was also the grand finale.

K took pleasure in giving. Having no money to buy gifts, she made little cards and crafts that satisfied her urge to give —not artistic achievements, just simple expressions of caring. She made Christmas cards for all the members of the Hooker family.

This was an extraordinary time for K. After years of confinement, she was out to soak up the special colors, flavors, and sounds heralding Christmas. As the holidays approached, these kindled memories of home, and she begged to contact her family. On Christmas Eve, Cameron again granted the supreme favor of letting her phone home.

Cameron and Janice stood listening to every word, ready to cut her off at any time, yet she was deeply grateful to be allowed to speak to her father. Just as before, K dutifully limited herself to only the sketchiest details and the vaguest descriptions of where she was and what she was doing. When her father asked for her phone number, she couldn't answer; when he asked when she would be returning home, she only said, "Soon, I hope." But this was the ultimate treat: to be able to wish her family a Merry Christmas.

To top it all off, when the Hookers were opening gifts the next morning, K was shocked to hear Jan say, "There is a present for you, too, K."

She received the large package with stunned pleasure. Opening it, she found a superbly practical gift: a new sleeping bag.

* * *

Regardless of the special favors and surprise Christmas present, a sinister and still undetectable shift was beginning, a shift within Hooker's psyche, a shift in Colleen Stan's captivity. Unbeknownst to K, her "year out" would shortly be coming to an abrupt end.

14

Cameron had forbidden more than superficial contact between Jan and K, and he paid the price in domestic strife. Jan bossed K around, the two women quarrelled constantly, and each complained to Cameron about the other. The tensions in the house reached such heights and irritated Cameron so much that he decided to take action. He took his wife and his slave, separately, out to Hogsback Road for disciplining. With ropes and whips, he made the point that he was going to wear the pants in the family, that he was going to be the boss, and that they'd better straighten up and try to get along.

When the situation didn't get any better, he started preparations for dramatic change.

He told his wife she would have to quit her job so she could take care of the girls. K was going back in the box, he said, and he wouldn't allow his daughters to be raised by another babysitter.

But he decided that K would be allowed one final glimpse of freedom: He told her that she would be the first slave ever permitted to visit her family. He'd already started making arrangements, he said, but the Company would probably want to test her in advance of granting final permission.

In the meantime, there were a few "obedience tests" that he needed to perform himself, in preparation for her encounter with the Company.

Cameron's parents were out of town, and their remote and ramshackle property offered an ideal site for one of

Cameron's "tests." The family drove out to Cameron's father's twenty-acre ranch, about fifteen miles south of Red Bluff. While the girls were napping in the house, the adults went out to the cavernous, drafty barn.

Cameron found a ladder and climbed up to the rafters with some chains, which he put over a beam. He locked the leather cuffs to the chains, and K, who had been ordered to strip off her clothes, was then brought up, strapped into the cuffs and suspended high off the ground. She dangled painfully there for some time, a bizarre sight several feet above the straw-strewn floor and an assortment of farm tools, barrels, feed bags, and disinterested hogs grunting in their stalls.

Cameron tied Janice up, too, but she wasn't hung. After a while he let her go, and she went outside.

About this time, Cameron's entertainment was interrupted by the sound of a car driving up. His parents! He grabbed the ladder and rushed up to release K.

"Go over behind the feed bags and hide," he told her, unlocking the cuffs. They climbed down and K ran across the barn.

Outside, Janice greeted her tired, congenial, and completely unsuspecting in-laws, and proceeded up to the house with Mrs. Hooker. Having seen Janice leave the barn, Mr. Hooker assumed Cameron would be inside. He headed in that direction.

K was trying to get dressed when tall, thin Mr. Hooker entered. She wasn't sure, but it seemed that he looked right at her.

Harold Hooker, who had expected to find his son feeding the pigs, was startled to see Kay struggling to pull up her underwear. He quickly closed the door so as not to embarrass her. Then he walked around to the back of the barn, expecting Cameron and Kay to come out. When they didn't, he proceeded up to the house and found them already inside.

Despite the awkward undercurrents, no one said anything about the incident in the barn. Evidently feeling self-conscious, K believed that Mr. Hooker kept staring at her. Her discomfort was heightened by the fear that Mr. Hooker, who Cameron had said was a longtime member of the Company, might realize she was a slave and want to "borrow" her.

To make matters worse, Cathy, with a child's innocence, kept pointing at K's reddened wrists and asking, "Did you scratch yourself?"

K tried to get her to be quiet. "They're okay, honey, don't worry about it."

Nothing more was said. The afternoon slipped by, they loaded the girls into the car, and returned to the mobile home. Though they'd come close to being found out, the incident passed, leaving in the mind of Mr. Harold Hooker only vague and unanswered questions.

With his secret habits still undetected, Cameron put the next step of his plan into action. K had become almost a standard feature in the neighborhood—taking the Hooker girls for walks, jogging down the lane or working in the garden—so now Cameron told her to say good-bye to the neighbors. He intended to take K down to Riverside himself, and he didn't want the neighbors to get suspicious. His strategy was to make it seem that K had left that weekend for Southern California; then, a week later, he could drive her down himself. He didn't want anyone—not even his children—to make the connection between K's departure and his own absence.

Dorothy Coppa, who had taken an almost maternal interest in the Hookers' companion, was especially sad to learn that K would be leaving. Characteristically, she worried about whether she would be all right. (Once she had given K a sweater; another time she guessed that she had no jacket—never having seen her wear one—and bought one for K at the local secondhand store.) Now, concerned that K didn't have any money, she pressed ten dollars into her palm and hugged her good-bye.

Cameron also told K to say good-bye to his two daughters, Cathy and Dawn. Then, as prearranged, they went out to the truck and she waved out the window as he headed toward the bus station.

But this was all a charade. K bought no ticket and boarded no bus. Instead, Cameron had her lay down on the seat and hide while they drove back to the mobile home. Once he'd made sure that the girls had gone to bed, he smuggled K back into the house and put her in the box, where she would stay for the next week.

Putting her in the box again would be good discipline, Cameron thought. It would remind her of her position. But before he could trust his slave to behave herself in the safe haven of her own home, he had to reaffirm his control over her with yet another obedience test.

He got his shotgun, got K out of the box, and ordered her to get down on her knees.

She kneeled.

While holding onto the butt of the gun, Cameron ordered her to put her mouth over the end of the barrel.

She put her lips around the cold metal.

He told her to pull the trigger.

She didn't know whether the gun was loaded, didn't even know what kind of gun it was. She only knew that if she didn't do as her master told her, there would be serious consequences.

With the barrel jutting toward her throat, she pulled the trigger.

It hit home with a metallic *click*.

The arrangements with the Company were nearly complete, Hooker explained. The phones of all her family members would be monitored. Their homes and cars were being bugged with listening devices sensitive enough to pick up even a whisper. Company surveillance teams would be watching her and her family at all times. These special precautions would cost a total of some $30,000, all of which was coming out of Hooker's Company account—money he had earned by capturing runaways years ago. He was making a tremendous financial sacrifice for her.

Since K would be the first slave ever to be permitted to visit her family, they would have to stop at Company headquarters in Sacramento so she could be evaluated before being granted final permission for her visit. Cameron was unsure what sorts of tests the Company would want to put her through. They might want to hang her up. Or they might take her through a Company "museum," showing her displays of skeletons of runaway slaves who had been tortured to death or the runaway who had been sealed in a jar of formaldehyde, "like a human pickle."

Finally, after K had suffered through a week of stultifying, monotonous confinement in the box, the day of departure arrived.

Cameron Hooker rose early on the morning of Friday, March 20, 1981, and called in sick. Before the children were up, he got K out of the box, snuck her out to the car, and told her to lie down on the floor in the back. He covered her with something and they drove off into the soft, morning quiet.

They stopped to get gas in Corning, just a few miles south of Red Bluff, then pulled onto the freeway, Interstate 5, heading south. Now Hooker told his slave she could sit up.

It was still morning when they pulled into Sacramento. Cameron stopped outside of some tall office buildings and told K to wait in the car while he went into Company headquarters to find out what they wanted to do with her.

K waited nervously, wondering what sort of painful test the Company might subject her to.

About fifteen minutes later, Hooker exited the building and came to the car with some papers in his hand. "You're getting off easy," he said. "They don't want to see you. You don't have to go in." The Company had granted permission for her to visit her family over the weekend.

"This will allow you to carry money," he said, handing her a typed, official-looking card with his seal on it. It was the same seal that had been on the slavery contract. She was to carry this card with her at all times, Cameron said, because if a slave were caught carrying money without it, the punishment would be harsh.

"Oh, and the secretary said to wish you good luck," he added.

It was a long drive to Southern California. On the way down Hooker had his slave rehearse the story she was to tell her parents. He was her boyfriend, Mike, and he was dropping her off in Riverside on his way down to San Diego, where he would be attending a computer seminar. They were engaged. And they were in the process of moving, so she couldn't give them an address or phone number just then, but would as soon as they were settled.

They drove all afternoon and into the evening before finally reaching Riverside, K giving directions as Cameron drove. On the way, she pointed out a street with several motels where he could stay. It was about seven P.M. when Cameron pulled over to a pay phone so she could call home and tell her stunned father that she would be there soon.

On the way to her father's house, K persuaded Cameron to stop at her grandmother's for just a moment while she ran in to say hello. Hooker waited in the car while the two women, delighted at this unexpected reunion, made plans to go to the Seventh Day Adventist church together the next morning. Then K rushed out and Cameron drove on.

As they approached Jack Martin's small, suburban home, Hooker pointed out that a surveillance team was stationed in a nearby trailer. He warned her again that if she said anything about the Company, they would rush in and not only take her away but also hurt or kill whoever she was with.

This was the most effective threat he could make. Knowing what she'd been put through, K couldn't bear to think of anything similar happening to someone she loved. She promised Cameron and herself that, no matter what, she would do nothing to endanger her family.

They pulled up in front of her father's house, and Cameron helped her carry her things to the door—a small suitcase with a few clothes and some gifts she'd made for her family. Without waiting to be introduced, he walked back to the car and drove away.

It was a whirlwind visit.

None of Colleen Stan's family knew what to make of her sudden appearance. Of course they were thrilled to see her, but behind the excited chatter were unspoken questions. Hurt and bewildered by her long absence, they felt they must have committed some kind of offense that had estranged her from them. Now they were evidently hesitant to make too much of her protracted silences for fear they might frighten her away. They wanted to welcome her home, not make her uncomfortable, so no one dared press her for reasons. At least not yet.

Jack Martin, a man of few words, noticed that his long-lost daughter seemed happy to be home but looked pale and tired and unhealthy. And when Colleen's younger sister, Bonnie, came home late that night and suddenly found Colleen sitting on the couch, she immediately noticed that Colleen's once-curvaceous figure was now angular, her handmade clothes hanging on her with little style or grace. And the shiny and luxuriant mane that Colleen had once prided herself on had turned dingy and thin.

It seemed that Colleen hadn't been taking very good care of herself, but with everyone so glad to see her and so much to talk about, no one guessed how serious her deprivation had been. They stayed up late and talked well into morning, sitting on the couch and pouring over photo albums, trying to catch up on years in just a few hours.

At one point twenty-one-year-old Bonnie got up the nerve to ask: "Why haven't you been writing to me?"

Colleen looked at her and answered simply that she couldn't. Watching her, Bonnie got a strange feeling that Colleen was trying to tell her something with her eyes. But Bonnie's nerve failed; she was afraid to pressure her older sister.

After a good deal of reminiscing, exhaustion finally overtook them and they had to go to bed.

Saturday started early and sped by.

Colleen was up and gone by seven-thirty, for she had phoned her mother the night before with a promise to come and see her before church. Her mother, an outgoing and talkative woman, lived just a few blocks away. Colleen walked the short distance to her house, then emotionally embraced the mother she hadn't seen or spoken to in nearly four years.

Her daughter was unusually thin and unkempt, but Mrs. Grant had also resolved not to push Colleen about where she'd been. Instead, she filled her in on recent events and listened attentively as Colleen told about her babysitting job at a place that sounded like some sort of religious commune.

After the church service, which Colleen attended in a borrowed dress and shoes, she, her sister, and her mother embarked on a day of marathon visiting. They drove to Sunnymead to see her sick aunt and visited with her uncle and cousins, the hours melting away.

Afterward, Colleen and Bonnie dropped their mother off at her house, Colleen promising to see her again before she had to leave.

Just a short while after Colleen and Bonnie returned to their father's, the phone rang. It was "Mike" calling for Colleen. "It's time to go," he said. "I'll be there in ten minutes."

Colleen was taken aback. She'd been promised a whole weekend at home, but barely twenty-four hours had elapsed.

The young man named "Mike" arrived and was introduced to the family. He was tall, wore glasses, and had stringy brown hair.

Someone insisted on a photograph being taken, and the two posed briefly on the couch, but "Mike" stayed only a few minutes, then said it was time to start the long drive back up to Northern California. With several parting embraces, Colleen Stan said good-bye to her family and got in the car with Cameron Hooker.

K was upset that her visit had been cut short, especially since she'd promised to say good-bye to her mother. She begged Cameron to let her stop by for just a minute, and he consented.

Evelyn Grant was surprised when Colleen appeared again that evening at about six-thirty. She met Colleen's boyfriend, "Mike," a computer programmer. The tall fellow spoke little before telling Colleen that it was time to go.

Saying good-bye, Colleen struggled to keep from blurting out the truth, but she held her tongue, and within minutes they were gone.

The drive back to Red Bluff pushed through the evening and deep into the night, K sulking about the brevity of her visit before finally dozing off. Hooker drove steadily, and they pulled up at the mobile home early Sunday morning. K

stirred, gathered her things and headed for the door, paying
little attention to what would be the last dawn to meet her
eyes in a very long time.

No one was home. Janice and the kids had gone to stay at
her parents'. Cameron told K to take a shower. When she
came out and he told her to vacuum out the box and put a
blanket in it, she realized he was going to have her get back
in. But after she put the vacuum cleaner away, he told her to
lie down on the floor. He raped her before putting her back
in the box, handing her the bedpan, and bolting the secret
door shut.

K's "year out" had come to an abrupt end. Perhaps
Hooker had decided that he'd made a mistake, that he was
losing control and needed to restore discipline. Perhaps he
saw no other way to put an end to the bickering between his
slave and his wife. And perhaps he felt it had become too
dangerous, with his children getting older and more neighbors moving into the neighborhood, to keep his slave so
openly. Whatever his motives, he slammed the door on K's
recent liberties. Except to eat and do Cameron's bidding, K
was scarcely let out of the box for the next three years. So
complete was her isolation that relatives, neighbors, even the
Hooker children who shared the same home, would not see
K again until 1984.

PART SIX

The Malleable Psyche

January–March 1985

To a terrorized person, an open door is not an open door.
Martin Symonds, M.D.
Victimization and Rehabilitative Treatment,
the American Psychiatric Association
Task Force Report on Terrorism

15

Deputy DA McGuire, who tried to immerse herself in the facts of the Hooker case, found that she could not simply file and forget what she learned. Instead, every incident lodged in her head and replayed itself, over and over, like some particularly loathsome song that she couldn't stop hearing. Details seeped into memory and then popped out again, demanding reexamination. And as she turned them over and over again in her mind, pondering the puzzle of the pretty, beaten, yet blasé Colleen Stan, it began to seem clear that Colleen's mental state was pivotal.

This wasn't a welcome prospect, but with so much hinging on the issue of consent—and therefore Stan's state of mind—Christine realized that the mind control issue was unavoidable. Worse, with that damned "year out" to explain, she scarcely had a hope of winning the case if the jury choked on the idea of brainwashing.

Legally, the argument of brainwashing was tenuous, and McGuire was concerned about the jury's possible reaction, particularly since in the previous case where brainwashing was a crucial issue—*United States* v. *Hearst*—the jury had remained unconvinced. McGuire thought both the jury and the general public saw Patty Hearst as a rich girl trying to buy herself out of a criminal situation by the use of some heavy-handed, expensive psychiatric testimony.

And here she was, ten years later, in the same state of California.

But McGuire had to swallow her misgivings and reconcile herself to the fact that in proving the case against Hooker, she would have to prove a little-understood phenomenon which many people scoff at—that malevolent bending of the psyche commonly known as brainwashing.

But how does one research such a condition? She was going to have to start from scratch.

The local libraries were struggling just to stay open, and Red Bluff's last bookstore was having a going-out-of-business sale. Luckily, the thirty-three-year-old prosecutor, who had little familiarity with the field of psychology, wasn't going to have to rely on the withering resources of Tehama County for background information. Experts came to her.

Having read newspaper accounts of this extraordinary case, they began to call from across the country. They were specialists who had worked with hostages, with cult victims, with Patty Hearst and other captives, and they used psychological terms Christine had never heard: coercive persuasion, the Stockholm syndrome, involuntary conversion, post-traumatic stress disorder. Some were connected with the FBI or the military, others were psychologists or psychiatrists who had testified in relevant cases. (McGuire was even contacted by a former kidnap victim, now working as a counselor in the Southeast, who wanted to offer her help.)

Experts consulted with her during lengthy telephone conversations and sent her stacks of reading material. One even sent a videotape. They opened her eyes to a field of specialization that had evolved around the treatment of traumas suffered by these particular types of victims, demonstrating that such brutality happens more often than most of us would like to believe[1].

---

1. A Michigan case emerged as one of the most significant parallels. Assistant U.S. Attorney Virginia Morgan actively sought McGuire out, sending her information about her role in the prosecution of the Kozminski case, in which a man and his wife were found guilty of holding two retarded men as slaves. She recommended the expert witness they had used in the prosecution, Dr. Harvey Stock, and even suggested the possibility of helping McGuire with Hooker's prosecution.

A cross-designated prosecution, in which a state and a federal prosecutor co-try a case, would have been appropriate if the attorney general's office had decided to charge Hooker with the federal crime of slavery. This was not done, however, and the idea of a cross-designated prosecution was later abandoned.

Perusing the information she'd suddenly accumulated, McGuire was relieved to learn that brainwashing wasn't just some fringe element of pop psychology or a stepchild of Richard Condon's 1959 best seller, *Manchurian Candidate,* but a bona fide field of study. As she read these psychological papers, the logic of it all was like an opening door.

It became evident to McGuire that the intense isolation and abuse Colleen had endured had done more than hurt her physically; it had shredded the very fabric of her personality. But while Colleen's brainwashing, or coercion, had become startlingly apparent to McGuire, she would have to prove this unwieldy theory to twelve skeptical individuals, the jury.

It would help if she could get an expert to testify at the trial, to explain coercion and resultant captivity syndromes to the jury. Whether the judge would permit expert testimony or not was an open question. Some judges are inclined toward experts, some are not. If the judge prohibited expert testimony, McGuire would be left with having to rely on the testimonies of Janice Hooker, the truculent wife who had turned state's evidence, and Colleen Stan, the placid woman who had apparent freedom yet claimed to be held captive—not a heartening prospect.

She decided to set up consultations with some of the experts. If one of them could testify later, great. If not, at least the investigation would be headed in the right direction.

She set up interviews with six specialists, mostly in the San Francisco Bay Area: Dr. Chris Hatcher, an associate clinical psychology professor at the University of California at San Francisco; Dr. Robert T. Flint, an Oakland psychologist; Dr. Margaret Singer, a psychiatrist with the University of California at Berkeley; Dr. Philip Zimbardo, a professor of psychology at Stanford University; Dr. Donald Lunde, a Stanford psychiatrist who had examined Patty Hearst prior to her trial. And later in the week, she and Lt. Jerry Brown would drive down to Davis to meet Dr. Phillip Morton Hamm, a psychologist at the University of California at Davis, who had been the expert witness in the Parnell case.

McGuire made careful preparations for her trip to San Francisco, but she hadn't counted on her baby daughter's coming down with a cold the night before her appointments. After a sleepless night and an early departure, she was already weary by the time she arrived at the Airport Executive Inn in San Francisco.

With little time to spare before their nine A.M. meeting, she reviewed Dr. Chris Hatcher's curriculum vitae. It was an impressive list of credentials, including considerable work concerning terrorism, the People's Temple/Jonestown, articles written on the psychology of hostages, and work with police and sheriff's departments regarding investigations into more than twenty kidnapping and hostage cases.

Dr. Hatcher arrived punctually, looking fit, trim, and younger than his true age of nearly forty. A high forehead added to an overall impression of intelligence, and he was immaculately dressed in a navy blue pin-stripe suit with white shirt and dark tie. After introductions, Hatcher and McGuire went to discuss the Hooker case over breakfast in the hotel's coffee shop.

Early in the conversation, McGuire expressed concern that, despite his ample background in serving as a consultant in hostage and kidnap situations, Dr. Hatcher had never actually offered expert testimony in court.

To this Dr. Hatcher replied, simply, "I am not a professional witness."

This made McGuire smile. Dr. Hatcher understood, then, the pitfalls of retaining someone who had been on the stand *too many* times. Testifying, for an expert, can be astonishingly lucrative, but those who regularly testify are vulnerable to accusations that they are less an expert than a paid advocate.

McGuire found Dr. Hatcher to be articulate and well informed. He absorbed information quickly, asked questions, and even offered insights into areas of the Hooker case that needed further investigation. He was sharp, no doubt about that.

Still, McGuire wondered if this well-dressed psychologist might be too slick for a jury in the rural community of Red Bluff. His tailored, polished look and his intellectual bearing might alienate them.

"To be honest, I'm not sure how a jury in our county will

take to an expert witness from the big city," she told him. Then, as a joke she asked, "You don't by chance own a pair of cowboy boots, do you?"

He surprised her by answering, "As a matter of fact, I do." Then he added, "And at times I can draw upon my Georgia accent," demonstrating a smooth Southern drawl.

McGuire laughed. It was difficult to find fault with this man.

When breakfast was over and the interview ended, Dr. Hatcher underscored an already favorable impression by asking to see a picture of McGuire's daughter, then sharing a picture of his own little girl. He was not only sharp, but warm.

It was early—she'd only had one interview—but McGuire wondered if she hadn't already found her expert.

Soon, she departed for an afternoon appointment with Dr. Donald T. Lunde, of Stanford University. He was the only one of the professionals she contacted who declined to meet with her at the hotel. After a tiring ninety-minute bus ride, McGuire arrived at Dr. Lunde's office, was greeted briefly, and was then kept waiting for twenty minutes while he left the office. She tried not to be offended, remembering the times she'd kept people waiting at her own office.

When Dr. Lunde returned, inviting her into his plush office, he immediately took control of the conversation. He spoke of his areas of expertise and consulted his files frequently, yet he seemed to recall little about the Hooker case, despite their correspondence. Clearly, this was not a big priority in his life.

Christine did virtually none of the talking, partly because she was exhausted and partly because Dr. Lunde overran her attempts to interject. Somehow, during this two-hour interview, she couldn't manage to get her questions answered.

The district attorney didn't know quite what to make of this short, talkative man suited in brown. Nevertheless, the interview ended amicably, with Dr. Lunde assuring her that if he could be of service, he would be glad to help.

Some months later, she would look back on her meeting with Dr. Lunde with particular interest.

* * *

Deputy DA McGuire interviewed the rest of the special-ists over the next week. All had much to recommend them, and McGuire wished the county could afford to retain two experts, but even hiring one put an extra drain on their already meager resources.[2]

She took her file of notes back home and roughed out a letter asking about fees. The trial date was now set for Feb-ruary 20, scarcely a month away, and she had to decide soon.

---

2. Since only one expert could be retained, McGuire had to rule out Dr. Singer because of her sex—ironic, given that Christine McGuire had had an active role in the local chapter of the National Organization for Women. But the reality was that a Red Bluff jury might not take kindly to Christine, Colleen, Janice, and Dr. Margaret Singer all work-ing to put Hooker behind bars. It would seem, she feared, a conspiracy of women.

16

Attorneys always try to figure out an opponent's case in advance, then build counter arguments and counter evidence, anticipating questions and distilling answers.

For the defense, this is less difficult because "open discovery" laws are on their side. Whatever the district attorney's office uncovers must be shared with the defense attorney—every piece of evidence, every police report, every statement. With a big case, the paper work swells as each move gets reported on, typed up, photocopied, passed on, and filed. It can be mountainous.

Though the defense knows every move the DA's office makes, the reverse isn't true. The defense isn't obligated to share any information with the prosecution. Anything unearthed that supports the defendant's position remains secret. And whatever the prosecution understands about the opposition's case is conjecture, supposition, rumor, a stray fact that someone lets slip, or information that the defense attorney shares out of courtesy or strategy.

While police were helping Deputy DA McGuire build the people's case, Rolland Papendick had hired his own investigator, Gary Kelley, to help with Hooker's defense. Kelley, a red-headed man with more than a decade of experience as a private investigator, set about making the rounds, asking questions of friends, neighbors and coworkers but found that many of these had had enough of strangers nosing around. According to Janice Hooker, some of her neighbors felt intimidated by him, and one got mad and "threw him out."

But Kelley had better luck in other areas, and the DA's office had no way of knowing what he and Papendick had discovered.

Meanwhile, with less than a month before the trial date, Rolland Papendick filed a change-of-venue motion. McGuire wasn't surprised. The story had swept Northern California, and the intensive coverage had left her half expecting a request for a change of venue. Her expectation was confirmed one afternoon when Papendick showed her the fat file of newspaper clippings he'd accumulated.

Despite the media saturation, a change of venue was controversial. One judge made a point of calling the two attorneys into his office to caution them against what he considered the "horrors" of an out-of-county trial—the length of time it might take, the strange place it might be tried, and the not insignificant cost of transporting staff, witnesses, records, evidence, and such to some unknown destination.

These would turn out to be more serious considerations than any of them guessed.

In the meantime, Papendick's motion had the effect of postponing the trial. A new date would be set only after the change-of-venue ruling, giving both sides more time to prepare.

They couldn't both be right, but while Papendick thought a change of venue would help the defense, McGuire thought it would help the prosecution. She believed that everybody in the county had an opinion on the case—mostly prodefense. Though she made little comment to the press, she personally hoped Papendick's motion would be granted and the trial would be sent out of county—far away from Cameron Hooker's sympathetic neighbors.

In January, Al Shamblin was promoted to patrol sergeant, requiring him to work nights, so he was taken off the Hooker investigation and replaced by Lt. Jerry Brown. McGuire liked Brown but was sorry to see Shamblin taken off the case. (She wasn't the only one. Janice Hooker had developed such an attachment to the gentle detective that when she had anything to add to her statement, she continued to ask for Shamblin rather than Brown.)

McGuire accompanied Al Shamblin on the last two interviews he conducted for the Hooker investigation. The two subjects were ages eight and six, Cathy and Dawn Hooker.

They were both lovely children, with long, straight, light brown hair cascading down their backs. Dawn, the younger, was missing two front teeth. McGuire had prepared a list of questions for Detective Shamblin, but she left it to him to conduct the interview, only stepping in from time to time.

Cooperative and sweet, both little girls revealed themselves as totally innocent of any peculiar goings-on at home, though they offered a few corroborations and didn't directly contradict anything Janice and Colleen had claimed. How was it possible that their parents had kept these girls so completely insulated from their father's strange habits?

Christine McGuire already had a warm relationship with Lieutenant Brown. A seasoned police officer with some twenty years with RBPD, Brown had a craggy, kind face and an easy sense of humor. In no time, he was calling the almost daily lists of requests that McGuire sent "my honey-do memos," because, he said, they reminded him of his wife: "Honey do this, honey do that."

Acting on Christine McGuire's edict: "The more visual aids, the better," Brown arranged to have diagrams drawn up of the Hooker property, the rack, and the basement. (The Red Bluff Planning Department, knowing the county was financially strapped, was kind enough to do the work for free.) Pictures of the slavery contract and the rack were also blown up, mounted, and readied for display. (A local photo studio, demonstrating true civic-mindedness, did that work for free as well.)

On Friday, February 1, Lieutenant Brown stopped McGuire just as she was leaving her office on her way to court. He wasn't the kind of man you'd expect to see bubbling over with enthusiasm, but here he was, practically bouncing with excitement: "Guess what we got back from the FBI lab?"

McGuire knew he meant the out-of-date film they'd seized at the mobile home—that was the only thing they'd sent to Washington—but she scarcely had time to speak before Brown went on.

"Slides of a woman in bondage," he pronounced. "They're not real clear, but they appear to be shots taken inside the trailer."

"You can't tell who the woman is? They're not Janice?" she asked.

"I don't know. The film was so old, the slides aren't that good. They may even have to be restored. But the woman has moles on one side of her body."

McGuire's pulse skipped. The implication was clear: They could have shots of Colleen.

Janice had told them that all the photographs of K had been destroyed one night when they'd burned slides, papers, photos, magazines, and bondage equipment in a barrel in their backyard. But Hooker had forgotten about the negative of the slavery contract; could he have overlooked this old film as well?

"I've got to be in court in a few minutes, Jerry. When can I come over and see these pictures?"

"Just give me a call whenever you're free. I'll set up a slide show for you. In the meantime, I'll contact Janice and Colleen and ask them if they have any moles."

She arranged to meet Lieutenant Brown on Monday, after the weekend. He had a projector and screen set up and waiting in a small storage room in police headquarters.

Brown switched off the lights and the show began.

The first shots were clearly of Janice being hung in the woods—probably taken before she and Cameron were married—and a few more were of Janice hung or bound in the trailer. Then the image of another woman flashed onto the screen.

It showed the woman from the waist up. She was hung by the wrists, naked, with her eyes closed and a thin metal ring around her neck.

"Oh my god, the slave collar! That's gotta be Colleen," McGuire whispered.

They stared at this slide for a long moment. Though the woman's face wasn't clear, there was no question in Christine's mind that this was not Janice, but Colleen: Her breasts were smaller, she didn't wear glasses, and her hair was much longer.

Then Jerry projected another, similar slide onto the screen. Apparently taken at the same time, this was a full-body shot.

"That's her, Jerry, absolutely. Look how bow-legged she is!"

In her mind's eye, McGuire called up a picture of Colleen the day before the preliminary hearing: tight pastel jeans, high heels, and bow-legged, like her father. But then Colleen was plump; in these pictures she was bony, her ribs and hipbones sticking out. Hanging there with her arms out to the sides, she looked as if she were being crucified. Her dull, dirty hair trailed far down her back, her face was upturned as if pulled back by the weight of it, exposing a long, thin neck with the slave collar encircling it.

There were four slides of Colleen in all, two of each view. Characteristically, Hooker had duplicated his shots. He was fanatical, obsessed with chronicling the pain he inflicted on others. Now this meticulous cataloging had provided not only a picture of the signed slavery contract, but, it appeared, a photograph of the slave.

Soon the show was over. The two rolls they'd seized were short, and not all of the pictures had come out. Brown switched on the lights and everyday reality flooded back.

"We need to get a positive ID that this is really Colleen," McGuire said, blinking. "Can you get Janice in here and have her take a look?"

"I sure will," Brown promised.

McGuire chanced across Janice Hooker at the police station the next day. They greeted each other warmly and chatted a minute, Janice saying she was on her way to view the slides. The meeting was brief, but Christine noticed a change in Mrs. Hooker. She seemed robust and spunky, and her mind didn't wander. She'd come a long way from the drugged and reluctant character the prosecutor had become so exasperated with during the preliminary hearing.

McGuire would have liked to sit in on Janice's session, but she had to get to court. The next morning, she rang Brown to get the full report.

Janice had been shy about viewing the slides and embarrassed about having to ID so many pictures of herself, he said. "She wouldn't let me project them on the wall. She said she wasn't ready for that." Instead, Janice held the slides up to the light, identifying them one by one. And, yes, the skinny woman with the slave collar was Colleen Stan.

They had positive identification, the most significant piece of evidence against Hooker yet.

Later that same day, she received an unexpected phone call from Colleen. In contrast to Janice, Colleen didn't sound as coherent as she had in prior conversations.

She'd called, first of all, because she'd read in the Riverside paper about some recent rulings concerning the Hooker case: that Defense Attorney Papendick had filed a change-of-venue motion, that he intended to file for dismissal of the charges, and that the initial February 20 trial date had been vacated.

McGuire tried to reassure her. "Those are just technical motions. Nothing surprising and nothing really to worry about. But I'll try to get a new trial date set as soon as possible so that we can get through this and you can put it all behind you."

As they talked, McGuire got the impression that nearly every area of Colleen's life was in upheaval, that she had problems at work, that she had serious financial troubles.

The best that McGuire could do to help was to tell her about California's Victim Assistance Program, under which Colleen could apply for compensation for lost wages and counseling. "I'll put the application forms in the mail today," she promised, adding that she would contact the Victim Witness Program for her.

As she hung up, McGuire frowned. She was worried about Colleen's evident lack of enthusiasm for seeking professional help. Counseling, it seemed to the DA, was exactly what Colleen needed. Her mental state seemed shaky, and her voice was dull and listless. If Colleen didn't find some means for healing her emotional wounds, McGuire believed she could have serious and lasting problems.

McGuire was also troubled to learn that Colleen had spoken to an attorney about filing a civil suit against Cameron Hooker. This seemed futile, even ludicrous. Hooker had no money.

It may have seemed like nonsense to McGuire, but Colleen was serious about it. All the Deputy DA could do was advise her that filing a civil suit might make her vulnerable under cross-examination. If she were asked on the stand whether she had filed a civil suit and the amount of damages she was seeking, Papendick could make it seem she had a financial motive to lie.

Shortly after her talk with Colleen, McGuire received a call from the attorney that Colleen had spoken to. He said that he'd already been retained, though this wasn't what Colleen had told her. In fact, the attorney called Colleen by another name and generally gave McGuire the impression that he knew little about the case. Despite this obvious lack of knowledge, he seemed eager to get on with the suit.

McGuire felt he was proceeding in a reckless manner and was rather brusque with him. "We're talking about involuntary conversion, victimology, and captivity syndromes here, and if you don't understand those terms, you may be doing your client more harm than good," she told him. Moreover, she emphasized that a suit against Hooker could be used against Colleen during the criminal prosecution.

In the end, the attorney said he would hold off on a suit until the verdict on the criminal charges was in.

This entire interlude left McGuire feeling unsettled. She had no control over what Colleen or her attorney might do, but it seemed all too possible that she could jeopardize her own case.

By chance, McGuire learned of a child molestation case that was lost because the jury, try as they might, could not reconstruct the crime described to them. They concluded that it was physically impossible and the "victim" was lying.

This reinforced the Deputy DA's belief that it was crucial that the jury in the Hooker case be able to reenact the crime. So she sent Lieutenant Brown more "honey-do" memos, asking that the bed and box be reconstructed. She determined to try out Colleen's prison to make sure it worked.

On the afternoon of February 6, Lt. Jerry Brown arranged to have the box and bedframe up in the squad room so the box could be tried out. The reconstruction of the large frame and coffin-like box created quite a scene. Various officers wandered in and out, commenting on the strange apparatus, stopping to watch its assembly if they had time, offering a joke or two before moving on.

Once it was assembled, the first person to get into the box was the dogcatcher (or, more properly, the Animal Control Officer), Don Hermann, a big, broad-shouldered man weighing 250 pounds. "I got in the box to see if I'd fit," he recalls, chuckling. "It's small, I'll tell you that."

He did fit, albeit snugly. But when they put the lid on he was stuck. He couldn't turn over.

A call went up for someone of about Colleen's size to try it out, so Jerry Brown fetched Janell Begbie, a meter maid. She agreed to climb in and found that she could turn over with the lid on, though with difficulty.

Then Christine McGuire wanted to try it to understand how it worked, how it felt to be shut inside.

At five feet two and about one hundred pounds, the prosecutor was the smallest person to try the box yet. She climbed in and lay down. The officers placed the wooden top over her.

"When they put the lid over me, I felt the sensory deprivation," McGuire said later. "I felt like I was in a coffin, though I was surrounded by the reassuring words of police officers and other onlookers at the time." And even as unnerving as this was, McGuire realized that when Colleen was in the box it had been caulked—there would be no air and no light seeping in around the edges.

McGuire wanted to demonstrate that all elements of what Colleen claimed had been her environment were operational. Officer Roger Marsh was sent off to the Tehama County Health Center to pick up a bedpan, and someone went out to the property room where evidence was stored to get the sleeping bag.

These were the meager comforts afforded Colleen, and with their addition, the attorney climbed back into the box. She wanted to make sure that using a bedpan in the box was feasible. In a prone position, she hiked it up under her backside. Then, using her hands and then her legs, she removed it to the end of the box. Awkward, but practicable.

Finally, she wanted to enter the box as Colleen had, through the opening at the foot of the bed. Prior to this, everyone had been entering the easy way, through the top, where the waterbed mattress would have been. Now, with the wooden top in place, Christine crawled in through the small opening at the foot of the bed and wiggled her way into the box. She ran her stockings, but was able to enter and exit without any problem.

At the time, this whole experiment lent itself to comedy: the squad room almost completely occupied by an awkward, wooden framework, the little, smartly dressed Deputy DA climbing in and out, police officers ambling in to sip coffee, watch, and exchange lively banter. But later McGuire reflected that this nervous levity had only partially masked an underlying unease. Beneath the humor lurked the ugly realization that the box was genuine. This was no joke.

17

Dr. Chris Hatcher was retained late in January. From the beginning, he impressed McGuire with his gung-ho attitude and how quickly he absorbed information about the case. First, he requested a copy of the three-hundred-page preliminary hearing transcript, then asked for copies of police reports, and now he was asking to come to Red Bluff to take a firsthand look at scenes of the crime. He wanted to review the evidence, peruse Hooker's reading material, and interview Janice. After that, he would interview Colleen in Riverside.

When Hatcher first walked into police headquarters, McGuire was relieved to see that the expert whom she'd feared was "too slick" was casually dressed in slacks and a sports coat.

After introductions, they drove with Lieutenant Brown to the Hooker residence. Without a search warrant they could only circle the empty mobile home. Dr. Hatcher paced its width and length, asking where the master bedroom would be, where the children slept, where the bathrooms were. Then he scrutinized the sheds.

After learning what they could, they headed back to the police station to review the evidence. The head box was pulled from the clutter in the property room. Originally seized from one of Hooker's sheds, it was dusty and littered with mouse droppings.

Hatcher picked it up, opened and closed it. "It's in a dilapidated condition—the neck holes don't even line up. It ought to be reconstructed, if possible, so that it's clear how it works."

"That's a good idea. I don't know why we didn't think of that," McGuire said. A useable head box would help the jury understand the sensory deprivation it caused.

They reviewed an array of items—the whips, handcuffs, and hooks; the S/M sketches Cameron had drawn; and the disassembled bed and box where Colleen had been confined. Hatcher asked how Colleen handled urination and defecation in the box, what the temperature would have been during the summer, what sorts of punishments she was subjected to. They went through a seemingly endless collection of slides and photos, mostly of Janice, since virtually all of those of Colleen had been destroyed. Looking closely, Dr. Hatcher pointed out whip marks on Janice's body that McGuire had never noticed before.

It wasn't difficult to see how Hooker got ideas for some of his equipment and techniques. Going through boxes of seized pornography, Hatcher suggested they be cataloged in terms of those having to do with slaves and masters, kidnapping, mind control, bondage, and sado-masochism. Cameron's collection was replete with such material. And Hatcher underscored the importance of these publications by suggesting they be combed for specific information which Hooker might have applied in his treatment of Colleen.

Mid-morning, Christine McGuire's husband, District Attorney Jim Lang, brought their baby daughter to the police station. It was Christine's turn to take care of her while he played his Saturday golf game, so now she carried eight-month-old Nicole around with her as she, Dr. Hatcher, and Lieutenant Brown went through the evidence. Pouring through it, McGuire was oblivious to the contrast she created: mother with babe in arms against a backdrop of hardcore pornography and bondage equipment.

Later that afternoon Hatcher interviewed Janice, then wanted to examine the basement of 1140 Oak Street.

It was McGuire's first visit to this particular scene of the crime—a cold, dark, damp, gray room. Until now, she'd only seen photographs, and she was stunned to find it so small. Breathing the musty air, she struggled to imagine the box, the rack, and the workshop all jammed into this meager space. It seemed inconceivable that anyone could have been imprisoned here.

Brown pointed out marks beneath the stairs where the workshop had been. "This is glue," he said, pointing to light-colored lines running across the cement. "It's like an outline. It shows where the workshop was glued to the wall."

They stared and murmured. It was tiny. Like a broom closet. A claustrophobe's nightmare. Yet Colleen Stan claimed to have spent hundreds of hours in this cramped little corner, working on crafts through the dead hours of night.

Back at the police station, they said their farewells and Hatcher prepared to depart. It had been a brief visit, but the psychologist had managed to refocus the investigation, initiating an important turn in its direction.

As he was leaving, McGuire asked, "What do you think. Doctor, now that you've had a chance to view the evidence and talk to Janice?"

"I'd rather not give you an opinion until I've had a chance to talk to Colleen and digest everything," he said, "but I will say this case exceeds common fantasy, and it's far beyond any typical B and D or S/M relationship."

At about nine o'clock on the morning of March 8, McGuire walked into the Tehama County Courthouse and climbed the wide marble staircase that sweeps up to the second floor, every footfall echoing through the halls and into the courtrooms. Here, she was in her element. She relished her work, and this morning she was looking forward to getting a favorable ruling on the Hooker case.

Attorneys McGuire and Papendick had been asked to meet with Judge Watkins in advance of a scheduled hearing on the change-of-venue motion. McGuire arrived to find the nattily dressed and always confident Papendick already waiting in a leather chair.

Judge Watkins, a fair-skinned man in his fifties, with a shock of red hair, a concerned look on his face, and a cigarette in his hand, greeted them and spread a copy of the previous night's *Daily News* across his desk. "Crime Expenses Could Bankrupt Tehama County," declared the front-page headline. Christine had already read the article, which warned of the financial consequences of prosecuting four major and expensive criminal cases—most notably the Hooker case.

The judge felt the article made it inappropriate for him to hear the change-of-venue motion. "If I don't grant it," he said, "the inference will be that I was influenced by concern over the cost of an out-of-county trial."

With Judge Watkins thus disqualifying himself, a visiting judge, Stanley Young, would have to step in to hear the case. Judge Young, whom Judge Watkins had already spoken to, was close at hand, and as soon as arrangements were made, both counsels left to take their seats in the courtroom.

The media was already there, and when Hooker was brought in, looking thin but well-groomed, a ripple went through the courtroom. McGuire noticed that he seemed cool and collected, unfazed by all the attention, and at one point even appeared to turn and pose for the cameras. His family sat behind him, and he smiled and chatted with them before the court was brought to order.

Papendick presented a convincing collection of newspaper clippings, showing that local coverage had been so extensive that it was unlikely many people in the county were unfamiliar with the case. This, he said, jeopardized Hooker's chance of getting a fair trial.

When it was McGuire's turn to rebut his argument, she simply said, "We'll submit it, Your Honor," leaving it up to the judge.

She still thought Papendick was making a mistake. Hooker was a local boy, with a job and general lifestyle that people here could relate to, whereas Colleen Stan was an outsider, and therefore suspect. For the most part, the people of Tehama County were absolutely incredulous of the charges against Hooker. And her husband and Hatcher had both agreed that jurors in a more urban locale would be more likely to understand psychological explanations, coercion, captivity syndromes, and the ticklish issue of why Colleen hadn't escaped when she'd had the opportunity.

To both attorneys' satisfaction, Judge Young granted the change-of-venue motion. A new trial date would be set when the trial site was decided.

Janice Hooker called that afternoon, anxious over the *Daily News* article about the cost of trying her husband. She understood that the state would absorb part of the cost of trying death penalty cases and, thinking of the Spannhake case, worried that the county's fiscal problems would push the DA's office into going after the death penalty. Apparently, she felt guilty enough about putting Cameron behind bars; she didn't want to feel responsible for his death.

McGuire reassured her that there wasn't enough evidence to charge Cameron with murder, and even if there were, the possibility of a death penalty was remote.

A couple of days later, Janice called to set up an appointment. Although emotionally stronger, she still seemed under Cameron's sway. At times it sounded as if she were operating as his mouthpiece, passing on information for him. And she played both sides: Apparently she wanted him locked up so he couldn't kidnap or torture anyone else, but didn't want to feel responsible for whatever justice might be meted out. It was difficult to know how much Jan could be trusted.

At times McGuire was appalled by Jan's docility. She'd signed no slavery contract, she'd believed in no Company, why hadn't she just walked out? Why had she put up with the pain and humiliation for so many years?

But today McGuire put her head in her hands and sighed, thinking: *How can I possibly criticize Janice? Am I so different? Aren't I just as afraid to leave a bad situation?*

Her relationship with Jim had steadily soured, and now Christine also found herself caught in an unhappy marriage —one she was unable to change but reluctant to leave. She tried to deny her marital troubles by losing herself in the pressing responsibilities of being a working mother, pouring her energies into her job, but the veil of activity she spun about herself couldn't hide the anger and pain that was slowly eroding the foundation of her marriage. "In some ways," thought Christine, "I'm as weak and dependent as Janice."

She rubbed her forehead and tried to put her personal life out of her mind, refocusing on Janice Hooker.

Christine couldn't help but feel pangs of sympathy for her, despite Janice's exasperating fence-sitting. Obviously struggling to come to terms with what had happened, Janice was going to counseling regularly, catching up on ten years of repressed emotions, grappling both with guilt and her own victimization.

Once she had shyly showed Christine a scrap of paper with a few phrases penciled on it, saying it was something she carried around with her for emotional support. It was a short list of encouraging phrases, such as, "I am not a bad person." Christine had been touched by the disclosure, by the poignancy of Janice carrying around little reminders of her worth as a person.

When Janice came in today she chatted awhile and then indicated, as McGuire had expected, that she wanted to make a statement. Shamblin was called in.

When he arrived, Jan explained she'd read in the newspapers that Colleen had denied wanting to have Cameron's child. "That's not true," she objected. "Colleen told me that she loved Cameron and that he was going to let her have his baby."

Further, Jan said she'd read the same thing in a "diary" that Colleen had written, but that the "diary" had been burned along with other items before Cameron's arrest.

But Colleen had denied ever having loved Cameron or wanting to have his child. During the preliminary hearing, she had insisted that, though she wanted to have a child, she had never wanted to have Cameron Hooker's.

So now one star witness's version of truth had cast doubt upon the other's.

This turn of events left McGuire even more unsettled when she heard a rumor that Papendick had acquired some secret and potentially damaging evidence.

He was heard gloating to friends that he had "love letters" written by Colleen to Cameron. He claimed the letters demonstrated that their peculiar relationship, including the bondage and discipline, was therefore consensual.

When McGuire checked with Colleen and Janice, neither

could recall Colleen writing any letters to Cameron during her captivity. Their responses were so low-key that the prosecutor simply discounted the reported love letters as idle gossip.

PART SEVEN

Return to Darkness

Spring 1981–Summer 1984

Sometimes I'm not very far from utter despair. No one knows I am alive any more. I'm given up for dead by now, I'm accepted for dead.

Miranda, *The Collector,* by John Fowles

18

K's imprisonment had come full circle. The darkness was again her intimate companion, a heavy shroud covering her days that lifted off only at night, when she was let out into the trailer's artificial light for a precious hour or two. Then she consumed her nightly meal, usually leftovers, at the foot of the bed or in the bathroom, where she emptied her bedpan, and, if they gave her some time, did deep knee-bends and read the Bible awhile before being locked again in the darkness.

With K passing day after day in the secret compartment beneath the bed, peace was restored within the Hooker household. As usual, Janice blocked out distasteful details, turning her full attention to the duties of being a mother and housewife.

Jan was, ironically, an expert at compartmentalization.

Spring edged into summer and local memories of "Kay Powers" evaporated like dew. If anyone asked, the word was that "Kay" was doing fine in Southern California.

Meanwhile, the searing summer heat penetrated deep into the mobile home, sliding into the box like licks from hell. Day after day, K endured the sweltering and inescapable heat.

Once Jan and Cameron left town for a weekend, leaving K to bake and sweat in the box. No food. No water. For three days she suffered through a delirium of unrelenting incarceration and nearly intolerable heat. Sweat wept from her pores till K thought she would die of dehydration. When the Hookers finally came home and let her out, she could barely stand.

This apparently made an impression; the next time they went away for the weekend, they left K with a quart of water and about a dozen chocolate chip cookies wrapped in tin foil.

Months dragged by, K suffering through the slow, flat oppressiveness of solitary confinement. At night, when it was very quiet, she put her ear to the vent hole and heard the hiss of the cars and the growl of the trucks as they passed on the freeway just a few hundred yards away. Through that hole, that pinpoint view of ground beneath the trailer, she perceived the slow brightening as dawn approached. She heard Cameron leave for work, the slam of the car door and the snarl of the ignition reaching her before the exhaust billowed beneath the mobile home and wafted into the box, filling her lungs with fumes.

The temperature left its nightly nadir and climbed steadily upward until the day warmed to full-force: the dogs barking, the girls running in and out and letting the door slam, their carefree laughter ringing through the air. K listened hard, picking up bits and pieces over the constant whir of the blower.

While that small vent was her access to the world, it served to let in more than simply sounds and smells and a patch of light. One night she had company.

It startled her with its tiny claws. Pricking and tickling, it raced across her skin, searching for an escape from the huge creature it had unexpectedly encountered. It scurried the length of her body, K writhing beneath its miniature feet as she tried to maneuver the furry intruder toward the vent hole. It balked and scampered back up her bare skin toward her face, finally fleeing out the hole, leaving her shivering in its wake.

In an existence of tedium and monotony, even the brief visit of a mouse was an event.

Prayers and dreams were K's primary diversions. Sleep was her only escape. For a while she could lose herself in dreams and distant, almost hallucinatory images of family, of children, of freedom. . . .

But K knew Cameron would never let her see her family again, and even these shimmering illusions crumpled beneath the weight of reality. Some nights, swept up in nightmares of slavery, torture, and pain, she'd wake with her heart pounding from dreams of her deepest fear: being sold to slave owners even crueler than Cameron Hooker.

Usually, K passively endured being locked inside that loathsome box, but once she succumbed to a fit of temper.

Cameron had left for work, Jan was in the hospital for a knee operation, and K was alone in the house. She knew there was no one to hear, and taking the opportunity to vent her frustration on the box, she began kicking at it. She stomped on the door as hard as she could, kicking with all her strength.

Suddenly, it broke out. To her astonishment, she'd kicked the particle board so hard the bolts pulled clear through.

She could have escaped. She could have climbed out of the box and run away . . . but K's reaction was not of liberation, but of fear. There was nowhere to go. The Company was everywhere, watching, and she was too afraid to test them.

She knew Cameron would be furious when he saw what she'd done. He would surely beat her. He might even kill her for this, with Jan and the girls gone and no witnesses. The thought must have made her shiver, but she lay there, cowering, until that evening when he got home from work.

He looked at the broken panel and got her out of the box. "What happened?"

She summoned her courage and confessed what she'd done. Amazingly, Hooker wasn't besieged by a murderous passion—he wasn't even mad. Instead, he busied himself with repairs. In no time, he'd rigged a board across the broken section, so that instead of bolting the box shut, he slipped the board snugly into its slots, like a barn door.

That done, the box was secure once again, with K shut back inside.

19

For the most part, K simply endured and prayed, but during her captivity she also gained firsthand experience at a little-known craft. It was hard, demanding work, yet this training was too special to qualify her for much in any job market. Few people have labored at such a peculiar project.

The first year they moved from Oak Street, Hooker had built a small shed abutting the first one, with a common wall and a cement floor. He had poured the cement over the section of ground where he'd had K bury the railroad tie. When the cement had set, he had both a floor and a ceiling.

It was Cameron Hooker's ambition to build a dungeon, and his slave would be his reluctant helper. They worked on it, off and on, for months, years.

No neighbors were near enough to worry about, but just in case, he took K out to the shed at night, under cover of darkness. Cameron had planned ahead when pouring the cement, leaving a rectangular patch of bare ground twenty-seven by thirty-four inches. This was designed to be the entrance to his dungeon, and this was where he told K to dig.

They dug a little each week, with K shoveling the dirt into buckets that Cameron dumped outside. Over time the hole got bigger, and as K shoveled deeper into the earth, she sank with her work farther and farther below the level of the floor, until Cameron had to rig up a pulley system to lift out the buckets of dirt.

Jan helped a couple of times, but Cameron generally told her to stay in the house with the kids and the phone. He and his slave labored together, silent and intent. A mound of earth appeared to the south of the sheds, steadily growing as the hole got deeper.

Working a couple of hours a night and as much as two or three nights a week over many months, Cameron and K enlarged the hole from the size of a footlocker to the size of a car and, finally, to the size of a small room. At last Cameron decided that, though it would only be a miniature dungeon, it was large enough. Now it was time to put in a floor and build walls.

Cement bricks would do. Cameron borrowed a cement mixer from his father, made a mold, and poured the bricks himself. The bricks had to set for twenty-four hours or so, and he could only make ten at a time, but Hooker was a man with patience. . . .

"You will have to cash your check at Raley's. K has already been fed today. She doesn't know I'm gone. Don't tell her."

Thus read the note that Jan left on the kitchen table. She didn't even tell Cameron where she was going.

This was the first time she'd ever left like this, but she needed to get away from Cameron, needed some time alone. She drove south to the San Francisco Bay Area and stayed with one of her older brothers for four days of reprieve.

Cameron's "sex slave" had done little to ease the physical hardship on Jan, though that had been the reason, initially, that he'd given for kidnapping another woman. Janice detested bondage, and Cameron knew it, but still he hung her up and whipped her on a regular basis. With the exception of the head box and the electrical shocks and burns, Cameron used on her all the devices he used on K, making her sweat and weep with pain. Jan was hung, whipped, tied in various strange ways, blindfolded, gagged, stretched on the stretcher, forced to wear the gas mask, and dunked to the point of near-drowning. And yet she felt powerless to resist.

This strange marriage was all she knew. And she believed she loved her husband, even though she feared him.

Keeping so much of her life secret from outsiders was a

constant subconscious struggle, but she pushed the bad parts
out of her mind, beyond the reach of even the most confidential conversations with siblings, parents, or friends. Besides having two daughters and a lot of years together, she
and Cameron had a strong interest in keeping their marriage
together. They were bonded by the conjugal glue of secrecy.

In 1982, in an effort to clear the air and start their marriage afresh, the Hookers had what they dubbed "a confession time." All the dirty secrets they'd hidden from each
other were dusted off and brought out of the closet to be
discussed. More glue.

Janice reached all the way back to 1974 and confessed to
Cameron that she'd lied about being pregnant so that he
would marry her. She even told him about two brief affairs
she'd had in 1980. He was unperturbed.

Then he dropped the bomb: He told Jan that he had sex
with K while preforming bondage on her.

Jan was devastated. All these years she'd foolishly believed that, for all their problems, at least her husband was
faithful to her. She'd been lied to, betrayed.

But after the "confession time," beyond these painful revelations, there began a healing process.

To a couple of souls as lost as Jan and Cameron Hooker,
the Bible seemed as likely a key to repairing their marriage
as any. It was a do-it-yourself approach, with no third parties asking questions, just the two of them, the Holy Book,
and God. At first, Jan read by herself, looking for answers.
Then Cameron, who didn't read well, asked Jan to read the
Bible to him, and in time, she had read the entire New
Testament aloud, with Cameron sitting and listening carefully for parts he considered significant.

Hard-core pornography fans don't usually have much interest in the Holy Bible, but Cameron Hooker was nothing if
not unusual. To his surprise, much in the Bible spoke directly to him. He paid particular attention to references to
husbands and wives or slaves and masters, and there were
many, especially in Corinthians, Ephesians, and Colossians.
Clearly, he and God were in agreement that a wife should be

subservient to her husband in all things.[1] He emphasized this to Jan, and she heard him: If she didn't obey her husband, she would go to hell.

Noting that the Bible indicates that women should pray with their heads covered,[2] he gave Jan a "prayer hat" to wear whenever she prayed. Actually, it was just an expensive, red, white, and blue knit ski cap, but Cameron instructed her to wear it as a sign of submission. And so she did.

With Cameron's encouragement, Jan began to read the Bible more often, not just aloud to Cameron but by herself and with friends, including Cathy Deavers, a neighbor who had moved into a house down the lane in 1981. Besides having their locale in common, Jan and Cathy were both mothers of young children, and Cathy's little son often played with Jan's daughters.

One afternoon when Jan was over visiting, their talk turned to a discussion of the Bible.

"Before we start, Cameron wants me to put this beanie on," Jan said, pulling on her red, white, and blue cap. Cathy thought it queer, especially since it was summer, but she didn't want to embarrass Jan, and they proceeded with their discussion.

Cameron gave K a prayer hat, too—hers was a solid gray. Sometimes she wouldn't put it on when in the box; it was too hot. But if she was out and reading the Bible, she pulled it on like an obedient schoolgirl. Occasionally Hooker had

---

1. "Wives, submit to your own husbands, as to the Lord.

"For the husband is the head of the wife, as also Christ is the head of the church; and He is the Savior of the body.

"Therefore, just as the church is subject to Christ, so *let* the wives *be* to their own husbands in everything."

Ephesians, 5:22–24.

Holy Bible, The New King James Version

2. "But every woman who prays or prophesies with *her* head uncovered dishonors her head, for that is one and the same as if her head were shaved."

1 Corinthians, 11:5.

Holy Bible, The New King James Version

her read passages aloud, again lavishing attention on any mention of slaves and masters.[3]

The Bible had become more than a source of spiritual consolation; now it was a tool in her enslavement.

Cameron also recommended that Jan and K pray together, and toward the end of 1983, these two women with so much in common finally began to spend amiable hours together, without Jan giving orders, without hostilities. About three times a week, Jan would take K out of the box while the girls were at school, and they would read the Bible in the bedroom—their caps on, their Bibles open, their hearts filled with prayer. They reflected on the meaning of those passages, turning them over, discussing them, relating them to their own lives, until, for the first time, they found themselves actually talking with each other. . . .

When the bricks were ready, Cameron and K carried them down a makeshift ladder into the hole. In time, they had laid a floor. Then the walls went up, and the hole was finally beginning to look like a dungeon.

Hooker had big plans for his secret torture chamber. He affixed a hook to the ceiling beam, for hanging, and even put in a drain for an eventual shower. He also put two odd "windows" in the north wall, recessed places about eighteen inches wide and twenty-four inches tall.

Now that Cathy and Dawn were getting older, it was difficult to practice bondage in the house, and Hooker hoped that eventually he could keep his slave and his equipment down here, secure and out of the way. He explained to K that the windows would leave room for expansion. They could dig an adjoining room beneath the other shed, turning the windows into doorways.

---

3. "Servants, be obedient to those who are your masters according to the flesh, with fear and trembling, in sincerity of heart, as to Christ; not with eyeservice, as men-pleasers, but as servants of Christ, doing the will of God from the heart, with good will doing service, as to the Lord, and not to men, knowing that whatever good anyone does, he will receive the same from the Lord, whether *he is* a slave or free."
Ephesians, 6:5–8.
Holy Bible, The New King James Version

"Later," he boasted, "I'll enlarge the dungeon so there'll be room for more slaves." He told K that it would be her job to prepare the dungeon for them and then to train them, an idea that left her horrified.

Hooker's plans had an even more critical effect on Janice. Guilt was already growing inside Jan like a tumor, and the idea of another kidnapping seemed a nightmarish possibility. Ignorant of his wife's increasing disquiet, Cameron confided that, ultimately he'd like to capture four more women. And these new slaves might even bear his children.

Both Jan and K believed that Cameron was capable of carrying out these plans. Once Cameron Hooker decided on something, he pursued it with a chilling single-mindedness, and slaves were his ultimate obsession.

This called for nothing less than divine intervention. The two women prayed—fervently, with their prayer hats on— that Cameron's plans would never materialize.

It took until November of 1983—when Hooker had just turned thirty—to complete the hole beneath the shed to the point of usefulness, though it still lacked a few finishing touches. It was cold in the dungeon, so Hooker installed a heat lamp. Now, with both electricity and a ventilation system, the hole was ready for trial occupation.

Cameron gave K some clothes to put on: shoes, socks, jeans, and a sweatshirt. He took her out to the shed, unlocked it, removed the heavy board that covered the entrance to the hole, and said, "Climb down."

He handed down her Bible and a cheap radio they'd given her the month before. Inside, she found a portable toilet and a lounge chair with the same sleeping bag she'd received for Christmas of 1980—a bit worn, because the family had been using it, but a welcome touch.

Cameron had lingering doubts about keeping K in the hole, since it was possible she might somehow be discovered, so he left her with final instructions. "If anyone happens to find you down here," he told her, "say that you want to be here because it makes you feel closer to God."

He placed a sturdy board over the opening of the hole and went away.

To see how secure her new prison was, K climbed up on the ladder and pushed hard against the door. It didn't budge. Something heavy had been set on top of it.

But after surveying the situation, K found that even this dark, dank dungeon was an improvement over the box. She had room to move around. And sleeping on the lounge chair with the sleeping bag was fairly comfortable. The heat lamp didn't do much to counter the chill, but the light was a bonus; she could read the Bible or work on macrame or crochet dolls while listening to KVIP, the local Christian station.

It seemed feasible to keep K in the dungeon indefinitely. Her daily meal had to be brought out to the shed and handed down, which was a bit inconvenient, but no real problem. Cameron periodically came to empty the Porta Potti, K awkwardly passing the tank up to him so he could dump it down the toilet inside the mobile home. He told her that he would even get a hot plate so she could cook for herself.

But this new arrangement proceeded smoothly only for about one week.

One afternoon, Jan brought something out to K, went back in the house to fetch something else, and neglected to cover up the hole and lock the shed. This would have been harmless enough—K was far too intimidated to try to escape—except that children tend to find whatever mischief is about.

Cathy, now seven, and Dawn, now five, were exceptionally well-behaved children, and they had been told to stay away from the sheds. But on this particular day, they had company: six-year-old Denise Hooker, their high-spirited cousin. They'd been playing in the backyard, and when Jan came back outside, she found Dawn and Denise in the shed, looking down the hole.

Alarmed, Jan shooed the girls away, scolding them for misbehaving. Once they'd gone, she covered the hole back up and locked the shed.

K had seen the girls; she wasn't sure if they'd seen her.

When Cameron came home, Jan told him what had happened. They couldn't be sure what the girls had seen, but they were both worried that Denise would say something to her parents. They decided to take K out of the hole and put her back in the box until this blew over.

They waited nervously. A week or two passed. No one mentioned anything about a woman imprisoned in a dungeon. K was put back out in the hole.

But then the rains came.

Northern California's fall and winter storms made up for the long, dry months of summer with bone-drenching cloudbursts. The sky turned to ink and for a moment seemed to test the air with a tentative drizzle before the heavens ripped open and anyone with any sense took cover.

The earth turned wet, and water gradually seeped into the dungeon. It went from dampness to puddles, getting K's feet just a bit wet at first, then inching slowly up the walls, lapping at the legs of her chair, moving toward her ankles as the hole flooded in earnest. By the time Hooker came out after work to check on her, the cold water had risen up her shins.

He gave her a scoop and bucket and together they tried to bail the water out, but this was only moderately effective. Finally Hooker went out and bought a water pump—noisy, but more successful. When the water had receded to a manageable level, he left K in control so that she could turn the pump back on when the water level rose again. But, at last, he had to admit it was a losing battle. Winter had arrived, the dungeon flooded badly, and there was nothing to do but take K out and put her back in the box.

PART EIGHT

Scandal

March–June 1985

You can't try a case in a vacuum.

Christine McGuire

20

Christine McGuire was anxiously awaiting her first extended interview with Colleen. Dr. Hatcher had said that, during his interview with Colleen, she'd impressed him as being cooperative and frank; McGuire hoped this was true.

Still, Hatcher had unearthed some worrying surprises in Colleen's history, and McGuire was concerned that these could be used to besmirch her character and cast suspicion on her testimony.[1]

She worried about Colleen's mother, too. Today would be her first meeting with Evelyn Grant, but she already had a vaguely negative impression of the woman. For one thing, she'd read an article in *The Globe* that Mrs. Grant had supposedly written, and it galled her to think of the possibility of Grant selling her daughter's story to a tabloid.[2] Moreover, it bothered her that when Hatcher asked what kind of "moral outrage" Colleen's parents had expressed upon her return home, McGuire had to admit she was aware of none.

Now Colleen's plane had landed, and Colleen and her

---

1. In rape cases, the victim's past has no bearing on the crime and is generally disallowed, but ultimately it's up to the judge to decide whether certain evidence is admissible. Since myriad crimes had been committed here, and since this was a highly unusual case, McGuire was unsure how the judge might rule. She resolved to do everything she could to keep Colleen's past out of the trial.

2. Though the article carried her byline, Grant later denied having written it. Colleen also insisted that her mother hadn't been paid anything for the article in *The Globe*.

mother were emerging from the arrival lounge. McGuire's
brow furrowed when she caught sight of Colleen. Here she
was again, wearing tight black cords and spike heels. She'd
have to advise Colleen to wear something conservative at the
trial.

In the car, Colleen seemed quiet, withdrawn. McGuire
was starting to wonder whether her star witness had become
hostile when Colleen abruptly pulled out a business card and
handed it to her: "Here's the card of my attorney, Marilyn
Barrett. You should know she's representing me."

Startled by Colleen's defensiveness, McGuire wondered:
Whose side does she think I'm on? As she accepted the card,
she said she'd received a phone call from Barrett a few days
earlier, adding, "She seemed better informed than the first
attorney you thought of retaining." McGuire hoped this
sounded reassuring.

Actually, she was perplexed that Colleen had retained a
tax attorney to represent her. While well-meaning, Barrett
hadn't impressed her as particularly knowledgeable about
Colleen's case, and her primary qualification seemed less her
legal expertise than her involvement in the California Com-
mission on Assaults Against Women.

In a few minutes, McGuire mentioned her daughter and
asked: "Would you like to see some pictures?" Colleen
smiled, her posture relaxed, and McGuire saw that she'd
touched a soft spot. She shared her photos of Nicole, then
was surprised when Colleen started pulling out her own pictures of nieces, nephews, and half-sisters. It touched her that
Colleen so clearly delighted in these children. This was a
side of Colleen she hadn't imagined.

The two-hour drive back to Red Bluff gave McGuire a
chance to get a feeling for this strange, sweet, submissive
young woman. She liked her but also found her disquieting
—at once shy, defensive, and oddly bland.

Meanwhile, the attorney in her couldn't help but wonder
how Colleen would come across to a jury. Traces of malnu-
trition and ill-health lingered, especially in her thin, dull
hair and her discolored teeth, but these were subtle. And
despite years of abuse, Colleen was a long way from emaci-
ated; she was a bit heavy around the hips, her skin looked

younger than her twenty-eight years, and her blue eyes sparkled.

When they arrived in Red Bluff, they stopped at a deli for lunch, and McGuire had more opportunity to observe Mrs. Grant, whom Colleen had described as "a people person." By the end of the meal, McGuire would beg to differ.

She found Colleen's mother superficial and wondered if Grant, who dominated the conversation and often answered for Colleen, was along more for the notoriety than as support for her daughter. Lunch seemed to take ages.

When they finally arrived at the police station, McGuire assigned Lieutenant Brown the task of interviewing the mother.[3] Meanwhile, Shamblin and McGuire took Colleen across the street to the district attorney's office.

They started at the beginning and covered areas they'd never gone into before: the events of the kidnap, the years of captivity and intermittent beatings, the escape. Colleen explained about the slavery contract, recounted stories Cameron had told her about the Company, and gave details of how she'd coped with confinement in the box.

As her story unfolded, McGuire found it more and more bizarre.

Throughout the interview Colleen answered without hesitation or evasion, yet she always spoke with the same dull monotone. She was so unemotional that McGuire resorted to asking her to quantify pain, fear, and humiliation on a scale of one to ten. The pain of being hung, for example, Colleen rated a ten. And while the humiliation of soiling the box by defecation or urination rated a ten, menstruation rated only a five. (Unknown to Colleen, this rating was Dr. Hatcher's idea. He'd cautioned McGuire about this "lack of affect," or emotion, and had recommended rating emotions on a descending scale.)

Beneath her general passivity, Colleen was absolutely ear-

3. The most significant information he learned was that when Colleen came home, she told her mother only the bare minimum of what she'd suffered over the past several years. This seemed to explain, to some extent, the lack of "moral outrage" that concerned Dr. Hatcher and Deputy DA McGuire.

nest about one thing: She had tried to be a good slave. When Cameron told her to do the dishes, for instance, she tried her best to do them quickly and well. But Hooker would time her, and hurry as she might, she couldn't get them all washed and dried in less than twenty-five minutes. Colleen insisted that she'd tried, she really had, but darn it, she just wasn't fast enough.

McGuire shuddered inwardly. There was something pathetic in this, and for a moment McGuire flashed on the image of a mistreated dog, eager for attention but afraid, wagging its tail, yet cowering.

Late that day, McGuire finally got around to asking a troublesome question: "During any of the seven years, did you ever tell Cameron you loved him?"

Colleen didn't flinch. "Yeah."

McGuire sighed. Damn. This was the major weakness in their case.

"At what point in time did you tell him that you loved him?"

"I don't know. It was probably 1980 or '81."

"Looking back at that time, what kind of feelings did you feel?"

"I don't know. I suppose I just felt that I loved him because I was glad to be out of that box, for one thing, and because he gave me a certain amount of freedom. I suppose that was why."

McGuire was acutely aware of the tape recorder whirring in witness to Colleen's words. The tape would be transcribed and passed on to Papendick, who would sift through it for information he could use in Hooker's defense. So, for whatever it was worth, she would try to dredge up something with which to counter Papendick.

"Did you feel as though Cameron had given you back your life again?"

"Yeah, in a way."

"Did you feel grateful that he hadn't killed you?"

"Yes."

"Did you feel dependent upon him?"

"Yeah, I did at that time."

McGuire only hoped she could get Dr. Hatcher on the

stand to somehow explain Colleen's weird "love" for Cameron Hooker. Even then, she dreaded the jury's reaction. This simple, four-letter word could nullify their entire case.

McGuire made thorough use of the time she had with Colleen. They reviewed the transcript of the preliminary hearing and came up with few surprises. They went over diagrams, Colleen making corrections and offering suggestions. They viewed slides Hooker had taken of Janice in bondage positions, Colleen pointing out previously unnoticed details. And when something reminded her of an incident she'd forgotten, she went off on tangents, the tape recorder turning in dumb witness while McGuire struggled to fit new information into set legal contexts.

They went through the boxes of photographs the police had seized—a massive collection that surprised Colleen. Hooker had taken photos of everything, but he had never shown them to her. It took hours, but Colleen examined more than five hundred photographs. Most of the shots were of Janice in bondage positions; Colleen indicated those similar to what Cameron had done to her.

They also went through a large number of hard-core pornographic publications, the Deputy DA asking Colleen if she could identify scenes Cameron had tried to duplicate on her. But Hooker was such a pack rat (he kept everything, including magazines and clippings dating back ten or fifteen years), they got bogged down and finally elected to send Colleen photocopies of the magazines later.

At one point, McGuire and Colleen got down on their hands and knees on the floor to make a chart. With more than seven years to cover, McGuire wanted a time-line showing all the counts and significant incidents from the kidnap in 1977 to escape in 1984. Using Magic Markers on three-by-five-foot poster board, they sprawled across the floor like children, inking in lines.

They also inspected Hooker's gadgets. Colleen showed them how to reconstruct the stretcher—a good thing, since it turned out that part of it was missing. And they examined the reconstructed box and bed, Colleen pointing out the discolored area where her head had lain. None of them had been able to understand the ventilation system, so Colleen explained that it required an old-fashioned hair dryer, the type with a hose and bonnet.

Next, they wondered how the head box worked. They measured Colleen's neck, but were reluctant to ask her to put it on. McGuire volunteered.

There was nothing appealing about putting on the head box—the foam and carpet insulation were decayed and still sprinkled with mouse droppings—but the prosecutor was determined to try it, make sure it fit, and learn how it worked. To keep her hair clean, she covered her head with a plastic bag with a hole cut for breathing.

With Colleen coaching, Lieutenant Brown shut the box tightly around her neck.

Colleen had said it pinched. It did.

McGuire knew she was surrounded by people she trusted, but "a terrible, horrible, helpless feeling" went through her. Then claustrophobia struck and she started to panic, afraid they wouldn't be able to get the box unlatched. Now she was nearly hyperventilating. Some mouse droppings went up her nose. "Get this thing off me!" she cried.

When the head box came off the relief was so extreme, she laughed. Then Jerry Brown chuckled, her tension dissolved, and laughter spread through the room.

The morning of Thursday, March 28, Colleen and her mother were driven back to the Sacramento airport, where they boarded a plane back to Southern California. McGuire saw them off at the airport and hugged Colleen good-bye. Later, during the long drive back to Red Bluff, she was left to ruminate on this still-enigmatic woman.

Over the past three days, Colleen had described her ordeal in blunt and specific terms. She had relived every turn in her captivity, dredging up the most painful and humiliating details of what Hooker had done to her, and through it all, she'd remained almost indifferent. She showed no real sympathy for Hooker, but little hatred, either, nor any great desire for vengeance.

Colleen seemed to perceive herself as doomed to misfortune. At one point she'd likened herself to her father, who,

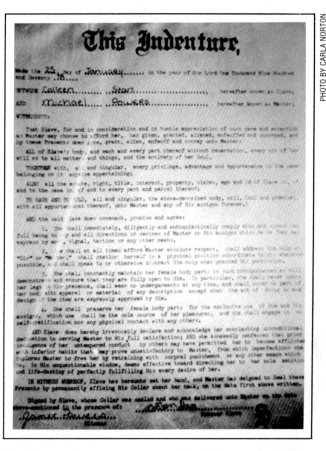

The Slavery Contract, supposedly drawn up by "The Company"

Cameron Hooker

Colleen Stan, "The Girl in the Box"

Janice Hooker leaves the courthouse after testifying

On display at the trial: the "Head Box" which was locked over Colleen Stan's head

Reconstructed by investigators: the box in which Colleen Stan was imprisoned

Police officer Al Shamblin leaves the mobile home in Red Bluff where Colleen Stan was held captive

Cameron Hooker (in handcuffs) after being arraigned on 18 counts

**Prosecutor Christine McGuire at work during the
trial of Cameron Hooker**

Colleen Stan (seated) with Christine McGuire

Cameron Hooker and his attorney, Rolland Papendick

she said, had been "ripped off all his life. Used, like me. We're two of a kind." Perhaps she felt the worst was only to be expected.

In some ways, McGuire thought, Hooker had found the perfect victim in Colleen Stan. She was naïve, pliable, and her history was tinged with tragedy—a broken home, a broken marriage, a few aimless years of young adulthood. Then, by a swift and cruel accident, she'd been standing at the side of the road when Cameron Hooker was hunting for a slave.

And she'd tried to be a good slave. She'd endured more than she'd resisted . . . and had survived.

However bewildering Colleen's apathy, however bizarre the details of her story, the prosecutor now felt positive that Colleen was telling the truth. She wasn't evasive, didn't contradict herself, take cheap shots, or try to make herself look good. And Christine McGuire, for all her meticulousness and despite the poker face she maintained in the courtroom, harbored a hot sense of justice. Over the past three days she'd come face-to-face with the gritty details of the crimes committed against this meek, obliging woman, and they left her outraged. They were beyond brutality, beyond reason, and they moved her to a personal vow that Cameron Hooker would be prosecuted to the full extent of the law.

But forces were already gathering to thwart that promise.

21

In mid-April, Christine McGuire and her husband took a long-anticipated vacation. Leaving Nicole in the care of her maternal grandmother, they flew to the Greek Isles.

They spent a rejuvenating two weeks away from the pressures of the office—hiking, sunning, sightseeing, and feasting. With the Mediterranean fluxing aqua-blue all around them, they rededicated themselves to their faltering marriage.

They returned to Red Bluff refreshed and optimistic—but they were kidding themselves.

Soon after their return, their familiar old problems resurfaced, and Christine and Jim again broadsided each other with accusations and threats. Christine threatened to leave. Jim didn't believe her.

She left and spent the night with a friend . . . but the next day she came back. Both of them genuinely wanted the marriage to work, but neither seemed able to halt its downward spiral. The cycle of pleading, promises, excuses and scolding resumed. . . .

Even as this private tempest blew, clouds were gathering around Christine McGuire and James Lang for a more public storm of controversy.

Tehama was a little county with big financial problems. Taxes in this county of 40,000 people, many of whom were unemployed, weren't yielding enough to support all the op-

erations of the government. Something in the budget had to
be cut.

Parks and libraries were first. County employees were
next. The Board of Supervisors announced that work weeks
were being cut back to four days, and not even the courts or
the DA's office would be spared.[1]

The cost of trying Cameron Hooker, estimated at between
$100,000 to $250,000, looked to be the straw that would
break the camel's back. Toward the end of May, members of
the Board had begun to grumble that if Hooker went to
trial, the out-of-county trial costs would force them to lay
off between twenty and fifty county employees.

Off the record, the word went out to District Attorney
James Lang that he ought to negotiate a plea for Cameron
Hooker because the county simply couldn't afford to try
him. At first, Lang thought the Board was crying wolf.
Moreover, he understood what the county bureaucrats did
not: a lack of funds was insupportable grounds for negotiating a plea.

But ultimately the DA has to answer to the Board of
Supervisors; they pull the purse strings. And they privately
made it clear that, in the county's best interest, Lang should
opt for a plea.

Meanwhile, innocent of these private exchanges between
her husband and certain members of the Board, McGuire
was fishing. She wondered if she could get Hooker to plead
guilty and avoid a trial. In court on another matter, she
approached Hooker's defense attorney and asked, "What'll
it be, Papendick? Are we going to try this case, or is your
client going to plead?"

Papendick grinned and unconsciously wrinkled his nose, a
characteristic quirk. He could work to persuade his client to
plead to the kidnap, he said, "but it's my understanding that
even though Hooker might have kidnapped her, the sex acts

---

1. Tehama County's judges and district attorney took the position
that the Board of Supervisors did not have the authority to control the
operation of the courts and that state law required they operate five
days a week. Therefore, while the Board announced four-day work
weeks, the courts continued to schedule hearings for a full five days.

were consensual. All the sex charges will have to be dropped."

"How the hell can someone be enslaved and validly consent to anything?" McGuire snapped.

But when she came back to the office and told DA Jim Lang of the ridiculous deal Papendick had offered, she was startled to hear Jim say: "Take it!"

Before she could protest he bluntly told her: "There is no money to try Hooker." She sat, stunned, as he explained the Board's position. It slowly sank in: They were going to have to negotiate a plea.

Hooker was going to get the deal of his life, and her hands were tied. If the county refused to pay for trying Hooker, she would have to form an offer that Papendick found acceptable—even if it meant dropping all the sex counts, which carried the most severe sentences.

She phoned Papendick, offering to drop the sex charges, leaving only the kidnap, abduction to live in an illicit relationship, and false imprisonment charges.

Papendick said he'd talk to his client and get back to her.

At 5 P.M. that afternoon, he strode into the DA's office to say that his client would accept.

The next day, while Deputy DA McGuire was in court on another matter, Judge Watkins asked to speak to her in his chambers. He'd heard the rumors of a plea negotiation and wanted to know whether or not Hooker was going to trial.

"I'm afraid not," she said. "We have to negotiate it because the Board says the county can't afford to try it."

He looked like he'd been hit in the stomach.

His first response, knowing that McGuire had been living and breathing this case for months, was to offer his condolences. Then he got angry. "The truly appalling thing," he said, "is that the Board is dictating to the criminal justice system."

Galling as this was, it seemed they were left with no alternative. If she stood up in court and gave the budget crunch as the real reason for negotiating, he would accept the plea —though with great reluctance.

The plea was scheduled to be taken the morning of June

10 in Judge Watkins's court. Deputy DA McGuire would
drop the sex counts, and Papendick would enter Hooker's
guilty pleas to the kidnap and the remaining minor charges.
The case would be referred to Tehama County Probation for
a sentence recommendation, and Hooker would be incarcer-
ated for a few years. That was all.

Originally, McGuire had calculated that if Hooker got the
maximum sentence on all counts, he'd get a hundred and
fifteen years. Now Hooker would be sentenced to ten. With
time off for good behavior, he could be out on parole in as
little as four and a half years.

What was she going to tell Colleen?

After all those months of preparation, the case against
Hooker would be decided not by a jury but by a bunch of
bureaucrats who cared more for economics than for justice.

In no time, the Hooker case was making headlines again.
It seemed the whole state was scandalized. If the very idea
that justice could be bought was repugnant, that Tehama
County wouldn't pay for it was worse.

PART NINE

Confession

December 31, 1983–November 19, 1984

The cruelest lies are often told in silence.

                              Robert Louis Stevenson

22

It was December 31, New Year's Eve, and as the last hours of 1983 slipped away, Colleen Stan turned twenty-seven. As the Hooker's slave, she had learned not to expect special attention or favors, but late that night, after the girls were safely asleep, Jan and Cameron got K out of the box and brought her into the kitchen. On the stove sat a birthday cake, iced and with candles. To her complete pleasure and surprise, the Hooker's sang "Happy Birthday" to her, and after she had blown out the candles, they all ate the chocolate cake with ice cream.

Thus 1983 elapsed, and this little celebration—which Cameron told her was a reward for being a good slave—marked not only K's birthday and the dawning of 1984, but the beginning of an era of freedoms beyond any K had experienced even during her "year out" three years earlier. It began gradually, with K being given just a bit more license —nothing extraordinary and nothing to presage the upheaval 1984 would bring.

Beginning in January, K was granted a few small liberties, special at first, but soon routine. Her nocturnal releases from the box elongated; most nights she was out for several hours. She was allowed to fix something for herself to eat, and afterward she could stay in the back bathroom to read or write poetry or do crafts. And though K was still required to call Cameron "Sir," she now called Jan by name.

The special relationship that had blossomed between Jan and K continued to grow, tentatively, in the quiet times when Cameron and the children were gone. The Bible was the root of their friendship, and their excuse, initially, for talking. Before their religious discussions, in all the seasons they'd passed under the same roof, they'd never engaged in real conversation.

Now Jan got K out of the box two or three times a day—not only for Biblical discussions but to help with housework or to chat over sandwiches and cookies.

The kinship that sprang up between them was evidently clandestine, a refuge in the midst of extreme circumstances, and their new camaraderie was nurtured by the many things they had in common. Both had dropped out of high school for quick marriages at a young age in Nevada. Both adored children, particularly Cathy and Dawn. Both were lonely, vulnerable, submissive women with terrible secrets and no friends with whom to share them.

And they were both deeply afraid of provoking the anger of Cameron Hooker.

K had been granted a long stretch of relative peace, with little physical or sexual abuse over the past several months. During this period, Hooker, instead, focused his attention on Jan. The incidents of hanging, bondage, and sado-masochism, which throughout their marriage had averaged about once or twice a month, started climbing in late 1983 and by 1984 had jumped to about six times a month.

Hooker had found it convenient to blame K's mistreatment on Company orders; now he hung and whipped Jan, he said, out of concern for her soul. He told her that she was possessed, and punishment was the only way to get the devil out.

Thanks to frequent meals, K's bony frame filled out from less than 100 pounds to a more respectable 110, 115, 120. She didn't realize at the time that the Hookers were intentionally trying to fatten her up.

Looking better nourished, cleaned up, and with some decent clothes on, she was ready to face the world again. Hooker had decided that, after three years of nearly continuous confinement, K was ready to be out of the box full time.

Now she no longer slept in the box beneath the bed, but in a sleeping bag on the living room floor. She was reintroduced to the Hookers' little girls and again entrusted with babysitting. Family members who stopped by found that "Kay" had returned from Southern California. And in no time Jan was steering her around the neighborhood saying, "Look who's back!"

But these were simply preliminaries. The real reason K was out of the box was that Cameron, obviously confident of his control over her, had decided to let her get a job.

"I'm sticking my neck out," he told her. "I don't have the fifteen hundred dollars to pay the Company's security fee, but I'll let you go out and work. The money you earn will be saved, and when there's enough I'll buy a little house trailer you can live in."

So in May of 1984, exactly seven years after Colleen Stan's 1977 abduction, K's increasing freedoms culminated in a job search. Jan drove her around to well over a dozen businesses to that she could fill out applications.

Motels seemed a good place to try. K opened the door of King's Lodge and asked, "Are you hiring? Do you have any work for me?"

The motel owner and manager, a stout, dark-haired woman by the name of Doris Miron, appraised this clean and smiling young woman, asked her to fill out an application, and hired her on the spot. K seemed happy to get a job and eager to work; that impressed Mrs. Miron. She was to start her job as a motel maid the next morning.

With her new employment, K settled into a routine. In the early morning she gardened, hoeing and weeding, planting and watering, working up such a sweat that the neighbors couldn't help but notice. She raised blisters long before any vegetables but never complained, for simply being outdoors again was an answer to countless prayers.

As dawn pushed into morning, K washed up and got ready for work. Sometimes Jan drove her, but more often K pedalled the three and a half miles into town on Jan's bike.

At King's Lodge, K worked so diligently that she earned the ire of some of her coworkers, who saw her as Mrs.

Miron's goody-goody "golden girl." And Mrs. Miron was indeed impressed. She soon gave her a promotion: "Kay" was the first maid Mrs. Miron ever asked to work at the front desk. She felt she could trust her.

Sometimes, if Mrs. Miron came into the office, they'd talk, and Miron learned something of K's situation at home.

At first K told Mrs. Miron that Jan was her sister; then she amended that, saying, "She's actually just a very good friend, but we're like sisters." They stayed up late together, K told her, making "strawberry dolls"—toilet tissue holders with crocheted skirts and cute little faces. They were trying to sell them for fifteen dollars apiece, and Mrs. Miron bought three.

It seemed to Doris Miron that money was a problem with the Hookers, and they were taking advantage of "Kay." Once "Kay" told her: "I give all my checks to Jan and Cameron to pay for room and board, and they give me an allowance of twenty dollars." That didn't seem right to Mrs. Miron.

When the maids took breaks and bought colas out of the vending machine, Lenora Scott, another maid, also noticed that "Kay" never seemed to have much money. Lenora, twenty-two, didn't like her at first, but one day the sky turned dark with clouds, and knowing that "Kay" had ridden her bike, she approached her after work.

"It looks like it's going to rain," she said. "Do you need a ride home? We can put your bike in the back."

K couldn't see any problem with that, so they loaded up the bike and Lenora drove her south of town, down the dirt road to the mobile home. No one was home, so K invited her new friend inside.

They chatted awhile. Lenora noticed a sleeping bag on the floor, where K said she slept. Motioning to a back pack, K said, "All my worldly possessions are in that pack." She apparently didn't consider that this would strike Lenora as odd, even though she'd said she'd lived here a long time.

Jan came home shortly and joined them in the living room. Lenora had met the plump, frizzy-haired Mrs. Hooker at the motel one day when she was picking up K after work. Now that they had a chance to visit they found,

as is often the case in a small town, that they had friends and
acquaintances in common.

It wasn't long until Cameron came home. He came in, sat
down on the couch, and stared at Lenora. He didn't say a
word, just stared.

Unsettled, Lenora said her good-byes and left.

Early in June, Cameron Hooker made a serious mistake.
K asked permission to go to church. He said yes.

The Church of the Nazarene stands on a quiet corner just
a few blocks from downtown Red Bluff. The church is a
large, airy structure with high, beamed ceilings. Broad steps
rise up to the front doors, and a sign out front announces the
service schedule.

The first Sunday K rode to church on the bus with the
children. The next Sunday Jan decided to go with her, so
they all went together in the car. From then on, Jan and K
attended regularly.

Had Cameron Hooker anticipated the effect these services
would have, he surely would have insisted that his women
stay home. But religion had served him well so far, and he
saw no reason why it shouldn't continue to do so. At least
Jan and K weren't fighting anymore.

Pastor Frank Dabney, a tall and distinguished-looking
man with an impressive girth and gray hair, led a devoted, if
not overly large or prosperous, congregation. They filed in,
smiling greetings to those they knew, then sat quietly on the
padded pews and skimmed hand-outs of church news while
waiting for the pastor to begin.

At last he ascended the pulpit, the assembly hushed, and
the service began.

It was a service not unlike thousands that take place every
Sunday across the country. The congregation sang together,
prayed together, and listened quietly as the pastor extolled
virtues and castigated sins in his "message," the spiritual
focus of the morning. As Pastor Dabney rocked back and
forth on his heels, his words resonating through the room,
he surveyed his flock, noticing two new faces among the
congregation.

There was nothing especially remarkable about "Kay

Powers" and Janice Hooker, except that Mrs. Hooker was often noticeably moved by the pastor's message. She wept. The pastor made it a policy not to pry, but it seemed clear this was a deeply troubled young woman.

Jan and K were now attending church regularly, so Pastor Dabney decided to pay them a call. They'd included their address when they signed the register, so one morning, unannounced, the pastor drove out to the brown and yellow trailer off Pershing Road.

It was just a brief social call. Pleasant, but unremarkable . . . except that "Kay" seemed a little nervous. When Pastor Dabney appeared at the door, she dropped and broke a dish.

One evening, on the spur of the moment, Lenora Scott and her husband, Tom, decided to stop by and see if K might like to go out with them. They pulled up outside of the mobile home and K hurried out to greet them.

"We're going out," they said. "You wanna come along?"

K asked them to wait, then rushed back inside the mobile home. Strange. It seemed she had gone in to ask permission.

When K came out she said she'd like to go with them, then invited them inside. They went in and spoke briefly with the Hookers. Lenora found Cameron only slightly less taciturn than the last time. He still just sat. Lenora thought he was weird.

They went to the Palomino Room, a popular after-hours place in the middle of Main Street. Each had a drink in the dimly lit bar, but they found it smoky and "full of drunks," so they only stayed a short time before taking K back home.

It wasn't much of a night out on the town, but even with friends in a bar, K divulged little about herself. "She was very meek," Lenora observed, "and she had no opinions. The only thing she seemed to feel real strongly about was religion." Not that K was preachy, but it seemed that religion was the only thing that meant very much to her.

Now Sarai, Abram's wife, had borne him no children. And she had an Egyptian maidservant whose name was Hagar.

So Sarai said to Abram, "See now, the Lord has restrained me from bearing children. Please, go in to my maid; perhaps I shall obtain children by her." And Abram heeded the voice of Sarai.

Then Sarai, Abram's wife, took Hagar her maid, the Egyptian, and gave her to her husband to be his wife. . . .

Genesis, 16:1–3
Holy Bible, The New King James Version

Cameron first brought up the story of Sarah[1] and Hagar in 1983, when Jan was reading the Old Testament to him. Now he began to reemphasize it, claiming that their three-party household was based on Scripture.

He tried to persuade his wife that with K out of the box, he ought to be able to sleep openly with her. "It's like Biblical times," he told Jan. "And you'll make it easier on yourself if you just accept K as my slave wife, because I'm going to sleep with her whether you like it or not."

Jan wrestled with this. She wanted to do what was right, and she knew the Bible said she should follow her husband's commands, but the idea of Cameron having two wives seemed blatantly sinful. With no one to turn to, she prayed for guidance.

But Cameron wouldn't wait for Jan to be granted divine inspiration. He started telling K that she needed sex, and that God told him that he should fulfill that need. . . .

The sex acts with K, which had lapsed during the past year and a half, recommenced. At one point, Hooker ordered his wife and his slave to entertain him with lesbian acts. And finally, with considerable effort, he succeeded in swaying Janice to his position: for the first time since 1977, he had both women in bed with him at the same time.

When Jan came down with a bad case of flu, K volunteered to take care of her. Mrs. Miron was disgruntled when

---

1. For some reason, the Hookers used this pronunciation and spelling of the wife's name. The husband's, they pronounced as "Abraham," so "Sarah" and "Abraham" are used hereafter.

K asked for time off to stay home with Jan—"Why can't her husband take care of her?" she wondered—but she granted her favorite maid some time off nonetheless.

While Jan recovered, K brought her refreshments, took care of the girls, and did the household chores. And instead of giving a large tip she'd just received to Cameron, she bought Jan some flowers.

Jan was so touched that when she was up and around again, she went out and bought roses for K, enclosing a card that read: "Hagar, I love you." She signed it: "Sarah."

23

As summer wore on, the three adults and two children living in the bucolic setting south of town presented the very picture of wholesomeness. The young and responsible father continued his regular working routine. The live-in babysitter rode her bike to and from work and exercised her green thumb in the flourishing garden. The two little girls, now nearly six and eight, played and laughed in the yard. But beneath this placid, sun-bathed surface, the twenty-six-year-old mother felt powerless and confused.

Anxiety was already eating away at the facade of normalcy that Janice had struggled for so long to maintain. She had blocked out as much as she could for as long as possible, apparently living her life in a daze, as if it were a bad dream. But now new conflicts rose to the surface.

She awoke to find that K had become her closest friend. Friendship demanded truthfulness, yet every offhand question or comment K made about slaves or the Company required some response, and no matter what Jan said, no matter how significant, it was a lie.

More than once, with K and alone, she sought out Pastor Dabney's advice, asking about roles of husbands and wives, and about Genesis, Chapter 16, the story of Abraham, Sarah, and Hagar. Without prying, he offered what guidance he could, but what he told Jan only heightened her dilemma. The compassionate pastor gave interpretations of the Holy Book distinctly different from those of her husband.

Cameron was using the Bible against her; Jan saw that

now. But despite this new glimmer of understanding that
Cameron was using fear to manipulate her, Jan was afraid to
stand up to him. She believed that if she made him angry
enough he would kill her. He had it in him, of this she was
absolutely certain.

Hooker meanwhile seemed increasingly committed to the
idea of capturing more slaves. The thought sickened her.
She'd had enough of kidnapping and lies, of snatching innocent lives off the street, of living with the fear of being found
out, of struggling to shield her daughters from what was
going on just beyond the walls of the room where they slept.

But what could she do? She couldn't tell anyone. She
didn't know whom to trust . . . and no one would believe
her anyway. And she couldn't go to the police because she
was guilty, too. Her daughters would be taken from her.
That was the most frightening thought: She would lose her
girls.

She wanted to flee, to leave her past behind forever. But
she had two young children to think of, nowhere to go, and
no way to support herself. She'd never even lived alone,
much less supported a family.

Now Cameron had a new plan which heightened Jan's
distress. He called it the "alternate night system," but no
matter what he called it, no matter how he tried to use the
Bible to justify it, it seemed sinful and wrong. He announced
to his wife and slave that under this new system, he would
sleep with one of them for two nights, with the other for the
next two nights, and with whichever he liked for the remaining three. He tried to pose this as a proposition, as if during
"their nights" they had an option to do as they pleased, but
both women knew that if they didn't do what Cameron
wished, they would be punished. With Cameron, there were
no alternatives.

Jan was at an impasse. The only person she knew in a
similar predicament was K.

At one point Jan confided in her that she was thinking of
leaving. K didn't want Jan to leave her alone with Cameron
—she was too afraid of him—but the idea of leaving with
Jan terrified her even more. "We can't go," K protested.
"They'll find us and torture us!"

There it was again. The lie.

By the end of July, Jan had played and replayed all her options. "I can't take it anymore," she told Cameron. "I want you to kill me."

She asked him to strangle her. He had experience at this. He'd choked Jan until she'd passed out at least half a dozen times in the past, though never at her request. Now he obliged her, placing his long fingers around her neck and squeezing hard.

It was not an unfamiliar sensation. She heard that odd crackling sound, like a TV had just been turned off, and she knew she was about to go out.

But then, with Jan still this side of unconsciousness, he relaxed his grip. He wouldn't do it.

She was still alive. And all her questions and problems came screaming back.

The blistering month of August broke, and Jan's anxiety boiled. She needed answers.

Her search for help moved her to approach other preachers in the area, but her questions were so oblique that she probably left them with the impression that she was struggling with problems of marital infidelity. She was advised to go home and try harder.

By chance, at the Church of the Nazarene, Jan met a couple whom she felt she could talk to—not telling the complete truth, of course, but for the first time in ten years, Jan opened up. They spoke of ethics, posing hypothetical questions to explore issues of right and wrong. Jan even asked the woman personal questions about how a husband ought to show love, for this was something Jan knew little about, Cameron being her only reference.

Jan evidently came away with new convictions. Battling with her conscience, wrestling with the wickedness within her life, she finally approached Pastor Dabney. In his large and comforting presence, she risked slightly more telling questions, though still presenting an impression more of a love triangle than of sexual slavery. The pastor told her they were living in sin and advised changes, scarcely realizing that his words were opening an irreparable crack in Cameron Hooker's iron control over his wife.

Jan's beleaguered spirit, wavering loyalties, confusion, and worry over the state of her soul finally reached a crescendo on Thursday, August 9, 1984. If the worst that could happen would be for Cameron to kill her, she had already faced it. She had to do something.

She arrived at King's Lodge at about eleven-thirty A.M. and asked Mrs. Miron if she could speak with "Kay." With the manager's permission she went down the slope to the main building and found K at work in one of the rooms. She had arrived at the moment of truth.

Jan screwed up her courage and finally spoke the words she'd contemplated but avoided for so long: "K, I need to tell you something. Cameron lied to you about everything. The Company, the slavery contract, all that he told you about me being a slave, all that was just lies. He lied to scare you, to make you stay his slave."

K simply crumpled. Stunned by the enormity of it, aghast that anyone could lie so constantly, so convincingly as Cameron Hooker had, she wept tears of shock and disbelief. Of bitterness. Of rage. Over seven years! A quarter of her life had been stolen from her!

Janice cried, too, saying over and over how sorry she was. "I hope you can find it in your heart to forgive me," she said.

They probably held each other, shuddering together in the middle of calamity. But now K finally saw that she was free. The door was open. The lie was over.

The two women needed to get away from Cameron, to escape together, but how? They decided to ask the advice of Pastor Dabney.

They walked back to the motel office. When they came in the door, Doris Miron noticed instantly that they'd been crying heavily.

"I have to quit," her favorite worker said, offering no explanation. Surprised, Mrs. Miron assumed it was some problem with the head maid, Heidi, but "Kay" looked so distressed that Mrs. Miron didn't press her for more information. Instead, she said she was sorry she was quitting, but asked that "Kay" finish her day's work first.

Jan called the pastor and set up an afternoon appointment and then left. K went back to making beds and cleaning bathrooms, tears streaming while she worked.

About two hours later, Jan came back to pick up K, who said her farewells and asked Mrs. Miron to please hold her next paycheck until she could send a new address. Cameron Hooker wouldn't be collecting any more of her money.

When they arrived at the church, the pastor had a hard time understanding these two very upset women, but he learned that K had been held against her will, that the two had been subjected to strange sexual practices, and that both were terrified of Cameron. Dabney advised them to pack up and leave immediately, suggesting they go home and stay with their parents.

But it wasn't that simple. It was getting close to four o'clock, Cameron's quitting time, Janice explained, and she was supposed to pick him up after work. There wouldn't be time to get their things before then, and they were afraid of confronting him.

The pastor suggested that they pick him up from work as usual, pretend nothing had happened, and then leave the next day, after Cameron had left for work. That's what they decided to do.

It occurred to K that Jan's will might falter and she might confess to Cameron what she'd done, but the cards had been dealt, and now, poker-faced, she and Jan had to play their hands.

They picked up Cameron as usual. They made and ate dinner and cleaned up afterwards. If Cameron thought it was odd that Jan didn't want to sleep with him that night, her excuse that she wasn't feeling well must have quelled his suspicions. Jan slept on the floor with K.

The next morning Cameron left for work at five A.M., and as soon as he was out the door, Jan and K started packing. When Cathy and Dawn got up, they were sent off to Bible school, and with no kids underfoot, the two women finished the job quickly. By noon they were done. They gathered up their belongings, picked up the girls, and fled to Jan's parents' home in the nearby town of Gerber.

Her parents were probably stunned to find their daughter, married now for ten years, on their doorstep with her two girls and the babysitter in tow, but they offered them a place to sleep.

Now it was up to Jan and K to figure out what to do next. They talked of staying together, of trying to make a good home for the girls. Because of her genuine affection for Cathy and Dawn, this seemed attractive to K. It also appealed to her selfless side: Oddly enough, she saw Jan as so dependent that she couldn't picture her taking care of her children and making it on her own. They discussed going together down to Riverside and staying with K's father or staying with Jan's folks. But in the back of her mind, K heard a voice urging her to go: *Don't stay!* it said. *Jan has to make it on her own. You can't help her anymore. Get away! Go home!*

K finally made her decision and called her father. She asked him to wire her a hundred dollars for the bus fare home.

Jack Martin, who hadn't heard from his daughter since her whirlwind visit of March, 1981, was stunned to hear Colleen's voice and thrilled at the prospect of seeing her again. Eager to do whatever he could to get his daughter home, he generously offered larger amounts of money: "Are you sure a hundred dollars is enough? I can send more, honey. How much do you need?" But Colleen finally convinced her bewildered dad that a hundred dollars was plenty.

The next morning, after K had her ticket in hand and was certain she would be boarding the bus for home momentarily, she phoned Cameron.

It was her declaration of independence. "I just wanted to tell you that I'm leaving, that I know you lied about everything, and you can't keep me here anymore."

Colleen doesn't remember all that Cameron said, but she does recall one thing: He cried.

24

Now with her parents, Jan was living several miles away from Cameron but hadn't escaped his pull. To her amazement, he didn't threaten her or come after her with a gun, but after sulking for a few days, he begged her to come back to him. He swore that he'd change, get counseling, give up bondage, *anything* if she'd just come home.

Janice wavered. She worried about how she was going to support her two daughters, about the police, and about whether she'd done the right thing in setting K free. She hadn't been very forthcoming about the real reasons she'd left Cameron, so friends and relatives, thinking this was little more than a marital spat, urged her to forgive Cameron, go back, and give their ten-year marriage another try. After a week of vacillation, she and the girls moved back.

Cameron started going to church with Jan, and she was encouraged when he even came forth for the altar call. It seemed to her that he was making a solemn vow before the Lord that he would change.

Together and separately, the Hookers also had private talks with Pastor Dabney. As Jan grew closer to the gray-haired avuncular clergyman, she confided that her husband was "a sadist," and that he kept an odd assortment of handcuffs, whips, books, and photos. This was so far outside the pastor's experience he could scarcely have imagined the full scope of Hooker's appetites.

When Cameron came in, he impressed Dabney as "mild and likeable," but the pastor found it difficult to tell what he

was really thinking. All he could do was advise him to be
true to his wife and get rid of his sexual paraphernalia. Cameron said he would.

But now Hooker's resolve seemed to falter. He refused to
go to counseling. Jan went alone. She wanted to give him a
chance, give him time, but now she felt a gnawing fear that
he was lying to her. And, worse, that he was lying before the
Lord.

One night in September Jan awoke suddenly. She instantly sensed that Cameron was wide awake beside her, his
muscles taut. She could almost smell the tension rising from
his body.

"What's the matter?" she asked.

"I don't know," he answered thickly.

He seemed so keyed-up it scared her. The lateness of the
hour, her imagination, or perhaps an almost clairvoyant understanding of this man she'd known since the age of fifteen
convinced Jan that he was about to do something terrible.

She had a flash of inspiration and clung to it: "Let's get up
and burn everything," she suggested. The pornography. The
bondage equipment the pastor had told him to get rid of.
"Do you want to burn that stuff?"

"I don't know." He paused. "Well, I guess."

It was only a distraction, but it worked. Cameron focused
all his energy on gathering up sado-masochistic magazines,
whips, leather cuffs, the gas mask, as well as the slavery
contract, slides of K being hung and stretched and dunked,
and things she had written. He heaped them all into the
burn barrel in the backyard and struck a match.

The barrel flared, the contents crackled, and smoke spi-
raled upward into the clear night air.

Meanwhile, Colleen Stan had rejoined her family in Riverside, a city as different from Red Bluff as it is far away,
with its palm trees, freeway loops, and the notorious smog
that characterizes Southern California.

Returning home, Colleen had called her father's number
from Bakersfield, mid-trip, to let him know when she would
be arriving, and a gathering of perplexed relatives had met

her at the bus depot. Years too late, they had demanded to
know where she'd been, what she'd been doing, and why she
hadn't written. Over breakfast, Colleen began to unravel the
story of what she'd suffered, and during the next several
days she revealed more, until her family had at least a superficial understanding of Colleen's ordeal—though it's doubtful any of them truly comprehended what Colleen had been
through.

Outwardly, Colleen approached her new freedom with remarkable clearheadedness, moving in with her father and
almost immediately setting about the task of finding work.
She seriously considered taking the civil service exam but
then landed a job in the housekeeping department of a hospital.

Beneath this composed exterior, "Kay Powers" struggled
to regain her identity as Colleen Stan. After spending so
many years as the Hookers' slave it was difficult for her to
completely sever those ties. They had formed her primary
support system, even if a negative one, and Jan had been her
only close friend.

These two troubled women, who shared problems no one
outside the situation could possibly understand, wrote to
each other sporadically but spoke on the phone almost daily
—sometimes twice a day.

It was so difficult for Colleen to extricate herself from
Cameron's influence. She spoke to him on the phone, too,
though it's unclear how often or what was said. (Once, while
Jan was still away, he simply called to ask how to make a
tuna sandwich. In some ways, theirs was a mutual dependency.) In any case, Colleen had several phone conversations with Jan and Cameron over the next several weeks.
Besides discussing mundane matters and simply touching
base, the Hookers gained Colleen's assurance that she
wouldn't go to the police.

Jan said she believed Cameron was earnest about trying to
change, and she told Colleen, "We owe him that chance."

In keeping with her almost pathological selflessness, Colleen agreed.

Though her family urged her to contact law enforcement,

she resisted, saying she wanted to put it all behind her and get on with her life.

For years, Colleen had suppressed her anger, knowing that if she offended Cameron she risked a beating. Even now, she scarcely recognized the rage locked within her subconscious. She expressed it in very indirect (and thus nonthreatening) ways.

In a casual, almost chatty letter, dated August 18, that she wrote to Cameron and Jan just after they got back together, Colleen made little direct reference to her captivity, talking instead of her new life at home and sending her love and greetings to those up in Red Bluff. Yet in the midst of this letter, apropos of nothing, Colleen inserted a powerful quote from the Bible, Psalm 64, which rings with a poetry of almost eerie significance:

> Hear me, O God, as I voice my complaint;
> protect my life from the threat of the enemy.
> Hide me from the conspiracy of the wicked,
> from that noisy crowd of evildoers,
> who sharpen their tongues like swords
> and aim their words like deadly arrows.
> They shoot from ambush at the innocent man;
> they shoot at him suddenly, without fear.
> They encourage each other in evil plans,
> they talk about hiding their snares;
> they say, "Who will see them?"
> They plot injustice and say,
> "We have devised a perfect plan!"
> Surely the mind and heart of man are cunning.
> But God will shoot them with arrows;
> suddenly they will be struck down.
> He will turn their own tongues against them
> and bring them to ruin;
> all who see them will shake their heads in scorn.
> All mankind will fear;
> they will proclaim the works of God
> and ponder what he has done.

Let the righteous rejoice in the Lord
and take refuge in him;
let all the upright in heart praise him!

Then, with the comment, "I just love the Lord. He's done
so much for me, and I know he's going to do so much
more," the letter goes on with its original breeziness, as if
this profound nugget hadn't been placed within the plain
black and white text. Colleen found the psalm meaningful
enough to quote yet inserted it abruptly, almost as if she
remained unconscious, even while writing, of any special
message it might contain. Interestingly, she accidentally
typed one line twice—"they shoot at him suddenly, without
fear"—as if her mind momentarily stuck on that idea.

Except to say, "I pray for you and Cameron that you will
never again get tangled up in a life of sin," she made only
one other reference to her former enslavement. At the close
of the letter, she signed with some hesitancy over her name:
"Love, Colleen (Kay)."

And on September 19, Colleen wrote to Jan: "If you get
any more angry phone calls from my cousins—I don't know
what to tell you except they are not forgiving. But I do not
want to play God, and I forgive you and Cameron for all
things—it's done."

Meanwhile, things weren't proceeding smoothly at the
Hooker home. Jan and Cameron had reached a stalemate.
The hangings, whippings, and abuse had come to a halt but
so had Cameron's apparent efforts to change. At one point
he told her he'd read in a magazine that his only problem
was a hormonal imbalance, and that it had a simple cure:
"The article said all I have to do is drink one beer every
night."

Jan despaired. She couldn't eat. She couldn't sleep. And
her waking hours were bedeviled by sudden panic attacks.
She feared it would start all over again, that Cameron would
kidnap someone else, and that his sadistic habits, now idling,
would soon slip back into gear.

As summer succumbed to the first morning chill of fall,
Jan took her daughters and left—finally and for good.

Unable to shake her dark anxieties, she sought solace in church. But now Pastor Dabney was on vacation, and though she tried to talk to his temporary replacement, the clouds over her head refused to dissipate.

Finally, fate put Janice Hooker in contact with someone who could help her.

Jan had driven up to Redding for a doctor's appointment. Afterwards, she struck up a conversation with the receptionist, Connie Fleming, a plump, blond woman with a warm and open manner.

They talked for two hours. Obviously nervous, Janice asked Connie many questions—some quite personal, others vague—large questions of initiative and strength. Connie understood they were important to Jan and didn't belittle or question. Instead, she responded with a sincerity that Jan apparently found as soothing to her psyche as salve to a wound.

At the end of this long conversation, Connie set up another meeting for the next week, when the doctor would be out of the office.

With Jan's conscience a spinning whirlpool, she clung to her new confidante like a lifeline, conferring with Connie on the phone a handful of times over the next few days as she grappled with questions of right and wrong, of accountability, of fear, of guilt.

Still, she had lingering doubts. Maybe Cameron really was trying to change. She ought to give him a chance.

One afternoon, Jan went back to the mobile home and looked around. To her dismay, she found he still had a collection of pornography—and was creating more. She found sculptures of nude women he was working on, and the footlocker in the bedroom still brimmed with hard-core magazines and bondage devices.

When Jan came in for her meeting with Connie on Wednesday, November 7, she'd done more than give her situation a lot of thought: She'd prepared a list of questions.

It was a single sheet, a short, handwritten list that reflected Jan's inner turmoil. She gave it to Connie, and Connie read:

Did any of your fears try and take you over?
Did you ever go and cry on someone else?
Did you ever say, "I can't"?
What made you change and where did you get the strength?
What does religion mean to you?
Are you afraid of your husband?
What gives you strength every day to go on?
Do you get angry?
How do you let that anger out?
Did you believe in God before?
What do you feel about the enemy of your soul?

Connie held in her hand a clear and powerful cry for help. And she wasn't one to leave such a cry unanswered.

It took hours. Jan was visibly upset, yet reluctant to reveal the cause of her problems. Connie probed gently, asking, "Jan, what is it you're afraid of?"

Gradually, Jan let the truth slip out. It was her husband. "He's evil," she said. "He gets off on sex games, on bondage. He ties people up and takes pictures of them." Eventually, she disclosed how they'd kidnapped Colleen Stan, locked her up, and kept her for seven years.

"Why didn't you do anything?" Connie asked at one point.

"I did," Jan said, "I let her go." She explained the events of the past few months, including the fact that she'd gone back to her husband, hoping that he would change, but that he hadn't, and now she was afraid of what he might do next.

Connie realized she was way out of her depth. She advised Jan to get counseling and go to the police.

But Jan was afraid to turn Cameron in because if he got out, he'd "get even." On top of that, "They'll say I'm an accomplice. I'll be locked up. I'll lose my daughters!"

That was the knot Connie had to untie. She tugged at Jan's sense of decency, her feelings of responsibility, but Jan was still afraid. Finally, Connie struck a chord: "You should turn him in because he might do something to your girls."

She could almost see a change come over Janice, as if she'd awakened to a new resolve. Connie suggested a talk with Pastor Dabney, who had recently returned from his long vacation. At a loss for alternatives, Jan agreed.

It was afternoon by the time an emotionally wrought Janice Hooker sat down in Pastor Dabney's office and started talking. She still harbored fears she was doing the wrong thing, but the dam had burst, and she let spill the chilling secrets that had for so long remained untold.

It was nearly four o'clock when, with Janice Hooker's consent, Pastor Dabney picked up the phone and called the Tehama County Sheriff's Office.

25

When Undersheriff Mike Blanusa arrived at the church he found Mrs. Hooker so overwrought she was almost unable to talk, so the pastor was obliged to tell Blanusa why he'd been called. As he was relating what he knew of the crime, Mrs. Hooker regained her composure and began filling in details.

What they told Blanusa, however, placed the crime within the city of Red Bluff, indicating that the police, not the sheriff's office, would have jurisdiction.

Police Detective Al Shamblin was dispatched to the pastor's office.

It was after five by the time Shamblin arrived at the church. The detective didn't know it, but he was going to be spending a lot of time with this woman who sat before him, red-eyed and with tissues in hand. She needed to talk, and he would be the man—more even than Pastor Dabney—to whom she would unburden herself.

More than Colleen Stan's 1977 abduction was troubling Janice Hooker, more than Colleen's imprisonment and enslavement, more than the possibility that Cameron Hooker would kidnap someone else. More, much more had been stalking her conscience over the past many years.

Verging on hysteria, Jan began to relate the story of a 1976 kidnapping. In late January of that year they had picked up a girl by the name of Marliz Spannhake in the nearby town of Chico. That night, she said, Cameron had murdered her.

When Shamblin clarified that Jan had been with Hooker at the time of the abduction, he decided it was time to advise her of her rights: "You have the right to remain silent. Anything you say can and will be used against you in a court of law. . . ."

Already panicky, she balked. Her worst fears had been realized: She was going to be prosecuted and her daughters taken away from her. Burying her face in her hands, she moaned, "I feel like I'm having a nervous breakdown."

Finally, she asked to see an attorney.

That put an end to Shamblin's questions, but by now, Jan appeared on the brink of emotional collapse. She was crying hard and talking in incomplete sentences. Her mental state was so poor that Shamblin and Dabney, worried about leaving her alone, discussed sending her to the county mental health unit.

Janice volunteered that she'd been seeing a counselor, Sally Leonard, at the Tehama County Mental Health Department. They phoned Leonard at home, advised her of Jan's condition, and put her on. Leonard spoke with Jan a few minutes and calmed her down.

Finally, with Pastor Dabney's assurance that he knew of a couple whom Jan could stay with overnight, Detective Shamblin returned to police headquarters to make his report.

Like a powerful locomotive groaning heavily to a start, the wheels of justice began to turn. Phone calls were made, computer files checked, reports passed. Cameron Michael Hooker's rap sheet showed him to be absolutely clean—no arrests, scarcely so much as a traffic violation. Ditto Janice Hooker.

Detective Shamblin's immediate superior, Lieutenant Jerry Brown, contacted the Chico Police Department, and by the next afternoon, two important points were certain: first, an eighteen-year-old by the name of Marie Elizabeth Spannhake (nicknamed Marliz) had disappeared from her Chico address on January 31, 1976; and second, investigating this dusty and forgotten case would be extraordinarily difficult without Mrs. Hooker's cooperation.

That understood, Lieutenant Brown and Detective Shamblin walked across the street to the DA's office, seeking immunity for Janice Hooker in exchange for her cooperation regarding the Spannhake and Stan cases.

District Attorney Lang, a man who had viewed the law both from street level as a Los Angeles cop and from the elevation of the judge's bench, was highly skeptical of Janice Hooker's story, particularly that unlikely business about Stan having been a slave. It took some time, but Brown and Shamblin eventually swayed him, and Mrs. Hooker was granted immunity from prosecution.

The next day, Friday, November 9, Shamblin called Janice advising her that she'd been granted immunity and asking her to come to police headquarters to make a statement. She agreed.

Jan came in appearing much calmer than she had two days before, but at first she was unresponsive. Still doubtful about the conditions of her immunity, she was cautious in her answers.

After reassurances from Shamblin, she gradually related a story—in fits and starts, with long pauses and many tears—that in many respects bore a striking resemblance to the tale of what had happened to Colleen Stan.

[Note to the reader: What follows is a summary of what Janice Hooker told police. This is only her version of the truth. Cameron Hooker has never been charged with this or any other murder. Little corroborative evidence was unearthed, and the investigation into the disappearance of Marie Elizabeth Spannhake remains open.]

Late in January of 1976, Jan and Cameron Hooker were driving the blue Dodge Colt in Chico, a town just forty minutes away from Red Bluff, when Hooker spotted a young woman with long, dark hair walking alongside the road. She was alone. He stopped and offered her a ride, and she got in and sat in the back seat. She told them her name was Marliz and asked them to drop her off at an apartment off of Rio Lindo Avenue. They drove in that direction.

When they arrived Jan opened the door to let her out, but as Marliz started to get out, Cameron grabbed her by the hair and pulled her back in. Jamming her head down between the car's bucket seats, he threatened her and drove off.

With some difficulty, he restrained her. Like Stan, she was driven down a dirt road, tied up, and shut inside the head box. Then the threesome drove on toward Red Bluff.

Before going home, Cameron and Jan stopped at Jolly Cone, a fast-food place, and got something to eat. By then it was dark, and Marliz was driven to the house at 1140 Oak Street.

Cameron parked in the garage, took the head box off Marliz, and left her with Jan for a moment while he went to unlock the house. Still tied up, Marliz pleaded desperately with Jan to let her go. Not knowing what would happen, Jan tried to reassure her, saying that everything would be okay.

Then Cameron came back, carried Marliz into the house, and took her down into the basement. Jan stayed upstairs while he stripped off his captive's clothes and hung her up by the wrists. For some reason, perhaps to stop her from screaming, perhaps because he wanted a silent sex slave, he decided to cut her vocal chords. He used a knife.

After this, weak and dizzy from loss of blood, Marliz indicated that she wanted a pencil and paper. She wrote a note that she was willing to call her boyfriend to get money for her captor. He refused.

As the night stretched on, Hooker shot Marliz several times in the lower abdomen with a pellet gun. Jan described this as "a torture thing."

Finally, he strangled her to death.

Shortly afterward Cameron came upstairs and told Janice, who was sitting on the couch in a state of shock, that Marliz had been killed. She cried, and Cameron held her.

At about two A.M., Cameron and Jan wrapped the body in a blanket and loaded it into the trunk of the car. They headed north to Highway 44 and drove into the mountains. Snow was falling lightly, and a heavy whiteness already covered the ground. They drove for some distance—Janice couldn't be sure how far—before turning onto a muddy side road and coming to a stop.

Cameron got out and walked several yards from the car. Using a shovel he'd brought along, he dug a shallow grave.

Then he came back and they got the body out of the trunk. Together, they carried Marliz over to the freshly turned earth and buried her.

It was nearly daylight by the time they got back to Red Bluff.

Later, Hooker burned Spannhake's identification, purse, and other personal belongings at Dog Island Park, just a couple of miles from 1140 Oak Street. The only thing he kept, Janice said, was a small gold watch, which he wore for some time before losing it on a conveyor belt at work.

Janice told police that she believes Cameron killed Marliz because he lost control of the situation.

Detective Shamblin elicited from Janice Hooker all the information he could about the alleged murder of Marie Elizabeth Spannhake, then turned her attention to other crimes. "Now," he said, "how did you meet Colleen?"

26

At times Janice was unintelligible. She rambled, cried, mumbled, took long pauses and side-stepped phrasings that she thought seemed incriminating. And the subject matter was almost as confusing as her manner of speaking: bondage, hangings, the workshop, the stretcher, leather cuffs, the head box, and references to "Kay," when Jan meant to say "Colleen."

From time to time she went off on tangents about God and religion, about right and wrong, about guilt and fear. Clearly, these were subjects she'd given a lot of thought. At one point, she offered: "If you work on somebody's fear, if you find their fear point, you can make them do anything."

Given the confinement and tortures Jan described, it seemed incomprehensible that Colleen Stan hadn't escaped at her earliest opportunity. For this, Jan offered an unusual explanation: "She was brainwashed," she contended. They both were. "One hundred percent totally brainwashed."

Comparing Cameron to Jim Jones,[1] Jan described the control he had in almost supernatural terms, saying that he used the Bible to reinforce what he told them. She said she felt powerless to oppose him, even when she thought he was wrong. "Lots of times," she said, "I felt like killing myself."

She recounted how she and Colleen finally escaped to-

1. Jones was the cult leader of the People's Temple who ordered some nine hundred followers to commit suicide in Jonestown, Guyana, in 1978.

gether, and then how, after going back to him, Jan finally left Cameron for good: "I do know one thing. I never had the courage in my life to convince him I was walking out. But I faced him, and for the first time, I acted like I wasn't afraid."

But Janice was still fearful of her husband. When some comment triggered the realization that she might have to testify against him in court, she protested that she couldn't, saying, "You don't know what he does to me when I see him. Something happens to me when I see him!" Shamblin comforted her and quickly moved on to another subject.

It was an exhausting interview, covering nearly a decade and a mind-numbing combination of circumstances, but finally Shamblin reached an end to this first round of questions. Then, with some last-minute reassurances, Shamblin sent an emotionally spent Janice Hooker home to her parents, with whom she and her daughters were staying once again.

The next day Lieutenant Brown and Detective Shamblin set about verifying parts of Mrs. Hooker's story. They met with Doris Miron at King's Lodge, who told them about Colleen Stan, or "Kay," her prize worker, who had abruptly quit after only three months. Then, search warrant in hand, they went to 1140 Oak Street, where a quick search of the basement lent further corroboration to Jan's story.

The next step would be to interview Colleen Stan.

On the afternoon of Monday, November 12, Detective Shamblin flew down to Riverside with Police Officer Mack McCall, a slim, good-humored fellow who few would guess holds a black belt in karate. They rented a car at the airport and found Jack Martin's address, a small house in a modest suburban neighborhood.

Colleen, her father, her stepmother, and her mother were all awaiting them. After introductions, Mrs. Martin bustled about in the kitchen, apparently uncomfortable yet faultlessly hospitable, while the others settled in the living room.

Initially, most people are apprehensive about having police officers in their home, so Shamblin set about trying to put them all at ease. Born and bred in Red Bluff, he possessed an easygoing, unaffected quality that stemmed partly from the fact that he wasn't a big city cop, and partly from training. Shamblin not only had twelve years of on-the-job experience, but had taken special courses on how to deal with victims in general and rape victims in particular.

After explaining that they would need to tape-record Colleen's statement, he turned the machine on, and they got under way. Again, Shamblin did the questioning, beginning with Colleen's background, then quickly going on to the kidnap.

Answering Shamblin's questions in a low, almost whispery voice, Colleen told about her captivity, the slavery contract, the Company, the boxes and the many devices Cameron Hooker had used to restrain and torture her. Her family listened quietly, her mother interrupting occasionally with a question that revealed gaps in her understanding of what her daughter had endured.

Shamblin found Colleen articulate, helpful, and lucid, but she had a disturbingly unemotional manner. In contrast to Janice Hooker's tears and near-breakdown, Colleen's responses to the officers' questions were peculiarly matter-of-fact. She spoke almost with an air of detachment—no dramatics, no flourishes, no tears.

The interview stretched on, covering year after year.

Then Shamblin asked the obvious question: "Why didn't you go to the police when you got back to Riverside?"

"Jan asked me not to," she said. She explained that they both had hoped that Cameron would change, echoing almost perfectly what Jan had told them earlier.

But here Colleen's voice cracked and her composure faltered. This was important to her; she wanted them to understand: "I'm not doing this for revenge, but only because I don't want it to happen to anyone else."

Later that week, Shamblin, McCall, and a matron, Katherine Engel, took Janice up into the mountains to try to locate the grave site of Marie Elizabeth Spannhake. They drove up and down the highway, turning down various likely-looking dirt roads, but Jan's memory was clogged by the cobwebs of time.

Nearly nine years had passed since the alleged murder. The dirt road could have been a logging road, long since overgrown, or it might now be paved. And though Jan said she remembered hearing a stream, up in these mountains, streams come and go. Further complicating the search, it had been late at night when they'd buried the body, and the ground had been snow-covered at the time. Jan seemed to be trying in earnest, but reality and her mental picture just didn't match up. They finally gave up and headed back to Red Bluff.

Without a body there was no evidence linking Cameron Hooker to Marliz Spannhake's disappearance. Since Janice Hooker was an accomplice, her testimony against Cameron would only hold up in court if it could be substantiated by other evidence. But the trail was ice-cold and, except for Janice's statement, there was nothing to suggest murder . . . outside the undeniable fact that Marie Elizabeth Spannhake had disappeared.

In the case regarding Colleen Stan, however, Janice Hooker's story was getting outside corroboration and was backed up by Stan herself.

In the meantime, Cameron Hooker was out and about, carrying on his life as usual, with no hint that the police were actively interested in him. It was difficult to say, in a town of ten thousand people, how long they could carry on an investigation without Hooker catching wind of it and perhaps fleeing. It was time for an arrest warrant.

Early on Sunday, November 18, Lieutenant Brown and Detective Shamblin drove out to the Hooker residence. They found Hooker at home and advised him of his Miranda rights. He invoked his right to remain silent, saying he wanted to talk to a lawyer.

He was handcuffed, loaded in the car, and driven to the Tehama County Jail. While booking Cameron Michael Hooker, Shamblin advised him that he had a warrant to search his property and asked for the key to his trailer. When Hooker handed it over, the detective noticed another, smaller key and asked for it as well. He'd recognized it as a key to a set of handcuffs.

PART TEN

The Machinery

June–November 1985

Surely the mind and heart of man are cunning.
But God will shoot them with arrows;
suddenly they will be struck down.
He will turn their own tongues against them
and bring them to ruin.

Psalm 64:6–8
As quoted from the Bible by Colleen Stan

27

Disappointed wasn't a strong enough word to express McGuire's feelings over the upcoming disposition of the Hooker case. *Indignant, devastated, frustrated*—these were closer.

She'd worked on this case for months. She had talked to neighbors and family and coworkers. She'd read bank statements, studied canceled checks, gone over department of motor vehicle, hospital, and work records. She'd had Hooker fingerprinted and had secured handwriting samples. She'd received late-night calls from Janice and from Colleen. She'd photographed the scenes of the crime on the ground and from the air. She'd handled every piece of evidence, even climbing into the box and having the head box shut over her. She'd charted the course of seven years of serious crimes. And through it all Christine McGuire had developed a deep, personal loathing for Cameron Michael Hooker.

She deemed him a sadist, the most detestable criminal she'd ever come across, and now, because of a shortfall in the county budget, Hooker could walk out of prison in less than five years. It made her sick.

On top of everything, she worried about Hooker's potential for revenge. When he got out, would Colleen be safe? Would Janice? And what about herself?

But with economics calling the shots in Tehama County, the only way McGuire could imagine the plea bargain being derailed would be if someone from the outside stepped in.

The plea was scheduled for June 10. She had a week.

McGuire got her information ready and placed a call to Colleen's attorney, Marilyn Barrett. She outlined what had happened, then told her: "Hooker could get off on a minor charge simply because the county can't afford to try him, even though this is in violation of penal code section 1192.7."

"What?"

"The penal code. It prohibits plea bargaining serious felonies for any reason other than insufficient evidence or because testimony of a material witness can't be obtained, or if the plea won't result in a substantial change in the sentence."

"It violates the penal code?"

"Right, Marilyn. In other words, having no money isn't an acceptable basis for negotiating a plea."

"What was that number again?" Barrett asked.

"Section 1192.7. Get a copy of the code and look it up."

Barrett took it all down, saying she intended to call some people. That was fine with McGuire, but she suggested that first of all, she ought to call Colleen.

When McGuire hadn't heard from Colleen by the afternoon of Tuesday, June 4, she phoned her. To her amazement, Colleen remained apparently unfazed in the face of all this. With uncanny passivity, she said she didn't care about the plea negotiation, that she just wanted to get on with her life.

To McGuire, this was as disturbing a response as if she'd shrieked and threatened suicide. Colleen was so damned acquiescent. Why?

A couple of days later, the Assistant Attorney General for the State of California, Arnold Overoye, phoned to ask: "What the hell is going on?"

McGuire explained the county's perilous financial situation, but Overoye was unimpressed. Courteous but brisk, he explained what McGuire and Lang already knew—that a plea negotiation based on a lack of funds was inappropriate. "If that's the basis for a negotiation," he said, "our office will step in and try the case. And in the end, we'll have to bill it back to Tehama County."

Well, this was an interesting twist. A plea bargain wouldn't save the county any money if the state used its own high-priced attorneys to try Hooker and then sent the county the tab.

With just a weekend between them and the scheduled plea negotiation, District Attorney Lang returned from a business trip, heard the news, and made a decision: "That's what we needed," he said. "The Board can't argue with the Attorney General's office. Hooker's going to trial."

The Board wouldn't be happy, and God only knew where the money would come from, but McGuire was elated.

By Monday the news had hit the grapevine. When McGuire walked into Judge Watkins's office, he looked up, smiled, and said, "Well, it looks like you're going to get to try the Hooker case after all, eh?"

Rolland Papendick was less enthusiastic. Minutes before the scheduled hearing, McGuire found him and told him they weren't going to accept the plea. He scowled but said nothing.

Cameron Hooker was meanwhile waiting in court. When Papendick told him the deal was off, Hooker seemed unconcerned. He only shrugged.

The summer brought an abundance of awful but somehow pertinent news. In Europe, a TWA airliner was hijacked, with several people taken hostage and flown to Beirut. In New Jersey, a man was convicted of imprisoning, beating, and raping a young woman, who was held for four years, forced to sign a document acknowledging her submission, and made to work twenty-hour days. In La Jolla, near San Diego, the FBI arrested a couple on charges of subjecting several women to involuntary servitude, battery, and forced labor. And in Calavaras County, when a mysterious man by the name of Leonard Lake committed suicide after being arrested, a story of multiple murders, sexual torture, and sadistic pornography came to light, launching a massive search for bodies.

In Tehama County, Christine McGuire watched these

headlines with a kind of gruesome reassurance. The Hooker case was beginning to seem less and less farfetched—or perhaps the world was seeming more and more deranged.

McGuire hoped the people down in San Mateo County were following the news. Because of the change of venue, some of them would end up on the jury, and she figured that any mention of hostages or sadism should leave some residue in their collective unconscious.

Moreover, McGuire worried that she couldn't count on Janice Hooker. Jan's attitude flip-flopped; she revised statements, sometimes seeming either defensive about Cameron or upset with Colleen, on whom she began to cast blame. Exasperated, McGuire wondered whether this was a result of Jan's therapy or merely her way of handling her own culpability. In any case, she was unsure whether to treat Jan as a victim or a hostile witness.

Then Papendick touched a raw nerve: He filed a motion to compel psychiatric exams of both Janice and Colleen, obviously so that he could have his own specialist examine the prosecution's two main witnesses. Further, when Papendick's motion arrived on her desk, she was appalled that he'd attached a copy of Dr. Hatcher's report.

The report was confidential, so she rushed over to Judge Watkins's office and asked the court to have it sealed.[1] At the end of the day she stopped by Papendick's office to let him know what she'd done and to point out that he'd risked letting Hatcher's report out to the press. Unruffled, Papendick apologized; the confidential nature of the report simply hadn't occurred to him.

Then he remarked, "By the way, I'm going to ask for a continuance on the Hooker case."

McGuire's face flushed. This would make the second continuance Papendick had asked for, and now the case would be nearly a year old by the time it went to trial.

---

1. Dr. Hatcher's twenty-three-page report on Janice Hooker and Colleen Stan summarized their personal histories, their perceptions of what had occurred between May of 1977 and the fall of 1984, and gave the psychologist's evaluation of the mental status of each.

"I decided the other night that I won't be ready," Papendick explained. "Dr. Hatcher's report was late."

"Rolland, I told you way back when that Hatcher's report would be late. You said it wouldn't cause you problems and that it wouldn't cause you to ask for a continuance. I can pull the records on it."

"Well, what can I do?" he asked innocently.

"Sure, I understand. If I oppose it and the court forces you to trial when you aren't ready, it's grounds for an appeal." She was provoked. It was less than a month before trial, and she'd already sent out sixty subpoenas.

Papendick coolly went on to say that Hooker's family had run out of funds, so he was going to ask the court to appoint him public defender for the Hooker trial. He was already so entrenched in the case, he said, a regular public defender would have a hard time catching up.

Great, Christine thought, *now the county would not only have to pay for Hooker's prosecution, but also for his defense.*[2]

Next, Papendick remarked that he was having trouble finding a psychiatrist to testify as an expert witness. She'd started her search for an expert *six months ago.* He'd been sitting on his hands!

She went home seething. There was no way she would be granted a continuance if she wasn't ready to go to trial—it was a government job; she was expected to be ready. Yet if she countered Papendick's request it would be interpreted as circumventing the defendant's rights. Well, what about the people's rights? What about the victim's rights?

McGuire hated to tell Colleen the trial was being postponed again, but when she did, Colleen responded with great equanimity—calmly, coolly, with as much emotion as a bank teller counting bills. So the last thing McGuire ex-

---

2. In a bill modeled after legislation that helped another financially strapped county (then faced with the burden of trying mass-murderer Juan Corona), the Tehama County Employees' Association asked Assemblyman Stan Statham to seek special funding of $120,000 for trying the "sex slave" case. Then, in an unexpected development, California Senator Jim Nielsen managed to slip an urgent request for $250,000 into a bill regarding the disbursement of offshore oil tax revenues. These unusual measures made funds available for trying Hooker.

pected, when Colleen called back a few days later, was a temper tantrum.

In a plaintive tone, Colleen began enumerating all the problems this trial was causing her. She was worried about getting laid off from her new job. And if she took time off to come up to Red Bluff to prepare for her testimony, as McGuire had suggested, she wouldn't be able to make her car payments—and then her credit rating would be shot!

To McGuire, who'd seen thirty Tehama County employees laid off and figured it would cost the county over $150,000 to bring Hooker to justice, it seemed ludicrous that Colleen was upset about missing one day's pay. And she said as much.

But Colleen wasn't one to be blunt with, and McGuire paid for this lack of tact. Colleen began screaming and crying into the phone. Then, abruptly, she hung up.

McGuire immediately called her back, but Colleen's temper was unabated. "Everyone's taking advantage of me," she screamed, "You're all using me!" And she slammed the phone down again.

McGuire called back; no answer.

A few minutes later, she called again, got a busy signal, and dialed the operator. "This is an emergency," she said. "Can you please cut into this call?"

Once she got through, using her most commanding voice, she said: "Colleen, don't hang up," and Colleen didn't.

"Now, let's take your problems one at a time, and we'll see what we can work out."

Basically, Colleen's anxieties boiled down to two issues: her family's support, and money. She didn't want to come to the trial without the comfort of having a few family members close by, but was concerned about how much Tehama County would pay for, and she was concerned about losing pay for taking time off work. With that understood, McGuire quickly worked out solutions and compromises, methodically addressing herself to each of Colleen's concerns: who could accompany her to the trial; how they would travel; whether the county could send her money in advance. And, since Colleen didn't want to take time off to

prepare for her testimony, the attorney would fly down to
Riverside on a Sunday.

Finally, with her problems ironed out and her voice at a
much more even timbre, Colleen rang off.

Colleen's ire had been misdirected at the DA's office, Mc-
Guire thought, but in retrospect, this was a red-letter day.
Colleen was getting healthier. Her flat, placid exterior had
finally given way to some emotion. For the first time, Colleen had shown anger.

As the trial date neared, McGuire took a renewed interest
in one aspect of Janice's story that had been hushed up and
apparently forgotten: the alleged murder of Marie Elizabeth
Spannhake.

Though Janice Hooker had told police a convincing version of Spannhake's 1976 kidnap, murder, and burial, she
was an accomplice, and her testimony alone would not be
legally sufficient to convict Cameron Hooker.

Some outside corroboration did, in fact, exist. Spannhake
had disappeared from the location, on the day, and at the
time that Janice said she had. She'd been wearing jeans and
a sweater, as Jan described. She had been living in the apartment complex Jan indicated and had come from Ohio, as
Jan had told police.

Jan told police that Cameron had burned Marliz's personal belongings, but had kept her gold watch, then lost it.

One of Cameron's coworkers told police she remembered
him wearing a woman's watch to work. She'd asked him if
he'd lost his and was wearing his wife's, and he'd said yes.
Later, she recalled. Hooker lost the watch on the conveyor
belt at work.

If Janice Hooker fabricated the murder story, this plain
and unimpressive housewife was either clairvoyant or extravagantly crafty. For instance, when shown a "photo line
up"—photographs of missing young women—her eyes immediately began to water. She stared, then correctly identified Marie Spannhake. Asked to rate her certainty on a scale
from one to ten, she said, "Nine. It's just something you
don't forget." Other details, such as Spannhake's nickname,

Marliz, Janice hardly could have learned without having met the eighteen-year-old.

Still, the evidence, as it stood, was slim, with most of it hinging on Jan's believability.

McGuire researched a *corpus delicti* brief, but without a body they had a flimsy case. No matter how real the murder was to Janice, no matter how convinced Deputy DA McGuire might be of Hooker's guilt, unless police could locate Spannhake's body, there seemed no way to prosecute Hooker for murder.[3]

Still, McGuire perceived a way to bootstrap in the limited but incriminating findings that pointed to Hooker's involvement in Spannhake's disappearance. Lacking enough solid evidence to formally charge Hooker with murder, McGuire considered a rather daring legal maneuver that would allow her to introduce the murder into the trial without actually charging Hooker with the crime.

In trial, the prosecutor must prove a defendant guilty *beyond a reasonable doubt,* but another, uncharged but related crime may be introduced as evidence if there is a simple *preponderance of the evidence.* This is done through an interesting device known as a "prior similar act motion."

A prior similar act is just what it sounds like, a crime committed previously, at not too remote a time, upon a similarly situated person. That crime is admissible to show a common plan or scheme. In other words, it's relevant to the limited extent that it sheds some light on the defendant's motive, intent, preparation, or disposition to commit such acts. His criminal style, as it were—his *modus operandi.*

In this sense, the alleged kidnap of Marie Elizabeth Spannhake was relevant because of several striking similarities to the kidnap of Colleen Jean Stan. Both were single young women, given a ride by Cameron and Janice Hooker,

---

3. Considerable effort was made to find a grave site. Not only the Red Bluff Police, but also the Redding and Chico Police, the Shasta County Sheriff's Office, and the Department of Justice participated in searches in the mountains. Using infra-red satellite photographs to pinpoint disturbed earth, teams of as many as twelve drove up into the mountains to probe the ground and dig at suspicious-looking sites. They found nothing.

with Cameron driving the blue Dodge Colt. Both were taken down a dirt road, threatened, bound, and shut into the head box.

Both were then driven to the Hooker residence on Oak Street, with the Hookers stopping along the way to get a meal at a fast-food restaurant. After dark, both were smuggled into the house and taken down into the basement, where they were stripped and hung by the wrists.

McGuire filed the motion, and the investigation into Marliz Spannhake's disappearance, long stalled, began to move again.

It was alleged that while Hooker had Marliz down in the basement, he had shot her in the pelvis with a pellet gun. McGuire remembered that Lieutenant Brown had mentioned seeing BBs in the basement at 1140 Oak Street, and now she asked him and Shamblin to check it out. They removed two BBs from the stairwell, then went about tracking down the pellet gun, which Hooker had apparently borrowed from his younger brother, Dexter.

They did ballistic tests on Dexter's gun, but these were inconclusive, showing only that the BBs *may* have been shot from that particular gun.

McGuire also made a point of contacting John Baruth, the man who'd been Marliz Spannhake's fiancé in January of 1976. Now married and living in Cleveland, he was shocked to hear that Hooker was suspected of murdering the woman he'd loved so many years ago.

Baruth related what he could about the day that Marliz had disappeared. That afternoon the couple had gone to a flea market where they'd had a spat. She'd left—angry and on foot.

He never saw her again.

Police had immediately suspected Baruth, but he was cleared after taking a polygraph test. Baruth said that, over the years, he'd feared that Marliz's parents still believed he'd killed her. Before hanging up he told McGuire: "I'll pray for you."

Cameron Hooker would be tried in Redwood City, the county seat of San Mateo County, in the superior court of

Judge Clarence B. Knight, a man of short stature and wide-ranging humor. On a hot August 16, Judge Knight heard arguments for and against the prior similar act motion.

McGuire's motion was granted. But the court also found that the motion was only relevant to the defendant's intent to kidnap. If Hooker admitted to kidnapping Colleen, the prior similar act would have no relevance and would be inadmissible.

Disgruntled, Papendick said he needed to discuss the matter with Hooker over the weekend.

On Monday, Papendick indicated that to keep the findings regarding Spannhake out, Hooker would admit to kidnapping Colleen Stan.[4]

---

4. Just before the start of the trial, Judge Knight reversed his ruling on the prior similar act motion, holding that it was more prejudicial than probative.

28

Downtown Redwood City, the county seat of San Mateo County, is geared for pedestrians, with brick walkways, strategically placed trees, and a few outdoor cafes that take advantage of the long, warm summer. But just a short walk away stands the imposing San Mateo County Courthouse, an eight-story cement structure with all the architectural charm of a jail—which is housed on the fourth floor. The courthouse dominates the skyline, making it easy to spot from the freeway.

Tuesday, September 24, media people milled around in the hallway, waiting for the courtroom doors to open. Though today would only be jury selection, the air buzzed with an opening-day anticipation.

The judge had rejected the Cable News Network (CNN) request to film the trial, ruling that no cameras, tape recorders, or video cameras would be allowed during the proceedings, but all of these were permitted when court was not in session. Now camerapersons maneuvered their bulky equipment into the aisles, hoping to catch a few shots of Hooker when he came in.

One outspoken journalist with the *San Francisco Chronicle* discoursed loudly on the subject of bondage. "There are lots of bondage societies in San Francisco, and they don't necessarily have anything to do with S/M. They even have a newsletter and a computer data base," he said, conferring an air of respectability upon them. His offhand comments set a tone. Throughout the trial, the media, like the jury, would be trying to judge whether Cameron Hooker was guilty of anything more than kinkiness.

Cameron's mother, looking gray with worry, was already resolutely seated in the audience, just behind the defense table. She would remain here during jury selection but, as a potential witness, would be barred from observing the proceedings against her firstborn son.

Rolland Papendick, in a light-weight suit and well-shined shoes, hurried in and took a seat at the long, curved defense table.

McGuire, all-business in a somber suit, entered and took a seat at the adjacent prosecution table, Investigating Officer Al Shamblin ambling in to sit next to her.

Hooker was brought in, and the cameras kicked to life, raising a low, mechanical racket. Dressed in a tweed sports coat, white shirt, tie, and gray slacks, Hooker probably looked better than he had on his wedding day. His hair was carefully combed, parted on the side, and while not handsome, he looked boyish and neat.

The bailiff warned the media people that proceedings would soon commence. Cameras dutifully stopped, the equipment was hustled out the door, and the bailiff called the court to order. "All rise. . . ."

Judge Knight, an articulate man with a clear voice and the alert, unflinching gaze of a hawk, entered and stepped up to the judge's bench.

He explained that this trial might take five or six weeks and asked the prospective jurors a few preliminary questions. He proved to be fairly lenient, excusing several people who said a long trial would cause them hardship.

Court was recessed so potential jurors could be called, one at a time, for questioning in the judge's chambers. Secluded from the group, they were asked about any pretrial publicity they may have heard about the case and whether they'd already formed an opinion. This was a way of weeding out those who were familiar with the case without tainting the others. For the most part, those who had heard of the "sex slave" case claimed not to have strong feelings about it.

Then the attorneys prepared to begin the *voir dire.*

Some argue the *voir dire* is the most important portion of

the trial. It's the sole chance the attorneys have to address the jurors as individuals, question them about their backgrounds and beliefs, and dismiss those who seem less than sympathetic to their side of the case. Although the stated objective is to choose a fair and impartial jury, both attorneys have a shot at slanting the jury in their favor.

The defense went first. One at a time, Papendick asked prospective jurors a list of questions about their jobs, families, educational backgrounds, and hobbies—and whether they read the Bible.

Among prospective jurors were mail couriers, retired architects, engineers, managers, housewives, and maintenance men. Some had lived in the area all their lives; others had recently moved from out of state. They were of all ages and education levels, with interests ranging from classical music to rollerskating. It was a smorgasbord of society, as it was meant to be.

With these thumbnail biographies established, Papendick's questions circled closer to the matter at hand. Shifting from foot to foot, he asked whether any of them disagreed with the California legislature that bondage between consenting adults should be legal. No one spoke. Saying that people have their own "peculiar needs" and their own reasons for staying in relationships "that some people may find abhorrent," he asked whether anyone felt they couldn't give the defendant a fair trial if his sexual preference were bondage. No one believed they would have any problem with this.

Revealing the skeleton of the defense strategy, Papendick took care to explain the statute of limitations, asking if anyone disagreed with the law that a case must be filed within a certain time. And he wanted to know if anyone believed that if someone were kidnapped, it meant that person could not subsequently consent to sex. He asked if they had ever heard of someone "bad-mouthing" a relationship after it had ended, and if any of them had strong feelings about lesbianism.

The prospective jurors sat quietly, taking it all in, nodding on occasion.

Papendick soon concluded his questions and took his seat. It was the people's turn.

Before starting, the prosecutor asked the bailiff to set a podium before the jury box, which gave her a place to put her papers, and made her seem more imposing, despite her diminutive stature. Her approach was more formal, more serious.

Reading from her notes, McGuire seemed stiff at first. She tried to educate and prepare the jury with her questions, asking if they'd heard the myths that women like to be raped, asking if it would bother them to view graphic slides and pictures or to hear sexually explicit language. She noted that the defendant sat before them looking like "a nice, clean-cut young man," and cautioned them not to feel that a person charged with serious crimes should look a certain way.

And she tried to prepare the prospective jurors for the testimonies of her main witness. Regarding Colleen's unemotional demeanor: "Do you expect a victim to become hysterical or cry while she is relating what happened to her?" Regarding Janice: "Will you be able to equally accept the testimony of a witness who has been granted immunity?"

She ended her remarks by asking each individual: "Can you think of any reason why you could not be a fair and impartial juror?" Each responded: "No."

Now each counsel was allowed to dismiss those who they felt wouldn't be favorable toward their positions. Papendick made sure to excuse those who were close to or had been victims of rape or wife-beating. McGuire favored those with college educations and avoided men with blue-collar jobs— those whom she felt would be most sympathetic to Hooker.

Prospective jurors were called, questioned, and excused all day, without much let-up or change in the script. But the solemnity was broken when Papendick asked one of the panelists, a middle-aged NASA employee who would later become jury foreman, if he had studied or had a special interest in sado-masochism. Mr. Hogan responded: "I don't even know what it is."

"You will after this case," the judge quipped from the bench.

The court rippled with amusement, Papendick smiled, even Hooker chuckled. But later Papendick would decide this wasn't so funny.

By late afternoon of the second day, Papendick and McGuire finally had a jury acceptable to them both.

A jury of five men and seven women were sworn to sit in judgement of Cameron Hooker. Eight of the twelve had at least some college education. Two others, women, were selected as alternates in case someone had to step down during this long trial.

The jurors were mostly middle-class, with white- and blue-collar jobs. They dressed informally. Mr. DeMarco, an engineer, favored T-shirts that revealed resplendent tatoos on both arms. (Many were surprised McGuire kept him on the jury—including DeMarco himself—but she was more impressed by the fact that his wife was expecting than by the ink designs on his skin.)

There was a wide range of ages, from mid-twenties to retirement age. Only two members of the jury were divorced, one was widowed, and one had never married. Two blacks, Mr. Fuqua, a scholarly-looking man who worked with Pacific Bell in marketing, and Mrs. Tamplin, an employee at a mint and the mother of nine, kept it from being an all-white jury.

Most described themselves as "not religious," and their hobbies were wide-ranging: square dancing, painting, sailing, gardening, and so on. They gave an impression of being an active bunch, well-rooted in their communities and happy with their family ties—with interests far removed from bondage and sado-masochistic sex.

On the third day, the jurors finally learned what they were in for. Judge Knight started off by reading the impressive list of charges against Cameron Hooker, a total of sixteen felony counts: one of kidnapping, with a special allegation of having used a knife; seven of rape; one of forced oral copulation; one of forced penetration with a foreign object; one of forced sodomy; three of false imprisonment; and two of abducting to live in an illicit relationship.

There were a few preliminaries, and then it was time for opening statements.

The prosecution went first. McGuire posted a list of the charges on the front wall, arranged her papers on the podium, and began to chronicle Colleen Stan's kidnap and captivity.

Her straightforward, cool presentation contrasted with the bizarre situation she described. She stood before the jury, smartly attired in her navy pin-stripe suit, the very picture of propriety, yet speaking of appalling tortures, describing how Colleen had been hung, whipped, chained, hurt, and humiliated by Cameron Hooker.

McGuire claimed Hooker had employed mind and behavioral control techniques, such as isolation and terror, designed to rob Colleen not only of her physical autonomy but of her will. Letting a note of anger slip into her voice, she declared that Hooker had kept Colleen "on an invisible leash."

In relating the principal events of those seven years, McGuire was careful to describe, count by count, each crime with which Hooker was charged. She also included the weakest portions of the people's case—the "year out" and the brief trip to Riverside, Colleen's declarations of love for Cameron, and Janice's jealousy. She didn't want the jurors to feel she was hiding anything.

In the state's interpretation, Jan's conscience motivated her to free Colleen and leave Cameron. Fearful of her husband's plans for taking another slave, guilty over her own role in Colleen's kidnap and imprisonment, Janice told Colleen the defendant didn't belong to the Company, there was no Company, it was all a lie.

McGuire explained Colleen's failure to contact police as the result of "seven years of attachment conditioning." She compared Colleen to "an infant who must cry for food, could not talk, and was bound. As Hooker intended, she became extremely dependent, just as an infant is. And just as an infant develops an attachment even to the worst of mothers, so did Colleen."

While she spoke, two sketch artists deftly rendered McGuire's likeness with charcoal pencils, while journalists madly scribbled in notebooks.

Few noticed, however, that in the midst of her opening statement the prosecutor surprised herself. Her voice didn't waver, but her eyes grew wet, and she came dangerously close to tears. After all these months of acclimatizing herself to this case, it still affected her.

McGuire concluded her remarks, rather anticlimactically, by simply listing some of the most convincing evidence. Then a recess was called, and a clutter of television cameras zeroed in on her for brief interviews in the hall.

When the cameras were shut off, a female television reporter commented to McGuire, "This reminds me of *The Story of O*. Have you read it?"

"That's reference material," McGuire joked. But the reporter's question triggered a recollection. She decided to ask Janice about it.

Defense Attorney Papendick presented a very different version of the relationship between the three main characters in this peculiar drama.

He began by casting doubt on Janice Hooker's credibility, noting that her November, 1984, statement to police was replete with "I don't knows" and "I can't remembers." "She was making changes in her statement as late as two weeks ago," he charged.

And he portrayed her as a clearly guilty party. He said, for instance, that it was Janice, not Cameron, who found the article on slavery and suggested making Colleen their slave.

Striding back and forth as he read from notecards, the defense attorney explained that Cameron and Jan had originally agreed there should be no sex with Colleen, only bondage. He granted that she was initially kidnapped and held against her will, but said that once the Hookers moved to the mobile home, "Kay," as Colleen was called, was no longer held captive.

She was free to go, yet opted to stay, becoming part of the Hooker household. Papendick enumerated her many freedoms: she attended family gatherings, made phone calls, babysat, and was often out on her own. She went jogging, shopping, and to bars where she met men. And wherever she went, she always returned to the Hooker home.

In 1981, Colleen was even taken to visit her family, alone, for twenty-four hours. She never complained about her living situation. And she voluntarily returned to Red Bluff with Cameron.

Papendick didn't deny that Cameron practiced bondage with Colleen, but this, he said, was consensual. Moreover, he announced, "the evidence will clearly show that Colleen *loved* Cameron, even promising she would give him the son that Janice never did."

Papendick explained that Jan became extremely jealous of Colleen's relationship with Cameron and felt threatened by Colleen's easy rapport with the children. In 1981, Colleen was put back in the box at Jan's insistence.

Emphasizing discrepancies in the stories of the threesome, Papendick said: "Cameron recalls she was out and free all night, every night. Jan recalls one to three hours. And Colleen recalls fifteen to thirty minutes."

By 1984, Colleen had resumed her status as a live-in babysitter and regular member of the household. She was included in family excursions, and even rode a bike to and from King's Lodge, where she worked as a motel maid.

Meanwhile, Papendick contended, Janice was on the verge of a mental breakdown and was in no condition to care for her daughters. Still intensely jealous over the sexual relationship between Cameron and Colleen, she now feared they would take her children from her.

By August of 1984, Janice badly wanted Colleen out of the house, so she told her the Company was a lie and that she had to leave.

It was significant, Papendick continued, wrinkling his nose with emphasis, that three days after her departure Colleen telephoned Cameron *at 12:11* A.M. and talked for seventy-six minutes! In fact, the defense would show there were *several* phone calls placed between the two over the next three months.

More than a lingering affection existed between Colleen and Cameron, Papendick said. They planned to be reunited:

Colleen's father owned land in Cottonwood, not far from Red Bluff, and she talked of moving there. Cameron volunteered to put in sprinklers and plant trees. In a letter, Colleen wrote: "I can't wait to get back home."

Janice panicked, went to the police, and Cameron landed in jail.

Returning to his seat, Papendick left in his wake the impression of a quirky—yet technically legal—living arrangement.

29

Janice Hooker, who had been waiting in the jury room while McGuire and Papendick give their opening statements, would be the state's first witness.

She emerged from the back of the courtroom looking decidedly undramatic, plain, and pudgy. But she'd cut her hair short since the preliminary hearing, and instead of her usual sweatshirt and jeans, she was wearing the simple cotton dress that McGuire had bought for her.[1]

Janice was sworn in, then seated herself in the witness box without even glancing at Cameron.

McGuire had watched Janice grow over the past months, watched her struggle with her own guilt, with her unhappy bond with Cameron, with worry over how all this would affect her children. Her private life had become painfully public—never a comfortable situation, but worse in a small town like Red Bluff. It took considerable courage for her to overcome the awful twin pulls of fear and loyalty in decrying the sins of the man who had been the center of her orbit for more than twelve years.

But McGuire knew the jurors might feel unsympathetic toward Janice. That she was getting immunity for her testimony rubbed some people the wrong way. After all, they said, she was guilty of everything he was, she ought to be on

---

1. She didn't know the source of the gift since McGuire, not wanting to embarrass her, had given it under the pretense that it had come from an outside donor.

trial, too. And there seemed something doubly suspect about a woman who would testify against her husband.

So McGuire tried to balance Jan's guilt against her victimization. She wanted to encourage her to be open, yet avoid appearing too chummy.

Gun-shy after Jan's horrible testimony at the preliminary hearing, McGuire asked: "Are you taking any medication today?"

"No." She was straight and clearheaded.

The prosecutor quickly delved into the evidence. First, a stack of photographs of Janice in bondage positions. (The whole courtroom was stunned to hear that some of these had been done to Janice as many as fifty or a hundred times.) Then McGuire had her identify the heavy, double-walled head box, which she placed on a table near the center of the room. Next, she had Janice describe how Cameron had constructed the head box in 1975 in the basement at 1140 Oak Street, and led into the agreement that preceded Colleen Stan's abduction.

Asked to explain, Janice said, "I wanted a child, and I pressed him many times about having a child, and he agreed, as long as he could have a sexual slave."

McGuire started to ask, "Was it your understanding that the sadism—" but Papendick shot out an objection over the word *sadism*.

Judge Knight paused to consider this, then said, "That's a matter of opinion, but I'll overrule."

It was a small victory for McGuire. They'd made the leap from bondage to sadism, from a legal form of sexual expression to one that, while not overtly illegal, was certainly more sinister.

McGuire asked, "Was it your understanding that this person would endure the sadism?"

"Yes."

"And that it would stop with regard to you?"

"I believe some things he might do to me, but the hanging he'd do to the sex slave."

"Was the hanging the most painful?"

"Yes."

"Did it end?"

"No."

"What do you understand a sadist to be?"

"A person who performs acts of bondage, hanging, whipping, and enjoying the pain that the other person suffers."

"And what about a masochist?"

"Sexual enjoyment from pain."

"Is the defendant a sadist?"

Papendick shouted out another objection.

The judge sustained the objection, barring Janice's answer, but the idea that Hooker was a sadist was firmly planted in every mind in the courtroom. Whether his wife was a masochist was another question.

Several of the jurors took notes as McGuire laboriously covered the events of the first several days of Colleen's captivity. She posted displays on a bulletin board, asking Janice to identify a picture of the rack, then a large drawing of the box that Cameron kept Colleen in. It "opened like a chest freezer," Janice said.

The courtroom sat transfixed as Janice described the nightly feeding routine, how Colleen was only allowed to use the bedpan once a day for the first few weeks, and the dunking incident when Colleen was given her first bath.[2]

"How long was Colleen kept in the box?"

"Maybe five months," Jan answered, raising an audible gasp from the spectators.

But the next day Janice corrected herself. Colleen's detention in the box had been even longer.

"We lived on Oak till April '78. She was kept in the box during that time. I thought you meant how long she was kept in there until the workshop was built," she said, and

2. This caused one of the jurors, Mrs. Carlton, an unforeseen problem, and she later asked to speak to the judge about it. With the other jurors excluded but both attorneys present, Mrs. Carlton told the judge that, though she hadn't mentioned it during jury selection, her daughter had drowned.

Judge Knight asked whether she still felt she could be a fair and impartial juror.

She said she believed she could and so remained on the jury.

then McGuire had Janice explain the workshop to the jurors.

This led to a new stage in Colleen's captivity, and McGuire put up another exhibit. All eyes strained to make out the writing on the poster-size photograph. Across the top was written: "This Indenture." It was a blow-up of a picture from the negative of the slavery contract.

Contradicting Papendick's opening statement, Janice said Cameron was the one who had found the contract in an underground newspaper.[3] He had showed it to her and asked her to type up the contract. She was unaware of the accompanying article, she claimed, until police showed it to her in 1985.

Papendick was right, however, that Janice had been changing her statement almost up to the last minute. She had finally decided to "come clean" and tell what she knew about the Company. For months she'd denied having heard Cameron tell Colleen about it. Now she started filling in gaps.

Jan said she heard Cameron tell Colleen that a Company messenger was waiting upstairs for the signed contract and that he'd had to pay a fifteen-hundred-dollar registration fee to the Company. Also, Cameron had threatened Colleen that she would be caught and "tortured almost to the point of death" if she ran away, and that "if she did anything wrong, her family would also be killed."

After signing the contract, Janice said, Colleen was known by her slave name, "K Powers." She and Cameron also assumed aliases.

---

3. Janice's description of the elaborate contrivance of the slavery contract wasn't the only part of her story that didn't mesh with Papendick's. During a break, McGuire and Shamblin searched through their several boxes of evidence trying to find some particular photographs of Janice. When Shamblin announced that he'd found some, McGuire asked, "Is she pregnant?"

Hearing this, Hooker looked over sharply.

Papendick had claimed that Cameron's sexual preference for bondage had been thwarted when Jan became pregnant. The photographs said differently.

"What happened to the original contract?" McGuire asked.

"I believe Cameron burnt it," she said, at which point Papendick leaned over and whispered something to Hooker, who nodded.

Under questioning, Janice carefully described the conditions of Colleen's enslavement over the next few months and how, in the spring, they moved to the mobile home where Colleen was kept in a box beneath the bed.

As she talked, a weird assortment of evidence gave mute testimony from a nearby table—the nightgown Colleen wore, the large and small head boxes, straps, the bedpan, leather cuffs, hardcore pornography, even a bright purple-and-pink afghan that Jan and K had crocheted.

The whips caused a stir.[4] "How many whips did he have?" McGuire asked.

"Four or five," Janice answered. He had several types—a bull whip, a cat o' nine tails, and other variations, some of which Cameron had made himself.

But the strange clutter on the table paled next to the spectacle that awaited.

After the lunch break those who entered the courtroom found, set up in the middle of the room, the box. The waterbed frame had been reconstructed and the steps placed in front of the opening, just as they had been at the Hookers' home.

The spectators were agog. The press was delighted. And the jurors stared.

The prosecutor had Janice explain how the box opened: "Move the steps from the foot of the bed and there's a cutout panel. I used to take, like, two knives and pry the front part down."

The bailiff and Officer Shamblin assisted as McGuire unscrewed the wing nuts and removed the panel, revealing the opening.

---

4. As McGuire stood talking with Janice, whip in hand, a sketch artist did a quick rendering of the scene. McGuire was amused to see herself on the television news that night, apparently brandishing this whip in the courtroom.

Jurors in the back stood to get a better look. Taking this as a cue, many spectators, unable to restrain themselves, also stood to see into the infamous box. If the box had been sordid in imagination, it had greater impact in reality. Sitting hard and cold and open in the middle of this carpeted court of law, the box seemed massive, chilling, and more obscene than even the worst of Hooker's pornography.

Just two weeks before the trial, Christine had finally made good on her tearful threats and left Jim. Now, on top of the stress of commuting a long distance to a demanding trial, she was juggling addresses and child care while weighing the prospect of divorce. Far from being relaxing, her weekend home in Red Bluff only added to her tension.

Back in court on Tuesday, October 1, McGuire took Janice through the remaining years of Colleen's captivity and entered more stacks of evidence.

Much of the evidence logged that day was pornography Hooker had collected, pornographic pictures he'd taken, and listings of pornographic movies he'd seen or wanted to see. In fact, there was so much of this pornographic material that, at one point, the judge asked its relevance, since Hooker had already stipulated to a preference for bondage. McGuire simply replied, "It goes beyond that, Your Honor." Only later would it become clear that these were more than just a collection of girlie pictures.

Just as the courtroom was getting bored with the tedious lagging of exhibits, McGuire exploded another bombshell: two large photographs of Colleen Stan, nude and hanging by the wrists, with the slave collar around her neck.

Everyone in court sat bolt upright, straining to see. Spectators buzzed. Judge Knight gave a long, hard look, pulling thoughtfully on an earlobe, as McGuire set the pictures on an easel at the front of the courtroom.

At the lunch break, reporters and photographers rushed over for a closer look, but once they'd scrutinized the picture, their enthusiasm waned. Colleen looked so malnourished and pathetic, even the old hands were shocked and appalled, and no one thought this appropriate for the nightly news or a family newspaper. It was too graphic.

Meanwhile, the prosecutor's entourage went downstairs to view something equally graphic, and also not family entertainment: *The Story of O.*

Following up on the reporter's comment, McGuire had learned from Janice that this was Cameron Hooker's favorite movie. She'd asked her secretary, Doris Gunsauls, to locate a VCR and a video of the film, and now Shamblin, Janice, her brother, Doris and McGuire found themselves in the sheriff's office training room, having lunch and watching Hooker's inspiration.

McGuire scratched notes about the similarities between the film and Colleen's enslavement: the slave collar; the rules forbidding "O" to look at her master's face, wear underwear, or put her knees together; the hanging and whipping; the piercing of her labia; the designation of an initial for a slave name . . . the list went on and on.

McGuire later asked the judge about showing *The Story of O* to the jurors, but he was reluctant, at a cost of three thousand dollars a day, to spend court time on a film. She would have to work it into the testimony.

McGuire's impressive display of evidence wasn't complete yet. When court reconvened, another large box, this one about four feet square, had been added. It was a scale model of the "hole," which Cameron and Colleen had dug beneath the shed.

Janice again took the stand, and McGuire asked why Cameron had left two "windows" in one wall when constructing it.

"He was going to make more dungeons," Janice replied.

"Why?"

"To be able to house more slaves." (This raised subdued muttering in the courtroom.)

"How many?" McGuire asked.

"Four." (More astonishment whispered through the courtroom.)

Sighing often, Janice explained that the hole had taken more than two years to build, and virtually all the work had been done by hand, by Cameron and Colleen. While Jan told about the hole and its construction, some of the jurors again stood to get a better view.

But bizarre as the hole was, and despite the extraordinary effort made in its excavation and construction, it had been put to little use. Janice testified that Cameron restrained her in the hole on only a couple of occasions. And except for two brief stays in the hole, Colleen was locked in the box almost without let-up from March of 1981 to May of 1984—more than a thousand days.

Not once did she contend that Colleen had been free to go. Even during the period of "freedom," in 1979 and 1980, when Colleen babysat the children and was allowed to stay out of the box, she was kept, Janice testified, "in the back bathroom, chained to the toilet."

While Papendick had said that Colleen had gone to numerous family gatherings, Janice testified that Colleen attended family get-togethers "infrequently," until June and August of 1984, shortly before the two of them escaped.

But if Janice portrayed Colleen as thoroughly enslaved, she also came across as pathetically cowed by her husband. She described a three-day period in 1983 when he made her fast, threatening to beat her if she ate or drank anything without his permission. And when McGuire asked Janice why she rarely spoke to Colleen, Janice answered, "I was too scared to. I was afraid to do or say the wrong thing. I was afraid that Cameron would become angry."

This prompted a dramatic sigh from Defense Attorney Papendick.

Janice testified that Hooker used the Bible to underscore his control, pointing out passages that said slaves and wives should be totally submissive. This made her feel "helpless," she said. Cameron also told her that if she didn't do everything he told her, she would go to hell.

(Everyone puzzled over the strange religious undertones in this three-way relationship. A Bible lay incongruously amidst the hard-core pornographic evidence, a moral contrast sharp as black and white.)

Finally, after two and a half days of draining testimony, Janice's direct examination was nearly over. Deputy DA McGuire was proud of her. She thought she'd tried hard to be clear and responsive and had withstood the pressure well. Though Janice may not have emerged as a very admirable character, she didn't hedge, even when it would have been easy for her to lie.

And McGuire was touched by small things, such as Jan's carefully thumbing through magazines or deposit slips to make *sure* she was identifying them correctly. She doubted that the jury understood the earnestness reflected in those small gestures, but she hoped they saw that Janice did not take her role lightly.

The most poignant moment came toward the end of Jan's testimony, when the long pauses were no longer sufficient for her to regain her composure, and her sighs melted into sobs.

McGuire was questioning her about the final rape count, in July of 1984, when the three of them were in bed together. Janice murmured that it was Cameron's idea, that he'd said "that he was going to sleep with her whether I wanted him to or not, so I could make it easier on myself by just accepting it." He again used the Bible as justification, saying that Colleen was like Hagar, the slave wife to Abraham.

Under questioning, Jan dutifully described the bondage and sexual relations involved, though this was obviously difficult for her. She spoke slowly, with gulps and pauses.

McGuire asked why she went along with it.

"I felt like I didn't have any choice."

"Why?"

Janice covered her eyes with her hand, and sobbed, "Because I was scared to go to hell!"

When Papendick began his cross-examination of Janice Hooker the next morning, his desk was yellow with legal pads. He sprang toward the witness stand and immediately came to the question he'd been waiting so long to ask: Had Janice told Colleen that she could go?

Janice said she had.

What exactly had she said?

"I just simply told her, 'go.' " The two had been arguing about something, she couldn't remember what. Colleen had

said something about going, and Janice had said, *"Then go!"*
They'd parted without further words.

Hearing this, McGuire and Shamblin exchanged worried
glances. But there was more.

Did Janice recall telling Al Shamblin that Colleen had
told her: "God doesn't want me to go yet?"

"Yes."

"Did Colleen tell you that God had put her there to
straighten out her life—drugs and stuff?"

"Yes."

The jury sat rapt as quite a different picture emerged under questioning by Defense Attorney Papendick.

"When did you first believe Colleen was becoming fond of
Cameron?"

(Sigh.) "About 1980."

Papendick asked what it was that made her think this.

"She would cook special things for him," Janice said.
"And before he came home from work, she would put on
makeup. That king of thing."

She didn't recall Colleen showing Cameron affection before the trip to Riverside, but specified that she'd seen Cameron showing Colleen affection as early as 1977.

Further, Jan said she saw the two "hugging and kissing"
in 1982 and 1983 "in the evening, after the kids were
asleep." And in 1984, she saw such displays of affection
nearly every day, sometimes in front of the children.

Papendick asked where.

"In the mobile home, in the yard, different places."

"Such as?"

"Burney Falls."

This was something Papendick had been waiting for. In
July of 1984 Colleen had gone with the Hooker family on a
trip to Burney Falls. He even had snapshots of them all
smiling together, which he entered as evidence.

His portrayal of Colleen as a happy family member was
amplified by Janice's testimony about the summer of 1980,
when Colleen had gone water-skiing with them at Black
Butte Lake.

McGuire cringed when she heard Janice describe how
Colleen and Cameron's brother and his wife had come with

them on an all-day outing. Colleen had even learned how to water-ski.

And like any member of the family, Papendick contended, Colleen was free to come and go. He established that the back bathroom where Colleen stayed in 1980 was directly across from an outside door, that Colleen was not always restrained, and that, in fact, Colleen had locked the bathroom door from the *inside*.

Papendick continued to emphasize the freedom Colleen enjoyed during her stay. In 1980 she went jogging nearly every day. Over the years, she frequently worked in the garden and babysat. She made phone calls to her family. Cameron took her on a trip to Reno and to visit her family in Riverside. She and Jan read the Bible together. And Jan took her on shopping trips, without Cameron, to the nearby towns of Chico and Redding.

Then there were those highly suspect evenings when Jan and Colleen went to bars.

"In 1979 and 1981," Papendick asked, "did you go out on dates with men other than Cameron?"

McGuire quickly objected that this was irrelevant, but she was overruled.

"Yes," Janice answered.

"How many men did you date?"

"Two." Under questioning, she said she'd dated one in December and January, and the other for a couple of months in 1980, though she couldn't remember the months.

Papendick asked where they went.

By now, Janice appeared near tears. "The New Orleans bar," she said.

With Colleen?

"Yes." She said they both had a couple of drinks, danced, and had coffee with a couple of guys. With great hesitancy, she related how they'd gone home with the two men, and she and her date had gone into a separate room, leaving Colleen and the other fellow in the living room.

Papendick asked if she had sexual relations with her date.

Looking pained, Janice said, "Not then, but later."

Papendick also established that the Hookers had a number of visitors, mostly family, who came to their home on a regular basis. Most of them had met Colleen, who was introduced as Kay, the live-in babysitter. (Though Janice didn't say that guests encountered Colleen every time they came over, it was hard to imagine that another adult could remain isolated in so small a home as a single-wide trailer.)

Papendick also managed at least partially to nullify McGuire's pornographic evidence by establishing that, despite the magazines he collected, Cameron had trouble reading. Jan said she assumed he looked at the pictures.

Papendick scoffed at Jan's contention that the bondage was painful and she'd done it unwillingly. Referring to their dating period, he asked: "Why did you accept the relationship?"

" 'Cause I was able to block out all the bad and only look at the good," she replied.

Still insisting that their relationship was completely consensual, he asked if they didn't have some kind of bondage "system."

"If you call begging to be let down a system, I guess that was true."

Some of Papendick's questions, while acknowledging the stories about the Company that Colleen had been told, cast blame on Janice. In general, Jan accepted her share of the blame, but sometimes she quibbled. For instance, Papendick asked if she had given Colleen orders.

"I *asked* her to do things," she said stubbornly.

"Did you order her?"

Janice said she had a problem with the term, *order,* but finally admitted that she sometimes told Colleen to clean the bathroom or clean the girls' room.

More often than quibbling, Janice would simply say, "I don't remember" or "I don't recall." She said this so much that the courtroom began to sigh at her unresponsiveness. And the less responsive she was, the less credible she became.

The defense attorney also succeeded in making Janice look cruel by getting her to admit that she'd whipped Colleen on two occasions. Papendick asked: "Why?"

"Cameron told me to," she said simply, as if this were unequivocal.

The lesbian acts with Colleen, she said, were also done under orders from Cameron.

But to everyone's amazement, when Jan described the incident of the final rape count she admitted that Colleen asked her permission to sleep with Cameron, and she had said yes. If Cameron was such a tyrant, why was Janice the one to grant permission?

The courtroom was utterly silent as Papendick drew out more testimony of this weird ménage à trois.

Speaking very softly, Jan conceded that she recalled Colleen saying that she enjoyed sex with Cameron. For instance, Colleen had said that when she returned from Riverside, Cameron had slept with her to make her feel better and that after her shower he had lain with her to warm her before putting her back in the box.

"Did she ever indicate to you that she wanted to have Cameron's baby?" Papendick asked.

"She said she wanted to have *a* baby, not specifically Cameron's."

"Did you believe that Colleen loved Cameron?"

"Yes."

"When was the first time?"

"In 1980."

"Did you still feel she loved him in 1984?"

"Yes."

"During 1980, did you feel jealousy toward Colleen?"

"Yes."

"When was the first time you felt jealous of her?"

"Probably May nineteenth, 1977."

"Did you always feel jealousy toward Colleen for the next seven and a half years?"

"No."

"When didn't you?"

"Before and after Riverside, both."

"Why were you jealous of Colleen?"

"I think that's a little obvious, why a wife would be jealous of another woman in the house."

But with Papendick hammering away at her, Janice seemed rather lame and unfathomable. McGuire could almost feel the jury's sympathy slipping away.

Now Papendick zeroed in on another weakness: "Did you feel that Colleen liked the children?"

"Yes," Janice answered.

"Loved them?"

"Sure."

"Took care of them well?"

"Yes."

"Did the children care for Colleen?"

"Yes."

"Refer to her as Mom?"

Icily, *"No."*

With at least the suggestion of a rivalry over the children established, Papendick went on to let the jury know that shortly after Cameron's arrest, Janice had come to his office to tell him that she could "destroy Colleen's story." Cameron's family, Janice explained, had told her that she should stand behind him. But Papendick dug for a deeper reason.

"In August of 1984, how did you feel about Colleen's desire to return to Northern California?"

"I felt threatened."

"Why?"

"That it would start all over again."

"Didn't you go to the police because you were afraid they'd get back together?"

"No."

"Because you were afraid they'd take the children?"

"No."

Suddenly, Papendick said, "No further questions, Your Honor," and sat down.

His abrupt ending left a sudden vacuum. The direct examination had taken two and a half days; Papendick's cross had taken just a few hours. McGuire had expected him to at least finish out the day, letting the jury go home with lingering doubts about Janice's veracity as a witness, wondering whether jealousy might, after all, be at the core of this bizarre tale. But now McGuire had almost an hour to rehabilitate her witness under redirect examination, and beneath her relief she was stunned by what she perceived as a major strategical gaffe.

* * *

First, McGuire clarified that when Janice told Colleen she could go, Colleen still believed in the Company. "When you let Colleen out of the box to read the Bible, why didn't she flee?"

"Because she was too afraid."

Regarding threats Cameron made about the Company, McGuire asked what would happen if Colleen didn't do as she was told.

"I don't think she ever did disobey," Janice said.

McGuire also established that Cameron had been calling and writing Janice, trying to sway her testimony. "Did he indicate to you that he loves you?"

"Yes."

"How does that make you feel?"

Softly, Janice responded, "Guilty, guilty."

Now McGuire came around to the "affection" between the defendant and the victim. "When Cameron was being 'affectionate' to Colleen that time in 1977," McGuire asked, "was she blindfolded?"

"Yes."

"Chained?"

"Yes."

"Roped?"

"Yes."

"And there was sexual intercourse?"

"Yes."

"Was it forced?"

Papendick objected, but Judge Knight overruled the objection.

"Yes," Jan answered.

"Is that consistent with your definition of affection?"

"No."

McGuire also established that Colleen had to ask permission to jog, go to church, or leave the mobile home. Moreover, the court heard, Janice had asked Cameron's permission to date those two men and to take Colleen to the bar.

McGuire moved on to conversations Jan had with Colleen about having been a slave. "Did one of those conversations involve the scars on your knees?"

"Yes. She asked me what happened to my knee. I told her I had a knee condition, that it was inherited." Later, Janice had mentioned the conversation to Cameron and he "got very upset because that wasn't the story that he had told her." Cameron had told Colleen that Janice had been crucified for having run away, and that she'd been nailed through the knees.

"Did you ever tell Colleen that the story about you was a fiction?"

"She never asked."

"Did you ever tell her?"

"No."

"Why not?"

"Because I was afraid to, afraid of Cameron."

Battered woman? Or jealous wife? The images fluxed.

Papendick only kept Janice on the stand a few minutes for re-cross-examination. All in all, Janice was less pliant this time around, but Papendick did manage to score a few points.

Focusing again on Colleen's freedoms, he brought out new information that she'd gone on a snow skiing trip with the Hookers in the winter of 1979.

And he dwelled on Colleen having said, "God doesn't want me to leave yet." Jan explained that she and Colleen were having a religious discussion when Colleen volunteered that "God was telling her that."

By the time Janice finally stepped down from the stand, Papendick had succeeded in sowing enough seeds of distrust that opinions in the courtroom were wavering. The salient points were that Janice *was* jealous and that perhaps Colleen really had loved Cameron. If the charges were rape and other sex acts, didn't that establish consent?

30

The morning of Thursday, October 3, the courtroom was
packed with a curious public, courtroom "groupies," and a
crush of media people, all eager to assess the woman known
as the "sex slave." Anticipation mounted, and now, as everyone hoped and expected, the prosecutor called Colleen
Stan as the state's second witness.

All watched as Colleen entered, swore to tell the truth,
and gingerly seated herself in the witness stand. With her
thin hair cut shoulder-length, wearing a pastel blue dress,[1]
Colleen looked demur, pale, and more fragile than she had
at the preliminary hearing. The eyes of the courtroom crowd
drank her in.

Their ears would have a harder time. Colleen spoke so
softly that the hum of the fluorescent lights nearly drowned
her out.

McGuire started, again, with the kidnapping. The courtroom strained to hear as Colleen Stan recounted the events
of May 19, 1977.

She took the listeners up into the mountains and down the
dirt road where Hooker had stopped the car, come around
to the passenger's side, and suddenly put a knife to her
throat.

Her tale turned to the head box, and on cue from Mc-

---

1. Another gift from Christine McGuire, who was convinced her star
witness needed a new dress to wear in court.

Guire, a woman[2] entered the court dressed much as Colleen had been on the day of the kidnap: in jeans and a T-shirt. Officer Shamblin swiftly opened the head box, and, to everyone's surprise, shut it over the woman's head. Whispers of "Jesus," and "Oh, Christ" rustled among the spectators as she staggered beneath the sudden weight of the box.

When the box was removed, its efficacy proved, Colleen went on with her testimony. The court sat engrossed as she described, step by step, how she'd been stripped, hung by the wrists, and whipped; the pain and terror of spending days chained to the rack, then being locked inside the double-walled, coffin-shaped box.

If there were any lingering doubts that she knew the box's measurement as "tall enough from my elbow to the tip of my fingers," and held up her forearm, to illustrate.

As Colleen told of her daily routine and explained the slavery contract, she was very subdued, with sad eyes that looked up when she thought, down when she listened, but never at those of the defendant.

She explained that she was too terrified to run away and that Janice Hooker, who was a much more malevolent character in Colleen's perception than she'd seemed on the stand, had told her "that if I ever stepped one foot out of the door, I might as well put a gun to my head and shoot myself."[3]

---

2. The volunteer was Debbra Hess, an employee of the Tehama County DA's office.

3. McGuire believed both her main witnesses were telling the truth as they saw it, but their perspectives varied. She was struck, rather, by the difference in their attitudes. Colleen now seemed hostile, especially toward Janice, who she believed was giving incorrect testimony. Janice was more introspective, probably because she'd been in therapy, and when she learned that Colleen was angry, she wanted to talk. Colleen did not.

McGuire endeavored to keep the two apart. But as they were leaving the eighth-floor courtroom that afternoon, they had an accidental brush. Along with McGuire and others, Janice and Colleen ended up going down in the same elevator. The air was electric—intensified since everyone in the elevator was aware of the tension between the two. No one spoke.

Hooker brought her upstairs to do household chores, but, Colleen testified, "he was never pleased with the way I would clean."

"How did you know?" McGuire asked.

"Because he would beat me and tell me."

"Why didn't you scream?"

"Because," she said dully, Cameron threatened that "if I screamed or talked too much he would notify the Company and they'd remove my vocal chords."

Besides the dual deprivations of hunger and darkness, she described being hung, whipped, sexually abused, burned with a heat lamp, nearly drowned, and having her ankles cuffed so tightly they swelled.[4]

Responding to a question about how she'd been marked "for identification," Colleen said Cameron had inserted a gold earring after piercing her labia "like you would pierce an ear." (This induced a pained gasp from the women in the courtroom.)

Throughout the day's testimony, no matter how terrifying the events she described, she remained outwardly unruffled, showing no hint of distress or indignation. At the end of the day, when the prosecutor fielded questions out in the hallway, reporters asked about Colleen's strangely unemotional manner.

Colleen didn't get upset, she replied, "because she'd been through it all." But McGuire read their questions like a barometer: If the press was bothered by Colleen's indifference, the jury must be, too.

The next day Colleen described her time under the waterbed and specific "punishments" Hooker had subjected her to—some of the most graphic testimony the court would hear.

Janice was hurt by Colleen's new coldness toward her—especially since when they'd met at the preliminary hearing they'd rushed together and hugged. But it was probably healthy for Colleen to finally express her anger, however mildly, by snubbing Janice.

4. Some incidents that Colleen described during the course of her testimony fell beyond the statute of limitations. Others, she had not testified to at the preliminary hearing, so they could not be charged.

Colleen told of being punished in 1978 or 1979 for doing a macrame project incorrectly. She thought it had turned out fine, but Jan got angry and told Cameron. When he got home he took her out of the box and put the cuffs on her. Then, she said, "I knew something really terrible was going to happen."

Hooker took her into the living room, hung her by the wrists on the frame, taped electrical wires to her thighs and breasts, "sat down on the couch and hit the switch."

Every time the current hit, she yelled, so he gagged her to muffle the sound. She began to sweat, and as her skin turned damp and then wet, the tape loosened. Hooker stopped and tried to reaffix the wires, but by then the tape wouldn't stick to her breasts at all. He gave up and settled for sending the current only through the wires taped to her thighs.

Hooker let her know she was being punished because she hadn't done as she'd been told. "He told me I'd better start obeying and show more respect," she said quietly.

The courtroom was solemn as McGuire took Colleen through several of the counts against Hooker, describing each in as much detail as possible. McGuire often referred to the time chart that she and Colleen had made to clarify the rather complicated sequence of events: the rape on the stretcher, the rape upon return from Riverside, the rape while hung on the frame, the sodomy occurring in September 1979. . . .[5]

McGuire also had Colleen identify some of Hooker's pornography, focusing primarily on articles concerning sexual slavery. As she pointed out scenes that Hooker had duplicated on his slave, her point became clear: This was his library, his field of study, and he'd applied what he'd learned in his treatment of Colleen Stan.

The Bible had been another resource. Once, Colleen said,

---

5. There is nothing in the California penal code regarding torture. "Mayhem," the closest, refers to maiming—putting out an eye, slitting a nose, ear, or lip. "Assault," another possibility, carries a light sentence. McGuire opted, therefore, to prosecute Hooker primarily on the sex counts, which carry severe sentences that can be stacked consecutively.

he'd asked her to read the entire Book of Revelations to him and mark all the sections that dealt with slavery.

McGuire asked whether Hooker had told her things about God.

Colleen thought a moment and responded: "Cameron drew a picture of a Y and said it's like a crossroads—one path to righteousness and one to hell—and that when he found me I was going the wrong way, that he had given me another chance, and now I had to decide to go the right way."

But when McGuire asked if she'd told Cameron, "God placed me with you to straighten out my life," she denied this. Rather, she said, Cameron had told her that several times in 1981.

Colleen's testimony contradicted Janice's on several points. She denied having asked Cameron to lie beside her because she was cold. She said Janice had never told her she could go. She denied cooking special meals for Cameron and said that she had put on makeup only for her own enjoyment, even when she was just babysitting. She never told Janice she enjoyed having sex with Cameron and denied having hugged or kissed him. And, she said, she'd never considered herself Hagar.

The Deputy DA spent a great deal of time going over Colleen's contacts with neighbors and visitors, being careful to weave Colleen's fear of the Company in with a recounting of the apparent freedoms she enjoyed during her "year out of the box." Colleen testified she was afraid of Cameron's family because he'd told her his father and brother were "heavy in the Company."

McGuire then moved to the touchy subject of Colleen's love for Cameron. The courtroom studied the witness as she stated that in 1980 she'd told Hooker she loved him "out of fear" and "because I felt that if I made him feel that I loved him, he would treat me better."

Had he treated her better?

"A little."

McGuire asked if Colleen had said she wanted to have his baby. The press and spectators sat very still, afraid a cough or rustling paper might make them miss a word.

"Cameron told me that someday I would have his baby," Colleen said. "I asked him if he was giving me a choice or if he was telling me. He said it was a choice. I said as long as I had a choice, I wouldn't have his baby."

Asked whether she felt love for Cameron, she paused and then responded that she "felt a kind of love, a thankfulness," then added: "I don't understand why I had those feelings, because now I feel that Cameron is a very terrible person."

Papendick quickly objected but was overruled.

Now McGuire turned to that worrisome but unavoidable trip to Riverside, beginning with Hooker's preparations.

The courtroom heard first of Colleen being hung in Cameron's father's barn, then of an "obedience test" with a shotgun: "He told me to get down on my knees. He was holding the gun and he told me to put my mouth over the end" and pull the trigger, Colleen said. "It clicked."

She testified that on the way down to Riverside Cameron stopped in Sacramento, near the capital, on the pretense that the people at Company headquarters might want to test her. She waited nervously in the car while he went into a "sky-scraper." When he came out, he told her she was lucky they didn't want to test her and handed her a permit to carry money.

Colleen insisted that fear of the Company prevented her from making what might have seemed the obvious move of asking her family for help. She stayed with them for twenty-four hours without even hinting that she was in trouble. As she was leaving, Colleen said, "It was very hard not to break down and cry and tell [my mother] what was happening."

Why didn't she?

"I was afraid to."

When they returned to the trailer, Cameron told her to shower and then raped her.

Why didn't she resist?

"I was afraid he would beat me or torture me or even kill me," she said softly.

"Is he strong?"

"Stronger than me."

But at the next break, some of the public in the back of

the room was heard to comment: *"Tsk,* what a fool." "She should have escaped." "She *liked* it."

From day to day, reactions among the courtroom spectators varied, depending on what portion of the proceedings they'd heard. But a CNN cameraman, who had been there from the beginning, told a colleague: "I think he's going to get off. She's just not convincing enough."

Her last full day of direct examination—with all the clocks stuck at 3:05, the air-conditioning blown out, and Judge Knight sweltering in his robes—Colleen Stan continued with her testimony.

She held the court spellbound with her perplexing tale of life with the Hookers. It was a story riddled with contradictions: love and hate, tedium and terror, autonomy and dependence, Holy Scripture and sleazy pornography, secret perversions within an apparently wholesome family. None of it seemed reconcilable, yet Colleen claimed it had all coexisted.

In a voice as flat and unemphatic as yesterday's beer, she described varying terms of confinement—three years in a box, vast new freedoms after January of 1984, and her apparently regular job as a motel maid at King's Lodge. Still, one part of her testimony remained constant: She said she was too afraid to try to escape.

If Colleen's monotone testimony wasn't totally convincing, it harmonized with the unmistakable strain of docility about her. Whenever court recess was called, for example, she hesitated even to rise from her seat to leave the witness stand until the prosecutor approached, then exited the courtroom with her. And when McGuire asked if she "had a plan or survival strategy," Colleen's reply was typically passive: "I figured that as long as I did what Cameron said, he wouldn't kill me. And I put a lot of faith in God, that He'd take care of me."

Further, Colleen said she never felt she had a choice except to do as Cameron told her, "because he told me I was a slave and slaves don't have a choice."

During the final summer, Colleen testified, Cameron began telling her that God wanted her to have sex with him,

and Janice, feeling that she had to obey her husband, added
to the pressure. They'd come to the controversial eighth
rape count—controversial because Janice had testified that
Colleen had asked her permission to have sex with Cameron. But in Colleen's description, both she and Janice were
tied to the bed, and penetration was forced.

At length, McGuire brought Colleen's testimony to the
time in August when Janice unexpectedly came to King's
Lodge, found her at work, and set her free. Colleen said she
was very upset and crying. "I was devastated because I had
believed everything he'd told me. He'd made it seem so
real."

"How did you feel?"

"I felt that I could go home. I felt that it was over."

But though Colleen was reunited with her family after a
long, mysterious absence, she didn't go to the police. Why?

Colleen claimed that Janice had asked her not to—a point
which Janice had denied.

McGuire then questioned Colleen point-blank about subsequent calls and letters to the Hookers. Colleen said she
was writing to Janice, not to Cameron, but since the two had
gotten back together, the letters were sent to them both. "I
don't really understand why I wrote the letters now," she
admitted, "but Jan wanted me to keep in contact with her,
and I wanted to know how they were doing."

The phone calls, according to Colleen, were mainly placed
by the Hookers, who wanted to know what she'd told her
family and whether she'd gone to the police.

Wrapping up a few final points, McGuire finished her direct examination and turned her witness over to Papendick.

Hooker's defense attorney immediately confronted Colleen with her contention that she hadn't shown affection to
the defendant. She maintained she had not.

Papendick then entered a photograph into evidence. It
showed Colleen with her arm around Cameron's shoulder,
both of them seated on a sofa and smiling.[6]

---

6. The photograph had been taken by Colleen's stepmother in Riverside in 1981.

This was passed around to the jury who, as usual, registered nothing but somberness on their faces.

Having punctured Colleen's credibility, Papendick pressed ahead. He asked if the witness remembered phoning Cameron just after midnight on August 14 and talking for seventy-six minutes.

Colleen said she didn't recall.

Did she recall saying she'd been looking at the photograph and decided to phone?

"No."

Didn't she remember sending the photograph to Cameron?

"I don't remember if I did or not," she said, but by now it seemed clear that she had.

Throughout the cross-examination, Papendick portrayed the story of the Company as ludicrous, contending that no one could be so preposterously gullible as to believe it. At one point, in a tone of conspiratorial hilarity, he asked, "Looking back on the story of the Company, isn't it the most bizarre thing you've ever heard?"

McGuire exclaimed: "Argumentative, Your Honor!" Her objection was sustained, but Papendick was laying a groundwork of skepticism, bringing latent doubts to the fore.

The defense attorney went on to point out the many opportunities Colleen had to escape but didn't. Paying special attention to the 1981 trip to Riverside, he listed place after place that she had ventured without apparent fear of reprisals by the Company and without asking anyone for help: How could the Company know the addresses of your aunts and uncles and grandmother? What about your father's car? Did you honestly believe the Company was monitoring these places? Wouldn't they think you were escaping?

Having presented the whole story of the Company and of slavery as absurd, Papendick shifted his attention to Janice: "Did Janice ever tell you that she was a slave?"

"I don't recall."

"Did you ever ask her?"

"I don't recall asking, but I do recall her telling me she was just as much a slave as I was."

"How frequently did you go shopping with Janice?"

"About half a dozen times."

"Did you ever suggest to Jan that you could both escape?"

"No."

Then, referring to a shopping trip to the Mt. Shasta Mall in Redding, Papendick asked, "Were there security officers around?"

"Yes."

"Did you believe they were members of the Company?"

"No."

What about the pastor of the church she went to with her grandmother in 1981?

"No."

"When you and Janice went home with the two men you met at the bar, weren't you afraid the Company would think you were trying to escape?"

"No, because it was Janice's decision."

"Did you ever inspect the phone on Pershing to see if it was bugged?"

"No."

Papendick listed numerous other phones and Colleen admitted she hadn't inspected any of them. On the other hand, she explained huffily: "I don't know anything about that stuff."

Asking how Colleen got to and from work, Papendick established not only that Colleen regularly traveled the three-mile distance unsupervised and under her own power on a bike, but that she once detoured to find 1140 Oak Street.

"Weren't you afraid the Company would think you were trying to escape?"

"No."

"Weren't you afraid you'd be punished?" he goaded.

"No," she answered flatly.

Again, after establishing that Colleen had visited a friend, Lenora Scott, after work, Papendick asked: "Weren't you afraid the Company would be angry with you?"

"No."

"Weren't you afraid that Cameron would be angry with you?"

"No."

Finally Papendick showed his hand: "Isn't it a fact," he said coldly, "that you used the Company as a *reason* to stay in the Hooker household?"

In her usual deadpan, Colleen replied: "I didn't want to stay."

Deputy DA McGuire listened with rising trepidation. She'd expected Colleen to do better than this.

Citing Colleen's testimony that she'd spent twenty-three hours a day in the box between March 1981 and December 1983, Papendick asked what she did in the box.

"Slept. Listened to the radio. Dreamed about going home."

"Did you do any exercise?"

"No."

Papendick asked her to recount what she did when she got out of the box. Besides "some knee-bends after I brushed my teeth," Colleen mentioned no exercise, a point that would come up later.

Papendick moved on, establishing that Colleen was aware that Janice was jealous of her, that Colleen was taking care of the children earlier than Janice realized, and that there was a strong bond between Colleen and the Hookers' daughters. "Did you believe Jan was a good mother?" he asked.

McGuire immediately objected.

Papendick exclaimed: "That was her motive for staying, Your Honor!"

Judge Knight sustained the objection, as there's no cause to show a *victim's* motive, but the defense attorney had succeeded in planting another seed of suspicion.

At times, however, Papendick seemed to be doing his client more harm than good. He stunned the courtroom by spending what seemed an inordinate amount of time in questioning Colleen about the electrical shock incident on the frame. He quibbled with her over whether the wire had been taped "tightly." Colleen, who averted her eyes from the defense attorney, looked pained at even having to discuss this, her words becoming very soft.

"How many times were you shocked?"

"I don't remember."

"More than once?"

"Yes."

"More than twice?"

"Yes."

"More than three times?"

"Perhaps."

"How long?"

"Maybe three or four seconds."

Surely this was not the sort of testimony Papendick was hoping to elicit, yet, to the court's astonishment, he continued.

"Where did you feel the pain?"

"In my entire body."

"Wasn't the pain more concentrated in one spot?"

"It shoots electric current through your entire body," she insisted.

Although Papendick must have thought he was helping his client by belaboring this, it seemed he was only making the incident more vivid to everyone in the courtroom. Worse, it was time for lunch and court was now recessed, leaving the image of Colleen being hung and electrocuted lingering in the minds of the jurors.

When Papendick resumed the cross-examination after lunch, he let loose with his biggest ammunition, a rapid-fire line of questioning that shot holes in Colleen's credibility.

"Did you ever tell Cameron that you would give him a son?"

"No."

"Did you ever tell Cameron that he spiritually inspired you?"

"No."

"Did you ever tell him that you were his spiritual wife?"

"No."

Here, Papendick handed Colleen a sheet of paper and asked her to identify it. It was a letter. Looking disquieted, she admitted it was her handwriting.

"Do you remember when you wrote it?"

"No."

He suggested she read it to refresh her recollection. After a moment, she said, "It says Christmas."

Papendick moved the letter into evidence and passed copies to the jury and the prosecutor. While the jury read, Papendick and Hooker sat whispering, Hooker looking pleased.

Resuming his questions, Papendick asked, "Did you ever tell Cameron that you felt more of a woman being a slave?"

"No."

"Did you tell him that he made you feel good about yourself?"

"No."

Now Papendick showed her a card. She admitted the printing was hers, and that she had drawn the picture of the leaf with a "K" on the front. It read: "Happy Third Anniversary," and copies of this, too, were passed to the jurors.

"Did you ever tell Cameron that your love was growing every day?"

"No."

Alluding to the car, he asked, "When you talk about 'just because I love you,' who are you referring to?"

"Could've been Jan," she said defensively.

Quoting again, Papendick read: "My love for you is growing every changing day—"

"I felt a love that he made me feel for him," Colleen objected.

"This card was given to either Cameron or Jan, is that correct?"

"Yes."

"And it expressed how you felt at that time, right?"

"Not necessarily. I used to write poems a lot."

"Do you recall writing a diary?"

"At Cameron's instruction."

"Did you prepare a document entitled 'Past'?"

"Not that I recall."

Papendick handed Colleen some handwritten pages. She flushed but said she now remembered writing it.

"Do you recall putting in the diary that you wanted to stay with Cameron, that he welcomed you into the family?"

She admitted that she recalled being welcomed into the family, though she couldn't remember when.

"Did you tell Cameron that you loved him?"

"Yes."

"When was the first time?"

"After he let me out of the box in 1980."

"Why did you tell him you loved him?"

"Because he treated me better, didn't lock me in the box, gave me more freedoms."

"Did you believe that Cameron loved you?"

"He told me he did."

"Did you believe him?"

"I didn't know."

While the defense attorney was pursuing this line of questioning, McGuire brooded over the new evidence Papendick had just dropped on her desk. This was a prosecutor's worst fear: unexpected evidence. The state is required to fully disclose its case to the defense, but since the reverse isn't true, there was always the danger of a sudden bombshell being exploded. And now it had. She recalled that she'd heard rumors of "love letters" months ago, but since Colleen and Janice claimed to know nothing about them, she'd put them out of her mind.

Now they lay inches from her fingertips, but she resolved not to read them until later. She didn't want the jury to realize this information was new to her, or to see how worrying it was.

Papendick asked Colleen a range of questions—about her diet, her encounters with family and neighbors, jogging—before coming back, again, to the letters. He quoted: "I seem to be falling deeper and deeper in love with you."

Colleen protested that Cameron had *told* her to write of her love for him.

Papendick, undaunted, pondered the letter in his hand and smiled, saying, "Sweet. Sounds like a teenager wrote it."

By now Colleen's eyes were red. She was sniffing as Papendick let loose with a barrage of questions about the eighth rape count. Specifically, he wanted to know whether she'd asked Jan if it was okay.

Colleen said she'd asked that because they'd been telling

her that she needed sex, that God had told them that Cameron was to be the one to satisfy her needs, that they'd pressured her for weeks.

Again, Papendick asked whether she recalled saying "okay?"

"I don't recall," she said, looking away.

Papendick questioned her rigorously on this count, having her describe again what had happened, getting her to contradict herself on a previous statement, and finally bringing her to tears.

The unemotional witness was crying.

Having made his major points, Papendick jumped around to various time periods, asking about the letters she'd mailed home, incidents of bondage she'd testified to, her relationship with Jan. Then, abruptly, he was done.

For a second time, McGuire was startled by the brevity of Papendick's cross-examination. Another thirty-five minutes, and the jury would have gone home to sleep on all the doubts he'd raised. Now she had a chance to dispel these.

Letting the "love letters" sit until she'd had a chance to read them, McGuire questioned Colleen about the damaging photograph of her hugging Cameron, giving her a chance to reassert that Cameron had told her to make it appear they were in love and that she feared letting her family know the true situation. Further, she hadn't told her family what was going on because Cameron had said the house and cars were bugged with minute and precise listening devices.

Only a few of McGuire's questions were hard hitting. She let the last minutes of the day elapse, still worrying about those unread love letters.

That night, the lights were on well past midnight in Christine McGuire's hotel room. She went over the letters in exhaustive detail with Colleen, who, shaken by this new evidence, apologetically explained that she'd simply forgotten about writing them, it was so long ago.

Long after Colleen had gone to bed, McGuire sat alone and read over and over the anniversary card Colleen had given to Cameron in May, 1980, three years after the kidnap. The outside, decorated with a leaf and a "K," said, "Happy Third Anniversary." Inside, it read:

Sometimes I feel that being your slave has made me more of a woman. But then there are other times when I feel it has made me less of a woman. You know how to make me feel good about myself. And I love you so much for it. I only wish that my dreams could be fulfilled with you. Because I feel a strong love and need to be with you. I'll always serve you with singleness of heart.

K

The Christmas letter was even worse:

This is my Christmas letter to express and give my love to my Master. You ask me to tell you how much I love you but I haven't ever been able to tell you because I don't know the right words to describe how much I love you but I seem to be falling deeper and deeper into love with you with each passing day. I find love hard for me to express with words. But you bring the passion out in me and it's a way of expressing my love for you. You've also spiritually inspired me and I can't tell you how much I love you for it. More than any words I know could ever tell. It's not easy being a slave but your love makes it worth being your slave. I hope that your right about how things will change for the better and that I'll have your child some day. I promise you I'll give you a son. I know you'll be proud of him and I hope you'll love him as much as you love me. I know that you know that I have great faith in God, I read this in St. Luke: For with God nothing shall be impossible. And I think you know how important it is to me to do everything with God in my heart, I need and want his guidance and strength. I can't explain how happy it made me feel inside when you told me that if I ever have your child that you would take me as your spiritual wife. I pray it will be someday. That God will recognize our love and commitment and that he'll join us to be one and that even though I'll be your bondmaid (slave) and second wife that no one or anything will ever

separate us. I wish you a Merry Merry Christmas and the
best of New Years. I pray that God will always hear your
prayers and always answer them. And that the Holy
Ghost will always be with you to guide you and to give
you insight and understanding so that you will always do
that which will make your soul feel good.

I love you more than words could ever say,

K

The third and last was another card. The outside read:
"Just because I love you. . . ." Inside, Colleen had written:

Love is not a single act, but a climate in which we live,
a lifetime venture in which we are always learning, discov-
ering, growing. It is not destroyed by a single failure, nor
won by a single caress. You cannot learn to love by loving
one person only, for love is a climate of the heart. My love
for you is growing with every changing day. You fill my
life with happiness and love. And I pray that that happiness and love will never end.

Love,

K

The next morning, McGuire opened by confronting the
"love letters" head on, one at a time.

Asked why she'd written the anniversary card, Colleen
said, "I suppose it was because I wanted to have something
to celebrate," since she didn't observe holidays or birthdays.

Then McGuire led her through the card, line by line, noting that Colleen had referred to herself as "your slave," and
had written: "I'll always serve you."

The Christmas letter was written around Christmas of
1980, just prior to her trip to Riverside. Why did she write
it?

"I believe Cameron told me to, because I write in the
beginning that he told me to tell how much I love him," she
said, then softly added: "I don't understand why I wrote it."

McGuire went through the letter highlighting each reference to slavery, noting that Colleen called Hooker "Master," and wrote, "It's not easy being a slave."

And what about writing that she wanted to have his child?

"Cameron told me that over and over," Colleen said.

Flipping through her notes, McGuire confronted the points Papendick had raised the day before, hoping her methodical approach could counteract the witches' brew of questions Papendick had splashed across the case. Cameron Hooker watched as she went over information as minor as that Colleen gave him the tips she made at King's Lodge, and as major as the several felony counts against him.

All the while, the jurors studiously took notes.

Defense Attorney Papendick began his re-cross-examination with a request to put some of his own markings on the time chart the prosecutor and Colleen had created so many months before. McGuire objected, since she hoped to use it in her closing argument, and a ten-minute discussion ensued about whether and how Papendick might be able to unobtrusively mark up this prop for use in his argument as well. They discussed little numbers, green as opposed to red or perhaps black, and considered larger or smaller markers. The judge, a natural comedian, couldn't help but see the humor in this, and while he joked about judicial function, the jury laughed at the spectacle of these dignified attorneys getting caught up in such trivialities.

With the details finally ironed out, Papendick had Colleen ink in the times she was out of the box, going to bars, jogging, or gardening. He quibbled with her about seasons, and she scowled but eventually the little numbers were in place.

This done, Papendick moved on to his last volley: phone records from Pacific Bell. There were a surprising number of calls placed from Colleen's father's residence to the Hookers', and these he listed one at a time, being careful to include the time and duration of each call. Many were more than twenty minutes long.

Papendick read these into the record, underscoring them in the minds of the jurors, interrogating Colleen on each. He asked to whom she spoke on each occasion. For most, Colleen could only weakly reply, "Probably Jan."

His point made, Papendick excused the witness and sat down.

31

With the trial into its third week and the sensational "sex slave" testimony over, the interest of the press slackened and the line-up of witnesses for the prosecution moved to those on the periphery, who have viewed the Hooker household from the outside. McGuire would call a total of nineteen witnesses—a few important neighbors and relatives, a doctor, and the expert witness, Dr. Hatcher—putting the strongest testimony at the beginning and end.

After Janice and Colleen's long stretches on the stand, the parade of subsequent witnesses went quickly. Neighbors and family members testified they'd known Colleen as "Kay," the live-in babysitter. They repeatedly stated they'd met her in 1979, 1980, or 1981, indirectly confirming she'd been in the box the rest of the time, but adding little substantive evidence.

Under cross-examination by Papendick, no one could claim to have seen any bruises or injuries on "Kay," nor to have witnessed any violent incidents. Only a few witnesses offered something fresh, a new angle, a possible insight.

On the heels of Colleen's testimony came a witness who didn't even have to speak to jolt the courtroom. The bailiff called Bonnie Sue Martin.

She entered looking so much like her sister it was as if Colleen had reappeared at a younger age—except for one stunning feature: her hair. Bonnie's gorgeous long hair fell well past her waist, full and luxuriant as a red-headed Godiva's.

The court had seen Colleen's thinning head of dishwater wisps. Now, as Bonnie swept across the room, she seemed the living, breathing example of how God intended Colleen to look: energetic and robust, with thick, rich hair tumbling down her back in shiny waves. Whatever words Bonnie might utter, nothing said more than the simple fact of her appearance.

She took the stand, and McGuire opened with a few questions about the three letters she had received from Colleen in 1979, then turned to the 1980 phone call from Colleen. Bonnie gave a moving narrative, her voice cracking as she described the brief, unexpected call from a sister so long missing that she couldn't even recognize her voice. "Her voice was very shaky," Bonnie said, "like she was being pressured."

Bonnie then described Colleen's short visit to Riverside in 1981. Glancing at the defendant, she said he was introduced as Mike.

McGuire asked how Colleen had acted around Cameron Hooker.

There were no hugs or words of endearment, she explained. And Colleen had oddly neglected even to mention "her fiancé" until just minutes before she left. "I didn't think they were boyfriend and girlfriend," she added.

Bonnie was shocked by the dramatic change in her sister's appearance. "I always called her Pudgy," she said tearfully, "but she was not the 'Pudgy' that I knew."

Struggling to regain her composure, she said that was the last time she saw Colleen until August, 1984.

Papendick spent very little time with this witness, probably believing it best to get her off the stand quickly. He showed her the photograph of Colleen hugging Cameron at her father's house in 1981, but Bonnie claimed she couldn't recall the picture being taken.

He also took this opportunity to try to work in some information about Colleen's past, but McGuire promptly objected, leaving the jury only with the knowledge that Colleen had been married at a young age, and that for some reason the prosecutor didn't want this discussed.

* * *

The testimonies of Mr. and Mrs. Coppa, the Hookers' next door neighbors, precipitated some controversial behavior on the part of Judge Knight.

McGuire's questioning of the matronly, retiring Mrs. Coppa uncovered little that wasn't by now familiar to the jurors—that "Kay" babysat the Hookers' daughters, worked "really hard" in their garden, and apparently left for an extended period and then returned.

Papendick's questions revealed little more, but then he asked, "Did Kay appear to be a regular member of the Hooker household?" to which Mrs. Coppa stammered the response: "Uh, well, yeah, I guess you could say that."

Judge Knight apparently felt this left an important question unanswered, so once the attorneys had wrapped up their questions he turned to Mrs. Coppa and asked: "Did it appear to you that she was like a servant?"

Seeming relieved at having been asked this, Mrs. Coppa replied, "I remember saying to a friend quite a while ago that she was like a slave."

Her words fell across the hushed courtroom like shattering glass.

This incident did nothing for Papendick's opinion of the judge. And following the testimony of Mr. Coppa, his smoldering displeasure with Judge Knight would spark into behind-the-scenes hostility.

Under questioning by McGuire, Mr. Coppa recalled most vividly that "Kay always seemed to be working in the garden."

"Did she work hard?" McGuire asked.

"She did it a lot harder than I would do it," he said, grinning. Then he added, "I was trying to figure out how to get my wife to work that hard."

As laughter wafted through the court, Judge Knight turned to Coppa and quipped: "I'll send you the transcript."

The spectators didn't hear this above their own chuckling. It was hard to say whether the jury heard the judge's comment, but Papendick did, and he was furious.

At the next break he came up to McGuire fuming: "Did

you hear that crack the judge made? I'm going to start keeping book on this guy!"

This was bad news. Papendick was going to try to make an issue of the judge's conduct.

McGuire had never come up against this before. Personally, she found Judge Knight efficient and astute and saw nothing improper in his rulings or his comportment in court. It was true he had a streak of the humorist in him, but they all made jokes back in the judge's chambers—it was a good way to ease tension—and Papendick laughed and wisecracked with the best of them. But if he took issue with Knight's conduct, there was a danger the judge could be disqualified, and McGuire had worked too long and hard on this case to have it declared a mistrial or reversed on appeal.

McGuire had resisted calling the Hookers' daughters, but since they were the only other people living in the mobile home at the time of Colleen's captivity, their perceptions were too important to skip.

The bailiff called Cathy Hooker.

Putting children on the stand requires special care. If testifying in court intimidates some adults, it can terrify a small child, so questions must be asked simply and gently, with no sarcasm or hostility. Kids must be handled with "kid gloves."

McGuire had learned from child molestation cases that having a trusted adult accompany the child on the stand lessens the anxiety, so Cathy was brought into the courtroom by her uncle, Janice's brother. Dressed in white tights and a pink skirt, with a long braid down her back, she looked absolutely angelic.

Cameron Hooker watched his daughter take the stand, a smile frozen on his face

Cathy said she was nine years old and told the court who her parents were. Since her mother was testifying against her father, the defendant, she could hardly have been in a more ticklish position, but she seemed unaware of this and answered with schoolgirl ingenuousness.

McGuire handed her a picture. "Who is that person?"

"Kay."

Cathy identified the blue terrycloth nightgown that "Kay" used to wear. She confirmed that Colleen had worked around the house, had one day left on the bus to go home, and had stayed away for some time. But Cathy sometimes seemed confused. When the prosecutor asked how long "Kay" had been gone, Cathy answered, "Three or four months."

McGuire skipped back to the period when "Kay" first babysat: "Is there a bathroom close to your bedroom?"

"Yes."

"Could you go in and out of that bathroom?"

"No."

"Why not?"

"Because it was locked."

"Are there a couple of sheds close to the trailer?"

"Yes."

"Could you get in and out of both of those sheds?"

"No."

"Why not?"

"Because one was locked."

Here, Cameron Hooker's smile faltered. He looked away.

"Were you supposed to go into your parents' bedroom?"

"No."

"Why not?"

"I don't know."

"Cathy, did you know about a box under the waterbed?"

Cathy's cheerfulness diminished. She looked nervous and sad. "No," she said.

"Did you know about the hole dug underneath one of the sheds?"

Also nervously: "No."

Having asked the hardest questions, the prosecutor shortly wrapped up her examination.

Rolland Papendick approached the witness in an equally gentle manner. "Was 'Kay' nice to you?" he asked.

"Yes."

"Did you love 'Kay'?"

"Yes."

Papendick set about illustrating Colleen's freedoms by eliciting testimony that "Kay" took Cathy and her sister for walks three or four times a month and for bicycle rides "most of the time." Diffusing some of the earlier testimony about Colleen's feverish labor, Cathy said that her mother, her father, and even she had worked in the garden.

Cathy was shortly excused. The bailiff next called the younger daughter, Dawn Hooker, and Cameron again had his smile in place.

All dimples, bangs, and nervous smiles, Dawn was brought in by the same uncle, who sat with her on the witness stand. When asked if she solemnly swore to tell the truth, the seven-year-old responded: "Yeah."

Dawn remembered less about "Kay" than her older sister, but the most important part of her testimony concerned the "hole." Colleen had testified that while she was kept there in 1983, Dawn and her cousin, Denise, had come into the shed and looked down the opening.

"What happened when you were back by the hole? Did someone come out and yell at you?" McGuire asked.

"No," Dawn replied, then quickly sucked in her breath, realizing she'd made a mistake.

"Did someone come out, do you remember?" McGuire persisted.

"Yeah."

"Who?"

"Mom."

"Did she get mad at you?"

"Yeah."

"For what?"

"Going back there."

Dawn remembered that she'd seen a light in the hole, but she hadn't seen Colleen, and in fact believed that "Kay" wasn't staying with the Hooker family at that time.

During his brief cross-examination, Papendick again highlighted the girls' affection for "Kay," in support of his claim that Jan was jealous over this bond.

By the time Papendick had finished his short round of questions, with Dawn again making simple mistakes and then sucking in her breath at the realization, the courtroom was completely charmed by her. Even the poker-faced jurors smiled.

The daughters had blown through the court like sudden fresh air, but McGuire's mind was always turning: She wondered whether their innocent appeal might backfire, eliciting compassion and sympathy for their father.

Another witness called by the prosecution clearly managed to make points for the defense.

Under questioning by McGuire, Doris Miron verified that "Kay" had come to work for her as a maid at King's Lodge in May of 1984, and identified several cancelled paychecks "Kay" had received. She also described how "Kay" had so few clothes that Miron felt moved to give her some, "because I just felt like she needed extra clothes to wear, like the other maids."

Papendick made the most of his cross-examination. He portrayed Colleen as a content and industrious worker, too well-adjusted to have been a terrorized and brainwashed slave.

First, he established that Colleen was such a good worker that she'd been promoted to a job at the reception desk, where she waited on customers.

"Was there a phone at the desk?"

"Yes, there was."

"There is a restaurant right next to your King's Lodge, isn't there?"

"Yes, there is."

"Is that a favorite hangout for the California Highway Patrol?"

"Yes."

"See a lot of Highway Patrol vehicles in the parking lot?"

"Yes."

"And you can see those right from the desk, can't you?"

"Yes, you can."

"Did you ever notice any bruises on Colleen, or 'Kay'?"

"No."

"Did she have any problem with her speech?"

"No."

"Any difficulty performing the tasks you assigned her?"

"No."

"When she referred to the trailer, she referred to it as her place?"

"Yes."

"Did she ever say that there was a discussion about adding on a room for her?"

"Yes. One evening before she left she was saying they were going to add on another room for her because she was sleeping on the floor in the trailer."

"Do you know if she ever went to anybody's house after work?"

"She said once that Mr. and Mrs. Hooker were in Redding and that she didn't want to go home right away, so she went over to one of the maid's home."

"Would you describe Colleen as the best worker you ever had?"

"Yes. She was very good."

Like most of the witnesses, Miron scarcely mentioned Cameron Hooker, but rather testified about Colleen and Jan. It sometimes seemed that Colleen Stan was the one on trial here and that the case hinged less on the actions of the accused than on the veracity of the victim. If one accepted Colleen's story, subsequent testimonies added foundation, but if her testimony was unconvincing, nothing the other witnesses said did much to dispel that skepticism. And some, like Miron, inadvertently made Colleen's version of the truth seem almost incomprehensible.

McGuire added to the visual impact of Hooker's handmade bondage equipment, which was strewn over the courtroom, by offering another visual aid: a videotape of a police search of the Hooker's property. Officer Shamblin narrated this video of the Hookers' deceivingly mundane single-wide trailer, backyard, and sheds. Though amateurishly made, the video gave the jurors an opportunity to see scenes of the crime—including the surprisingly deep dungeon—that distance prohibited visiting firsthand.

McGuire also asked Shamblin to testify about the seizure of sketches, slides, and various pornographic publications. While he identified these, Hooker fidgeted with a pen, shifted in his seat, and tensed his temples. It apparently unsettled him to have his private life dissected and paraded before the jury, and nothing seemed to upset him so much as people riffling through his artwork.

Papendick wasn't going to let this sleazy collection move into evidence without a fight. With the jury excused, he disputed its relevance, maintaining there was little probative value in establishing that Hooker liked to view adult films, read bondage publications, or draw, especially since he'd already stipulated to a sexual preference for bondage.

McGuire contended that this collection contributed to Hooker's plan for abducting and enslaving Colleen Stan. Out of the stacks of pornographic magazines seized, McGuire said, only those with stories showing a "how-to" for capturing and keeping a sex slave had been selected as evidence.

After hearing their arguments, Judge Knight admitted some of the evidence, excluded some, and withheld judgement on the rest until McGuire and Papendick could present the relevant parts more specifically.

It was a draw for now, but the pornography issue wasn't dead.

32

McGuire had saved the medical doctor and the psychologist for last. Twin punches—the outside examined, the inside explained.

The state called Dr. Michael J. Vovakes, a Red Bluff physician. After establishing the doctor's extensive background in treating child abuse and sexual assault victims, McGuire turned his attention to his December 4, 1984, examination of Colleen Stan.

Dr. Vovakes noted first that Colleen's hair was thinner than one would expect for an adult female, though he didn't speculate on what would have caused this.

While other witnesses gave subjective observations, his were scientific and measurable. He noted a very pale, flat scar on her left breast, about one-quarter inch by three-quarters inch but couldn't offer an opinion on what had caused it.

McGuire put up a diagram of the human body and asked that he mark where Colleen had scars.

The doctor also said Colleen had scars on the bony parts of both wrists, which were consistent with the use of handcuffs. He noted there were more scars on the right wrist, that Colleen was right-handed, and that "a right-handed person would struggle more with their dominant hand if they were restrained."

He also described scars on both ankles that were consistent with the use of cuffs—again, with more scars on the right side.

Dr. Vovakes then described scars on both of Colleen's inner thighs, high up and near the groin, with "rather unusual configurations." On the right side, she had a rounded scar, approximately one-third inch by one-half inch, which appeared to be a burn-type scar. Beside it was a Y-shaped scar. "The head of this Y had two round balls or round shapes of scar," he said. On the left side Colleen had a slightly longer scar with a similar configuration and texture, "as if it were some type of burn."

At the prosecutor's request, he marked these, also, on the diagram.

"Are those scars compatible with electric burns?" she asked.

"They certainly appear to me to be."

"Why is that?"

"Because burn scars have a distinct appearance," he explained. "Electrical burn scars round up the skin and make a smooth surface to the scar. These scars were very unusual with the little rounded areas at the top portion, as if that could have been made from wires or something touching the skin."

McGuire showed the doctor a wire that had been seized at the Hooker residence, and he confirmed that "something like this could make a Y-shaped appearance with the rounded areas at the top."

Lastly, McGuire asked about Colleen's pierced labia, and Dr. Vovakes confirmed there was a hole through the right labia.

Again, he marked the diagram, and the prosecutor, having produced another convincing exhibit, turned the witness over to the defense.

Papendick did his best to undermine the doctor's testimony. Showing him the leather cuffs, he asked if Colleen's scars would be consistent with their use.

"Not really," Dr. Vovakes said. "These are small linear scars. This cuff could distribute pressure on a wider area, much wider than the scar."

Papendick next produced a series of photographs and asked the doctor whether the scars depicted in the photos were similar to Colleen Stan's.

Vovakes seemed to have a difficult time with these. His replies were along the lines of: "It's hard to tell . . . that could be. . . . There may be two small scars on this one. . . . It's so light, I can't really tell."

Meanwhile, McGuire tapped her foot and fumed. She knew these photographs. Officer Shamblin had taken them during his first interview with Colleen, and they were abysmal—poorly focused and terribly exposed. Irritated that Papendick was using these to try to make Colleen's scars seem less severe, McGuire attacked the accuracy of the photographs on redirect examination. She asked the doctor if they were "accurate depictions" of Colleen's scars, and he concurred they were generally overexposed or out of focus.

Now that the medical doctor had described Colleen's physical scars, the state called a psychologist to describe her emotional ones.

When the prosecution called its expert witness, Dr. Christopher Hatcher, few realized it would take him about ten minutes simply to present his credentials.

Dr. Hatcher was an associate clinical professor and the Director of the Family Therapy Program at the Langley Porter Institute in San Francisco. He'd served as a consultant to universities and organizations from London to Hong Kong. His background included training programs involving hypnosis, terrorism, and victim behavior, and he'd received grants to research hostage behavior, as well as to study the People's Temple and its members. He belonged to a host of professional associations and had authored papers relating to hostage behavior, violent behavior within adults, and persuasive ability. He had worked with the U.S. Department of Justice, Scotland Yard, Hong Kong Police, San Francisco Police Department, Los Angeles Police Department, the U.S. Secret Service. . . .

By the time Dr. Hatcher finished, if anyone listening remained unimpressed, they'd probably stopped breathing. His diction and demeanor added to an impression of erudition.

When Dr. Hatcher mentioned that he'd studied sado-masochism and bondage/discipline behavior, McGuire asked that he explain what he meant by those terms. Finally, after hearing so much about the practice, the jury was to learn about the theory.

"The definition really requires that we look at a dimension," he began. "For example, some behavior that involves a person who is dominant versus a person who is submissive would be very much within the normal range. On this end, we might see a couple shopping for groceries. One person is making decisions, another may be bringing packages. This is on one end of the dimension.

"As it moves into the sexual side, you will see, in a lot of sexual behavior, a degree of tension, a degree of excitement that's involved; and of course, that's a part of something we all know about. That degree of tension, when moved into what's called bondage and discipline, means that you are magnifying that tension by physically restricting someone's movement. In other words, you are going to tie them up or require them to do certain types of acts of submission; and for the people who are involved with that, that forms a pattern of excitement. Individuals who are generally involved in bondage and discipline in this part of the continuum are involved in consensual activity.

"We then move farther over to sado-masochism. More than just bondage and discipline, it's actually the giving and receiving of pain that is involved in generating sexual excitement. Now, those types of individuals, again, form largely a consensual relationship. There are various types of ways of agreeing to participate in this activity.

"Then, at the far end of this continuum, way out on the other side, we see those types of individuals where their drive is so strong, the stimulation of sado-masochism is so strong, they will take an individual, imprison them, and sometimes kill them in the process of completing their various fantasies; and this category of individual is way out at this end of the stream," he said, completing a line in the air.

With this understood, McGuire asked about the psychologist's professional experience in captivity, kidnappings, mind control, and coercion. Among other things, Hatcher had participated in over twenty investigations involving kidnap and hostage cases, including a handful involving the three elements addressed here: imprisonment, involuntary servitude, and sado-masochistic behavior.

Since having been retained by the Tehama County District Attorney's office, the doctor told the court, he'd familiarized himself with the *People* v. *Hooker* case in the following ways: one face-to-face interview and several hours of telephone conversations with Colleen Stan; five hours of interview and five hours of telephone interviews with Janice Hooker; on-site visits to the Oak Street house and Pershing Road mobile home; a personal review of all evidence; a review of five ninety-minute and three sixty-minute tapes of police interviews with Colleen and Janice; a review of the preliminary hearing transcript, police reports, and interviews of approximately three thousand pages, as well as a telephone interview with Pastor Dabney.

By now, a collective "whew" was all but heard in the courtroom.

McGuire then asked Dr. Hatcher to explain the meaning of "coercion."

Again, he used the analogy of a continuum: "On the one hand, we might have pressure exerted to do all types of things every day. Moving somewhat farther, toward the center, we have coercion. In coercion, extraordinary pressure is being brought upon an individual to perform or do an act. This can be physical pressure, it can also be mental or psychological pressure. Of course, there can be many degrees and variations of coercion or extreme pressure.

"But, on the far side of that, keep going out on the dimension, then we have something referred to as 'brainwashing,' and the actual term 'brainwashing' comes from a journalist who published a book in 1951. It's really not a legal term or psychological term for diagnosis.

"In brainwashing, what theoretically happens is not just that a person is pressured to do something or not to do something, but in fact their whole adult processes, their values, their way of looking at the world is changed completely. In my experience with a wide variety of individuals, I can only report five or six cases in which you could make a pretty good objective case for a brainwash.

"So that what we are talking about here is not brainwashing, which is a relatively rare phenomenon, but simple coercion."

Summing up, McGuire said, "Doctor, let me see if I have this straight. We are talking about a continuum, and you have persuasion at one end, coercion in the middle, and brainwashing at the far end, is that right?"

"That's right." And by now the whole courtroom had surely grasped this.

Because of Judge Knight's ruling, McGuire could not ask the psychologist to speculate specifically about this case. Instead, she would have to base her questions on a hypothetical situation. She asked the doctor to assume certain facts, then meticulously outlined the elements of Colleen Stan's first six months of captivity: the kidnap, hanging, whipping, imprisonment in a box, deprivation of food and light, lack of hygiene, dunking, burns, and so on.

"Now, Doctor," she concluded, "assuming those facts, based on your experience, training and education, do you have an opinion as to whether those facts are sufficient to coerce a person?"

Papendick promptly objected to the hypothetical. He was overruled.

Dr. Hatcher said the facts "would be sufficient to coerce the majority of individuals into a desired behavior pattern and to give up any overt resistance."

McGuire then asked: "To 'break' a person—is that the same thing as coercing a person?"

Hatcher said the term, accepted within psychological literature, usually referred to "techniques initially developed by the Soviets and Chinese to establish coercion [to a degree that] you are able to extract a behavior or a confession, to the point at which a person essentially gives up their overt resistance and will do what you ask them to do."

"Is that what we're talking about here, given those sets of facts?"

"That's correct."

McGuire then asked the doctor if there were specific steps which could be followed to break a person. Dr. Hatcher began an explanation so closely related to Hooker's treatment of Colleen Stan, everyone in the courtroom seemed to lean forward to listen.[1]

The first step, he said, is a sudden, unexpected abduction, followed by isolation as soon as possible. "Refuse to answer questions, place them in a cell-like environment, remove their clothes, and begin humiliation and degradation."

Asked to apply this first step to the hypothetical example, Dr. Hatcher said: "We have an individual who is initially in a situation in which the average person would feel somewhat comforted, in that it is a family in a car with a small child. The captor then not only displays the knife, the first point of danger, but rapidly puts a device upon the head which is beyond the realm of most people's experience or ability to comprehend, so the degree of isolation imposed would be greater than, for example, a kidnapping in which someone puts a bag over their head or pushes them down in the seat and says, 'Don't look up. Don't ask me any questions.' "

Dr. Hatcher went on to explain that a cell-like environment stimulates a feeling that one's worst fears are being realized, raising the level of fear and anxiety. Removal of clothes magnifies the feeling of vulnerability.

The second step in breaking someone, the doctor continued, is to physically or sexually abuse the person, to expose the captive's vulnerability and shock her or him. "In other words, not only has the victim been stripped of their clothes and placed in a physically vulnerable position, but you are going to whip or abuse in some other way, specifically with sexual manipulation, to illustrate just how exposed and vulnerable they really are."

Applying this to the hypothetical, Dr. Hatcher cited the sexual manipulation, and the exposure in terms of hanging and whippings, in which there is no perceived way of escape.

"The third step is extremely important," he said, "and

---

1. Later, it was clarified that these were more accurately "techniques" rather than "steps." Dr. Hatcher pointed out that not all the techniques need be applied, and they needn't be applied in any particular order. "The degree and intensity" of application of these techniques is "so variable that you could take three or four of them and, with particular individuals, achieve the result," he said.

that's to remove normal daylight patterns. All of us, both biologically and psychologically, are used to a certain day and night kind of sequence, and this has been well-documented in various types of scientific literature." Removing this, either by placing someone in a constantly lit or constantly dark environment, "is very disorienting, and is a rather standard part of the techniques employed."

The blindfold and boxes of the hypothetical, of course, accomplished this purpose excellently.

The fourth step, Dr. Hatcher explained, is "to control urination, defecation, menstruation, and to be present when these activities are performed. Basically, what you want to do here is destroy a person's sense of privacy."

He also pointed out that "if a person soils himself, and isn't able to clean that up, the sense of shame in sitting or lying in their own waste product is really quite extraordinary, and individuals become very motivated to do what they can to get permission to clean themselves up. Most people have not had the experience since being a small infant, of sitting or lying in their waste product over a period of time. It takes you back to a period of vulnerability."

The fifth step is to control and reduce food and water. Hatcher stated the obvious: "If you don't get that food and water, you are going to die. So, on the one hand, they may be torturing you and preventing you from leaving, but on the other hand, they are bringing food and water." This helps make the captive dependent upon the captor.

The sixth step is to punish for no apparent rhyme or reason. Initially, the captive tries to figure out some rationale to the intermittent beatings but, finding none, eventually has to simply accept that punishment will occur with no reason.

The seventh step is to "require the victim to constantly ask permission for anything or any behavior. This would involve asking permission to be able to speak to someone, permission to take a tray of food. It is a type of training procedure."

The eighth step is to establish a pattern of sexual and physical abuse. This "indicates to the person that this is what their new life is now going to be like." It's a way of "getting the person to realize things have changed in a permanent sense."

The ninth step is to "continue to isolate the person. The captor has now become the source of food, water, human contact, as well. That's important—information, as well as pain. All of us are information-hungry people. If you put us in a restricted environment without newspapers or magazines or television, that's real nice for a while, but if it happens [that] you are totally cut off and weeks pass, all of us get a little hungry to find out what's going on.

"Cut that off and tie it to one person. Being a source of information is extremely important. As well as human contact—the captor has a tremendous amount of power because he's the human being that you see, he is that only point of contact."

During his explanation, Dr. Hatcher spoke clearly, usually addressing himself to the jury. He wasn't a man of few words, yet no one yawned.

McGuire next asked how someone might learn the steps of breaking a person.

Dr. Hatcher listed three sources: the study of psychology; the law enforcement and military forces of "countries who have a rather low regard for human rights"; or, the most common, sado-masochistic and bondage and discipline literature.

"How are people initially attracted to this S/M and B and D literature?" McGuire asked.

Hatcher's answer must have been more interesting to Cameron Hooker than to anyone else in the room. He'd surely never heard himself explained so clearly.

"The consistency is rather interesting," Hatcher said. About the time of puberty, a boy finds himself stimulated by images of people being tied up or tortured. "It's initially extraordinarily disturbing to them. They tend to feel there's something wrong with them." And so this is suppressed; they don't talk about it.

Instead, they eventually find S/M and B&D literature, which also isn't talked about. "But the impulse and stimulation of this after a while just becomes more than they can keep to themselves," so, at an older age, the boy perhaps approaches girls, showing a picture and saying, "Would you like to try something like this?"

"The literature provides the stimulation, which doesn't cause the behavior, there's no mistake about that," but it also shows "how you can hang someone up, how you can put them in certain types of positions of torture, how it's been done before."

Now McGuire wished to introduce some of Cameron Hooker's S/M and B&D literature. Papendick objected, and again, the jury was excused while the two counsels argued about the relevance of Hooker's collection of hard-core pornography.

Judge Knight finally ruled that "any literature that either has instructions or rules or suggestions on captivity and any literature that contains ideas that were communicated by the defendant to the victim is admissible."

With the jury ushered back in and Dr. Hatcher again on the stand, McGuire introduced another of her impressive exhibits: an enlarged reproduction of the graphics for an article in the June, 1976 edition of *Oui* magazine, entitled: "Brainwashing: How to Fold, Spindle and Mutilate the Human Mind in Five Easy Steps."

If the jury had thought McGuire a prude, taking umbrage at Hooker's prurient interests, the colorful illustrations before them now presented an interest less in sex than in control. While provocative and lurid, the drawings depicted the "five easy steps," which McGuire asked Dr. Hatcher to review.

As Hatcher pointed out, it wasn't necessary to read the article, written by the Harvard-trained psychologist, Dr. Timothy Leary,[2] to understand the "five easy steps." The pictures were sufficient:

Step one: "Seize the victim and spirit her away."

---

2. Dr. Leary expressed astonishment upon learning that this article had been introduced as evidence in the Hooker trial. He said that, following the Patty Hearst case, he wrote the article "to warn people" how easily they could be brainwashed. Though he said he had "nothing against things being sexy," he disavowed any responsibility for "those horrible illustrations," which he called, "disgusting."

Step two: "Isolate the victim and make her totally dependent on you for survival."

Step three: "Dominate the victim and encourage her to seek your recognition and approval."

Step four: "Instruct the victim and re-educate her to think and act in terms of your ideology."

Step five: "Seduce the victim and provide her with a new sexual value system."

The scene in the courtroom was now a weird tableau: the thoroughly dignified Dr. Hatcher, in his somber, dark suit, surrounded by poster-size pictures of the slavery contract, of the basement, of the rack, of the *Oui* illustrations, and of Colleen, stripped and hung. And still, the heavy bed and box occupied much of the courtroom floor.

(It doubtless required great restraint on the part of the jurors to be confronted with such images and information day after day, yet never discuss it. Every time court was adjourned, the judge asked that they please remember the "admonition of the court" and refrain from reading about, talking about, or viewing programs about the case. They bottled it up and took it home, without disclosing what they'd learned even to their spouses.)

Some of Dr. Hatcher's testimony, while phrased in academic language, was explicit—shocking. For instance, he said that places where a customer can rent sado-masochistic paraphernalia and perform various acts on a prostitute, which Colleen had described as "Rent-a-Dungeon," actually exist in cities such as New York, San Francisco, and Los Angeles. And he briefly analyzed a selection of articles from Hooker's library, including such literary gems as "Captive Maid," "Sex Slaves for Sale," and "Actual Case Histories of Sexual Slavery."

McGuire asked Hatcher if, in addition to the nine he'd already outlined, there were other coercive techniques.

There were, and the psychologist related these now.

The tenth technique, he said, is to "present a goal or a model of future behavior, a model of how to please the captor."

The eleventh is to threaten family and relatives with a similar fate.

The twelfth is to threaten to sell the captive to an even worse master.

The thirteenth is to continue to beat and torture the captive at irregular intervals.

The fourteenth, called "irrelevant leniency," is to allow small privileges for no reason, making the captive more confused and more pliant.

The fifteenth is to obtain further confessions and signed documents, having the captive give over more and more control in writing.

And the sixteenth and final technique is to incorporate new behavior goals. Dr. Hatcher pointed out: "It's enormously time-consuming to carry out a successful coercion. It takes a lot of time, a lot of thought, a lot of energy, and people have difficulty doing that over a period of time. They have to attend to other processes of life, and I'm speaking of the captor. So, you need to establish some type of pattern where you won't have to be constantly physically monitoring this person." Some ways to do that are to allow the captive to tend to personal hygiene, allow clothes, some privacy. And, Hatcher explained, it's important to permit the captive some degree of freedom, without the captor's constant presence, and then suddenly appear, giving the captive a feeling the captor is omnipresent.

Dr. Hatcher added, "There are many historical examples where slaves not only outnumbered their masters in terms of manpower but also had the opportunity to attempt an escape, and yet that's done in only a very small percentage of cases." The significance of this surely wasn't lost on the two black members of the jury.

With these sixteen coercive techniques understood, and with Hooker's research into coercion presented, McGuire returned to her nearly forgotten hypothetical.

Again, she asked the psychologist to assume certain facts, then outlined the conditions under which Colleen was kept during certain periods—the next six months, the next year, then each subsequent year. At the conclusion of each period, the doctor enumerated which of the coercive techniques had been applied during that time, giving special attention to important aspects, such as the slavery contract and the story of the Company.

Dr. Hatcher shed illumination on Colleen Stan's darkest hours. He took the components of her captivity—the workshop, the "attention drills," the slave name, the slave collar, the box—and distilled them into elements of power and control.

Even the freedoms that Colleen was later allowed—to brush her teeth, shower, wear clothes—the doctor explained as giving the person some remnants of self-esteem, with the reminder: "If you displease me, I can remove any shred of personal privacy or personal identity, with the exception of what I have chosen as your slave designation."

As the prosecutor continued with her hypothetical situation, Papendick fidgeted. He objected to each stage of her hypothetical, but the judge consistently overruled his objections.

Commenting on the captive's being allowed to do new activities in new settings where other people are present, the psychologist said, "the fact that these situations do not result in discovery" or in anyone interfering, "begins to reinforce, in the majority of captives' minds, that this is the way life is, and they are going to have to accept that."

Dr. Hatcher also commented on the gift of the Bible: "Part of Christianity emphasizes that you are going to suffer and that God will provide, that no matter what type of disaster or terrible situation may befall you, if you maintain your faith in God, God will get you out of it. Some captors use a religious tract, they want to assist the captive along the pathway of believing they should have faith in God, and that God is really part of all this, that this is not alien from Christianity. It incorporates [the captivity] within the framework of what's normal and serves often to make the person more religious. The sad part is that it does make the captive easier to control."

It seemed a shame that Colleen Stan couldn't hear this. Instead, Cameron Hooker, along with the rest of the court, was treated to an educated view of what made him tick.

Addressing himself to periods of greater freedom allowed the captive, Dr. Hatcher undertook an explanation of the captor's motivations: "The main thing here is that the captor is not necessarily an individual of extraordinary intelligence. He doesn't necessarily have to have a comprehensive kind of knowledge as, for example, Dr. Leary might have in constructing the article we talked about before. What comes across consistently, however, is that the person, to some extent, has a feeling that is like a hunter. Think of the person in your acquaintance who is the best hunter. It usually isn't the chief executive officer of the bank, a person who has a very high degree of status. It's a kind of sense or skill that makes them a particularly good deer hunter or duck hunter —a certain amount of patience.

"The analogy drawn for me by the individuals I have interviewed is that they see themselves in a similar way as a hunter. Initially, they are concerned with the stalking and the capture. Then, rather than killing the prey, they see how far they can train this person.

"After a while, curiosity sets in to see just how far he can let this person go and still have control. There is a certain risk or gamble there, but [this is outweighed by] the value or degree of enjoyment and satisfaction, the sense of being able to hunt with higher stakes. The gratification from being able to allow the person contacts with outside people and still know that you have enough coercion and pressure upon them, that's an extraordinary reinforcement and overcomes some of the other concerns about apprehension."

One couldn't help but wonder what Hooker thought of this.

Dr. Hatcher's direct examination took nearly two days.

He seemed to sort through every aspect of Colleen's captivity and place it in context: The "love letters," he pointed out, were consistent with types of statements in S/M literature, and it was common to have the captive echo the captor's belief system. He reviewed the letters, citing Colleen's repeated references to her position as a slave.

Still posing a hypothetical situation, McGuire asked if the doctor could account for the calls and letters to the captor and his wife.

"There is a great deal of dependency upon the wife in the

situation you've described," Dr. Hatcher explained. "It's not as if there was a relatively rapid, clean escape without having the possibility [the captor might come after her]."

By talking with the captor, yet experiencing that this doesn't result in being put back in the box, "the person gradually begins to feel they have a greater degree of control, that they have reestablished themselves somewhat."

Further, the psychologist said, it's common that captives, once free, express the idea "that they want to let God or someone else take charge of retribution or punishment," and he quoted sections of Colleen's letters to Cameron and Jan saying, for example: "I don't want to play God and I forgive you and Cameron for all things." Additionally, Hatcher said, victims are often averse to pressing charges because criminal proceedings would force them to relive the experience.

Hatcher made comparisons with several other cases in which the victims were "mentally restrained," fearful of attempting escape, and then, once free, reluctant to go to police. These cases shared many elements in common with Colleen Stan's, but by the time the psychologist concluded his remarks it seemed clear that Hooker's coercion of Colleen had been uncommonly intense.

Dr. Hatcher said as much: "The circumstances as you have described them to me, with the possible exception of issues that go farther back in time (such as black slavery in America), would be unique in recorded literature. There would not be a similar situation in which this degree of captivity and of sado-masochistic torture of a human being had existed in a previous case."

After nearly twelve hours of eliciting expert testimony—an outpouring of information—the prosecutor at last came to the end of her questions, took her seat, and handed Dr. Hatcher over for cross-examination.

Defense Attorney Papendick opened by trying to belittle psychologists as opposed to psychiatrists (since the expert witness for the defense, Dr. Lunde,[3] was a psychiatrist), but Dr. Hatcher's answer was so complete it seemed only to emphasize his competence.

Papendick persisted: "You are not a licensed physician, are you?"

"No, I am not."

"You are not an expert on the physical effects of diet control, are you?"

"No, I am not."

"Or the physical effects of lack of sleep?"

"I would have a degree of expertise in the physical effects of lack of sleep, but as it pertains to captivity."

From here Papendick launched an extensive examination of Dr. Hatcher's experience in related cases, such as the Parnell case and the People's Temple and Jonestown. Though Hatcher's accounts of these were informative, they served more to showcase his experience than to discredit it and seemed far from the matter at hand. It was difficult to understand what Papendick was trying to get at. Judge Knight finally stepped in: "I fail to see the materiality of this rather detailed questioning about Jonestown. What are we getting to?"

Still, Papendick continued his questions about tangentially related cases, such as Patty Hearst and Korean prisoners of war. Since it was late in the day, McGuire privately wondered if he were simply trying to kill time so he could prepare overnight for the beginning of his case tomorrow.

At length, Papendick referred to the spectrum Dr. Hatcher had described: from persuasion, to coercion, to brainwashing. Specifically, he wanted to know at which point persuasion ended and coercion began.

The doctor naturally said there's a gray area here, and that, for example, some people would call a military draft persuasion, and some, coercion. But, he added, "a person in a captive situation against their will is in a coercive situation."

---

3. McGuire was astonished that Papendick had retained Dr. Donald Lunde, the Stanford psychiatrist she had interviewed for the prosecution months before.

"In your opinion," Papendick asked, "can a person involved in a captive situation be subjected to persuasion?"

"Yes."

This was the answer Papendick wanted to hear. He brought up the example of a prisoner in a Nazi concentration camp having relations with a guard or officer. "Is that an example of persuading the person as opposed to coercing the person into a sexual type of relationship?"

Hatcher wouldn't grant those kinds of liberties with the term. He pointed out that, while there may not have been a specific beating or incident preceding the development of a relationship, the guard or officer was nonetheless perceived as a person in authority who had the power to protect the prisoner from torture or death.

Here the defense attorney asked Dr. Hatcher if he were familiar with the term "coercive persuasion."

The psychologist said the term had arisen in the 1950's, but had fallen from use and was no longer a common psychological term.

"Does coercive persuasion have a generally accepted definition in your field?"

"No, it does not." Dr. Hatcher explained that it had never gained general acceptance, and that it wasn't listed in the index of the *American Psychological Association Psychological Abstract,* or the *Index Medicus.*

(Terminology later became a sticking point. Dr. Lunde would use this term in his analysis of the Hooker case, attempting, in turn, to discredit Hatcher's use of the term *coercion.*)

Overall, Papendick seemed unable to take control of this witness. He unwittingly gave Dr. Hatcher the opportunity to further assist the prosecution when he asked: "What are the effects that one would expect to see in a coercive situation?"

"There are several," the psychologist said. "The most interesting one is a numbness of affect. You may, for example, ask someone to describe something related to their captivity, and they will describe something that is, by most objective standards, truly appalling, yet it is not expressed with a great deal of emotion. There is a flatness or blunting of affect."

The meaning of Colleen Stan's indifferent manner instantly clicked into place.

Hatcher explained another effect might be "intrusive images," something like nightmares in the daytime. McGuire hadn't asked if Colleen experienced this, but it seemed a reasonable guess.

A third characteristic, Hatcher said, "is that they want to try and get their lives back to normal. Before they can begin to deal with the images and impact of this, they have to put a great deal of effort into creating what is almost a veneer of a normal life. To have a job, to have some friends, to have some activities, is almost like a kind of teddy bear. It's a security, and they will work to do that before they start to go back and, in depth, deal with the problems they have had in their captivity."

To McGuire's mind, this fit Colleen perfectly. She wondered if the jury perceived this.

Papendick then switched to another line of questioning, and here he made headway. He asked Dr. Hatcher whether, in order to judge a person in a coercive situation, it would be important to know the person's background.

Hatcher said, "It would be contributory."

"What do you mean by 'contributory'?"

"Helpful, useful."

"Would that include social history?"

"All history."

"Social, family, marital, medical, sexual?"

"It would be useful."

McGuire's hackles went up. After having successfully countered Papendick's motion to admit the victim's prior sexual conduct, she was alarmed that Papendick might work it in. She only hoped it wasn't as glaringly apparent to the jury as it was to her that Papendick had uncovered some evidence about Colleen's past which he believed would help the defense.

But Papendick miscalculated when he handed a magazine to Hatcher and asked him to tell the court which of the sixteen coercive techniques it covered. He apparently remained unconvinced that Hooker's pornography collection could be used as instruction for coercion.

The psychologist promptly responded: "Page thirty-two in *Captive Maid,* we have sudden unexpected abduction."

"Which technique is that?"

"That's number one. Sudden, unexpected abduction. The isolation is begun as soon as possible. You begin the humiliation, degradation, sensory isolation. You remove the clothes."

"That's number one?"

"That's all number one. Fairly clearly, I think, both illustrated and in text. I can quote from the text if you like."

"No. I just want to know what number techniques are included."

Dr. Hatcher then mentioned number six, creating an atmosphere of dependency.

"How is that illustrated in that article?" Papendick protested.

"Well, it's illustrated by saying whipping and degradation are always accompanied with sex."

"How is that dependency? Didn't you talk about that before as dependent for food and water?"

"You are also dependent upon the individual whether or not they are going to beat you anymore."

This clearly wasn't developing as Papendick had hoped. He snatched the magazine away and, to McGuire's amazement, continued with this line of questioning. He handed the doctor an article which was, essentially, a pornographic movie advertisement, surely believing this illustrated no coercive techniques whatsoever.

The doctor appraised the article and listed techniques eight, nine, ten, and thirteen.

Still, Papendick didn't abandon this line of questioning. He handed Dr. Hatcher the article that accompanied the slavery contract. This was a mistake.

He'd given the prosecution's expert full rein, and Dr. Hatcher made excellent use of it. He listed techniques ten, sixteen, eight, and six, giving detailed explanations of how these were illustrated in the article.

Papendick seemed to realize his error in trying to fight Dr. Hatcher on his own territory and concluded this line of questioning by turning it to his advantage: "Are any of those sixteen techniques used by, say, the Marine Corps in boot camp training?"

Dr. Hatcher admitted that "some of the behaviors" were.

Completing his cross-examination, Papendick asked, "Do you know Dr. Donald T. Lunde?"

"Yes, I do."

"Would you consider him an expert in forensic psychiatry?"

"Yes, I would."

And with that, the psychologist was excused.

33

Anticipation had run high before the sex slave's testimony, then tapered off during the prosecution's string of less spectacular witnesses. Now the halls were again packed with television cameras, for today, Friday, October 18, there would be big news: The slave master was going to speak.

After nearly a month of sitting in silence, smiling or sulking, always enigmatic, Cameron Hooker was going to testify in his own behalf.

Throughout the trial, Hooker had always made sure his hair was neatly parted and combed before entering the courtroom. Today he was particularly meticulous. Dressed in the same tweed sports jacket he'd worn from the first, a gray tie, a white shirt, and shiny shoes (Janice said they were the first dress shoes he'd ever owned), Cameron Hooker entered the packed courtroom.

The defense attorney lost no time in getting to the matter at hand. He asked Hooker about May 19, 1977, and with a small-town-boy earnestness, Hooker related his recollection of that day.

He said he'd picked up Colleen Stan on Antelope Boulevard at about three P.M.

"Did Jan know what you were going to do?"

"Yes."

"Do you remember what you were doing prior to that?"

"We were going to go up into the hills and practice bondage," Hooker said, as if this were a most ordinary afternoon activity.

In most respects, Hooker's account of the kidnapping closely followed that of Colleen and Janice. At first it appeared that, relying on the protection of the statute of limitations, he was going to confess to the entire incident, but his version soon diverged from the one presented by the prosecution.

Though he admitted kidnapping Colleen at knifepoint, he denied having held the knife to her throat. Instead, he said, he held it to her "chest and stomach area."

Papendick asked, "Why did you kidnap her?"

"I had a fantasy of practicing bondage on a girl who couldn't say no."

Hooker said he and his wife had "kicked around the idea," and had even considered running an ad in a magazine, but he hadn't had any particular plan. The idea had occurred to him after they'd picked up Colleen, while they were riding in the car. (He interjected that he and Jan could "communicate without words," which explained how she knew what he was going to do when he'd only just realized it himself.)

Going back to the kidnap, Papendick asked, "What was Colleen's demeanor?"

"What does that mean?"

"How did she act?"

"Real spacey," Hooker said. She would jump when he spoke to her, and this, he contended, had "a great deal" to do with his decision to kidnap her. He said he thought he "wouldn't have any trouble" doing it.

By the time he'd gotten Colleen home and into the basement, she was "plenty scared" and shaking. He hung her up only "for a little bit, till she started crying," about five or six minutes.

Hooker admitted committing the crime yet softened it, making it less severe in its details, presenting himself as somehow boyishly mischievous, even caring.

That first night, he said, "I was beginning to feel real bad about everything I'd gotten myself into."

He put Colleen in an old crate he and Jan had used for S/M, checking on her several times throughout the night because he was "worried about her."

He couldn't remember if he'd gone to work the next day. He planned to let her go, he said, but he couldn't take her "for some reason," and so he was stalling until the next day.

In the meantime, he built a table and moved her onto that so she could lie down.

"Did you hang her up?"

"No."

By the third day, Hooker said, he felt it would be safe to let her go. "She was hitchhiking, on drugs, had drugs in her purse," and he decided she was probably no threat since she didn't know who they were or where she was. But later, when he went downstairs and unlatched the head box, she proceeded to describe almost exactly where they lived.

Hooker went back upstairs and told his wife. "We didn't know what to do," he said sadly.

Did he hang Colleen that day?

"No." In fact, Hooker contended that he hardly ever hung Colleen. The bondage with her "didn't work," he said. And he protested that he "had no interest in having sex with her."

Colleen was still "scared to death," and he couldn't let her go. "It tore me up inside to leave her secured," he said. "It wasn't what I thought it would be."

Meanwhile, Hooker told the court, Colleen was "down-right sick." He spent several hours with her in the basement, talking with her and holding her hand. She asked him "about drugs and stuff like that," but he knew nothing about drugs. She told him she was afraid she was going to be sick and asked for the drugs that were in her purse, but he'd already thrown them away.

She continued to get sicker over the next two weeks, sweating and shaking.

In Hooker's story there was no bondage, Colleen was unrestrained, and he spent many hours down in the basement with her. "Sometimes we'd hug," he said. And sometimes, after talking, she wouldn't let go of his hand.

Hooker claimed he talked about himself very little, but Colleen was quite talkative. "She was down on everyone—her parents, her past. She talked to me about most of it—just about everything."

But Cameron was stuck. "I was afraid to let her go. All I wanted to do was get her out, I just couldn't figure out how," he said, presenting his predicament with an "aw-shucks" chagrin.

After the second week, Colleen was better. By now Cameron had built the box, and she was kept in it unrestrained until he came downstairs after work and let her out. Then she would be out of the box and unbound for four to six hours, he told the court.

She slept a lot for the second and third months, and by then "me and Jan had faced the fact that we were stuck with her for a long time." He considered sound-proofing the whole basement, but decided it was too expensive. Again, he explained, "I didn't know how to let her go without ending up in jail."

Did she bathe? Papendick asked.

"Not the first two weeks," Hooker said. "After that, once or twice a week."

"Was she still blindfolded?"

"Yes."

After about three months, he and Janice built the workshop together so that Colleen wouldn't be "stuck laying down during the day, and she could do what she wanted."

He gave Colleen some walnuts to shell because "I asked her and she said she'd like to have something to do."

During the first three months, he hung her only twice. "Me and her'd become very close, and she asked about my interest in bondage." He hung her up but she started crying so he let her down. She asked how long she'd been up, and when he told her only five or six minutes, she asked why it was so short. It was because of her tears, he said—just like with Jan, when she cried, he stopped.

But there was no sex. Hooker was emphatic about this; he'd promised Jan there would be none. But Colleen, he said, kept asking him: "Why?" "She just couldn't understand that," he said, shaking his head.

The second time, he hung her for about fifteen minutes.

Papendick asked, "What's the longest period you would hang Jan?"

"Twenty minutes."

"Why?"

"I'd seen in a Boy Scout book or a first aid book that tourniquets are only supposed to be used a maximum of twenty minutes."

(The press and spectators, unable to contain themselves, reacted with soft guffaws.)

Papendick plunged ahead. When he asked the defendant about other bondage he'd performed on Colleen, Hooker described something far outside any Boy Scout manual: the dunking incident. He admitted tying her up and putting her face in the water, but, he said, "I was careful not to let her choke."

Asked why he'd done this, Hooker matter-of-factly responded: "I'd done it to Jan before, and I just tried it."

Just like that. Perhaps, since these were uncharged offenses and bondage between consenting adults is legal, he felt there would be no harm in openly describing these incidents. Or perhaps, having already said, "it tore me up inside to leave her secured," he believed he'd established himself as a warm and feeling person who simply had kinky tastes.

It wasn't long, however, until Hooker slipped badly. Papendick asked if Colleen were allowed upstairs the first six months.

"No," he said, "except the time she took a bath." Hooker forgot he'd testified just minutes before that she was allowed to bathe "once or twice a week."

But no one seemed to catch this, Papendick let it drop, and Hooker continued with his narrative.

Having Colleen sign the slavery contract was Jan's idea, he asserted. Cameron first found the article in *Inside News,* but when he showed it to Jan, she said, "Wow, what if something like this really existed!" and suggested that if Colleen were afraid of retaliation by a "company," she wouldn't go to the police.

After Colleen signed the contract, she was allowed to come upstairs every night. She did a few chores and joined them at the dinner table. It sounded quite homey.

Hooker admitted, without the slightest note of contrition, that he'd started subjecting her to "attention drills," during which she had to strip off her clothes and stand at attention in a doorway. He began the drills one day after his brother came over unannounced, and she "didn't move quite as quick as I wanted" when he rushed her down to the basement.

The drills, he said, were "to impress the fact that the contract wasn't just a piece of paper by itself."

But her attitude "started going downhill really fast" after she signed the contract, Hooker said. Unlike previous times, when she had a "sweet attitude," now she was depressed. He blamed this partially on Jan, who "was treating her like a slave," giving her orders and yelling at her.

Did Hooker ever punish her?

"No."

"Why not?"

"I always talked to Colleen with a soft voice. All I had to do was raise my voice or talk to her harshly."

Worried about the dramatic change in her attitude, Jan and Cameron came up with another plan. They decided to tell Colleen that, though it had never been done before and it was expensive, they were going to "buy her out" of the Company.

"At first she didn't know what to think," Hooker said. But once he told her the buy-out had been accomplished, she cheered up.

Not long after this, Cameron told her they were planning to move in a few months and asked if she would "hang around" and help. She said that would be fine.

Still, he conceded, Colleen slept in the box or the workshop, and she was treated like a slave.

But when they moved to the mobile home Cameron found putting Colleen into the box inconvenient. Except when they had visitors, she was kept unrestrained in the back bathroom, since he was "about to let her go anyway to see if she believed in the Company."

Hooker blithely went along with his story, apparently unconcerned by the apparent contradiction that though he had told Colleen he had bought her out of the Company, he was still, as he put it, "trying to drive the Company down her throat." He admitted telling her "little stories" to remind her of the threat of the Company, but denied having threatened her family.

Meanwhile, he and Colleen were taking regular excursions up into the mountains to cut posts, and, he claimed, Colleen's attitude was "really happy." During this time "everything was really perfect" in Hooker's opinion. He was delighted to have Colleen as his slave—"what I really wanted out of Jan." He practiced bondage with her in the woods a couple of times, and they hugged, kissed, and indulged in a little petting.

"Was this affection part of her slavery?" Papendick asked.

"No."

"Why was there no intercourse?"

"I was still trying to keep my promise to Jan," said Hooker.

By now, in Cameron's narrative, he'd already agreed on a time to set Colleen free, and they were counting down the weeks. To his surprise, Colleen came into the kitchen one Sunday, sat down, and asked if her current freedom would continue if she stayed. He told her it would, and she told him she wanted to stay.

"I was kinda shocked," he said, "but he opened his arms and said: "Welcome to the family!"

Hooker testified that Colleen told him she didn't want to get back into drugs, "plus I'd promised she could have a baby." She only asked that he guarantee he "wouldn't make her go home." She said every time she got close to someone, they ran her off."

"What was Jan's reaction?" Papendick asked.

"She wanted Colleen to leave, but I pretty much shined her on because I'd fallen in love with Colleen very deeply."

In Hooker's version of the next several months, Jan treated Colleen "really rough, trying everything to get her to leave." It was Jan who usually punished Colleen; he only did on rare occasions under pressure from Jan, because, he said, "I had to live with Jan, too."

Once when he'd hung Colleen up he left briefly to look for some straps. When he returned he found Jan had taped electrical wires to Colleen's thighs. She held a switch in her hand. Cameron pulled out the plug, then suffered recriminations from both women: Colleen "got after me for interfering," and Jan "told me it was none of my business," he said. "I was stunned."

Shortly after this episode, Jan burned Colleen with matches. But by now Cameron had learned his lesson: "I just stayed out of it."

Jan was now working at various jobs, and "she went out drinking after work," Hooker told the court. "She wasn't home much." Colleen took care of the children "all day and night," while Jan was dating other men, drinking, and going to parties. "At first it bothered me a little," he said, "but I was in love with Colleen, and I figured Jan would find someone else."

He said he and Colleen were having sex and "light bondage" on a regular basis, but insisted this wasn't forced. "She was willing to have my child, and we were talking about possibly getting married."

The slave collar "kinda became a wedding band." When the collar came off he pierced her labia, he said, adding casually that this is "fairly common among S/M and B and D fans, and that's what we worked out."

On that note, the judge declared the noon recess, and journalists, nearly jubilant over Hooker's colorful testimony, rushed up to Defense Attorney Papendick to garner quotes. Papendick obliged, saying that Colleen "was a willing participant" in the relationship, and that a "turning point" came when Hooker had offered to take Colleen home but she'd opted to stay.

After lunch, Papendick asked Hooker whether Colleen showed him any affection after she was out of the box.

"Yes, she met me at the door with makeup on and hugged me."

"Did she ask you to have sex with her?"

"Well, in some ways. I'd be sitting, watching TV, and she'd sit on the floor, put her hands on my knees, her head on her hands, and look up at me," he said, smiling. "She knew what that did to me."

"Did you talk about the Company during this period?"

"No, not unless she asked." Still, she believed he was a strong member in the Company. He didn't want to tell her the truth because, he said, "I was afraid I'd lose her. She looked up to powerful people."

Hooker's narrative continued in its same unrepentant and slightly cocky tone. McGuire meanwhile madly scribbled notes. And the jury listened impassively, betraying nothing.

Cameron testified that about a month before the planned trip to Riverside, Janice heard their older daughter call Colleen "Mommy." She "blew up," quit her job, and stopped dating.

Cameron told Colleen it might be best if she left, so she went around and said good-bye to the neighbors. Then, for a week, she was in the box, "out of sight of the kids," he said.

There was no obedience test with a shotgun, and no talk of the Company. Still, he admitted taking Colleen over to his parents' barn to hang her up. It was "good for pictures."

The original plan was to take Colleen home for good—spending one last night together—but on the way down, they had a change of heart and talked of Colleen coming back to Red Bluff. Once Colleen got down to Riverside and called home, she became so excited that they forgot about spending the night together, and Cameron took her directly to see her family.

He was left to kill time alone. The next night he called at about nine P.M., and Colleen said she was ready to go. He went to pick her up and was introduced to the family as "Mike" because "I had one mother-in-law enough, and I didn't want them dropping in on me."

After leaving, they stopped at a 7-Eleven store and Cameron explained to Colleen that Jan was really upset, and "things might get rough" because Jan didn't want her around the kids anymore. While Colleen considered this, he went in and bought a couple of Cokes. When he came out, she put her arms around his neck, told him she loved him, and said she could handle Jan.

When they got home, Hooker testified, there was no one there. They made love on the floor and then he put her in the box while he went to get Jan and the kids, who were at her parents'.

Janice was so insistent about keeping Colleen away from

the girls that they wouldn't see her again for three years. During that time, Hooker testified, there was no sex and virtually no bondage between him and Colleen because "she wasn't free anymore, and it just wasn't the same."

"Did you complain to Jan?" Papendick asked.

"Yeah, but Jan was really fixed on the idea of not letting Colleen around the kids." It was a long time until they stopped asking about "Kay," which made Jan only more hardened in her resolve.

But in 1982, while Jan was in the hospital for a week, Colleen was out of the box most of the time. He hung her up, but there was no sex. Rather, Colleen got angry at him for "not doing enough to push Jan" about letting her out of the box, and they had a fight. He put her back in the box, went to pick up Janice from the hospital, and when he got back found that Colleen had kicked out the bottom of the box . . . but it was "designed to be that way," he added. "Particle board won't hold wood screws."

Papendick asked if Colleen stayed in the box.

She was out at night, Hooker said, and she helped Jan when the kids weren't around.

Gradually, the two got over their hostilities and became friends. While Hooker was at work and the girls were at school, Colleen was out of the box, and the two women spent more and more time together. They cleaned, did macrame, and read the Bible.

Hooker added that he'd never ordered Colleen to do anything that he didn't help her do, but Jan would order her to do anything she didn't like.

In 1984, Colleen gave Cameron an ultimatum, he said. "She couldn't handle the way things were going," and since Jan said it was okay for Colleen to be around the girls now, she was let out once again. She got a job, and she and Jan started going to church together.

"What was Jan and Colleen's relationship?" Papendick asked.

"Good. They were getting along better than ever."

The defense attorney asked about their financial situation, and Hooker explained they were short of cash at that time, so most of Colleen's paychecks went into a general fund, used to pay bills. She kept twenty dollars out of each paycheck, but "that was about what me and Jan had to spend, too."

Papendick asked if he had intended to get more slaves.

Hooker said that he'd threatened to at one time, but he didn't really *intend* to.

Papendick turned to some of the physical evidence. He carefully took Hooker through it, asking about piece after piece. Cameron had fairly innocuous explanations for most of it. The knife, for example, wasn't the one he'd abducted Colleen with, but was instead one he used for carving plaster of Paris sculptures. And he picked up the 1976 issue of *Oui* magazine (with Dr. Timothy Leary's article) at the dump in 1984.

Papendick now led the defendant up to the day in August when Colleen and Jan left.

They had "asked if they could have that night to themselves," Hooker said, and they slept together on the floor. To Cameron's surprise, Colleen called him from the bus station the next day. She said she was leaving, that she knew the story of the Company wasn't true, and she didn't want to cause a divorce. It was time for her to go home, she told him.

"I told her I loved her and stuff like that," he said, and asked that she call when she got home. "I was crying. Saying good-bye was hard."

A day and a half after she returned, Colleen phoned after midnight, "and told me she missed me." She encouraged him to get back together with his wife "for the kids' sake." Five or six days later Janice moved back in with him.

Papendick asked if, after Jan moved back, they continued to practice bondage.

"Once or twice," Hooker said.

"Did you promise to stop?"

Hooker said he had. "After I went to the pastor, and he told me it was wrong and everything, I tried to back off on it."

"Did Colleen indicate that she wanted to come back to Red Bluff?"

Colleen wrote that she did, Cameron said. Her father had some property nearby, and Hooker volunteered to put in a drip system for some trees.

"Did you talk about seeing each other again?"

"To a point," he said. Colleen was going to come up and see them, but she didn't want to come between him and Jan, who "was scared" about Colleen moving back. "She said it would end our marriage," he said.

Hooker's first day of testimony came to a close, propelling the "sex slave" case back into the headlines. Newspapers were splashed with stories about the "hen-pecked husband" caught between a jealous wife and a slave who refused to leave.

It made good copy, but Deputy DA McGuire was dismayed that the news coverage cast Hooker in such a positive light, especially in Red Bluff, where many were still convinced of his innocence. She heard that many of her colleagues believed she was losing the case—even Lt. Jerry Brown thought so.

Hooker began his second day on the stand on Monday, October 22. Under questioning, he maintained that Colleen had willingly posed for him in bondage positions. And he portrayed a strange but legal bondage triangle—with Colleen staking out Jan, and Jan hanging and whipping Colleen and Cameron.

Hooker declared that Colleen was in love with him (telling him this almost every day), and was content with her position as a slave. He'd told Colleen she could leave—on the condition that she tell no one about the Company—but she'd stayed because she was grateful to get off drugs and have a home and because she wanted a child.

Finally, Papendick asked: "Did Colleen ever refuse to have sex with you?"

"Yes, in '82 and '84."

And did Colleen consent to have sex with him?

"She showed in about every way imaginable that she was willing," Hooker stated.

* * *

Papendick's direct examination of Cameron Hooker had taken just slightly more than one full day. Now it was the prosecutor's turn.

Her approach was bitingly sarcastic.

She attacked his story of having been innocently driving when he picked up Colleen, accusing him of carrying the head box for the express purpose of kidnapping someone. "You were out hunting, weren't you?"

"No, I was not."

"You took Jan and the baby with you to lure a woman, didn't you?"

"No."

"Why did you build the head box?"

"So Jan could scream and yell without everyone in the neighborhood hearing her."

"Why didn't you use a gag?"

"They don't work that well. You ought to try them and see how they work."

Jaws dropped and chuckles rippled through the courtroom.

McGuire retorted, "Thank you, but I don't think I will," and carried on.

The tone of the cross-examination had been set: McGuire mocking Hooker's story, Cameron sticking to his version every step of the way.

"It excites you to see a woman hung, doesn't it?"

"Yes."

"Does it cause you to have an erection?"

"Yes, it can."

"On Friday, you said that when you used your whips, you didn't hurt Jan or Colleen, just played, is that right?"

"Yes."

Showing Hooker a photograph of Janice, McGuire spat out: "Those marks on her back—are those from 'playing,' Mr. Hooker?"

"Yes, they are."

McGuire attacked his version of Colleen's first months of captivity. "You had a young, naked woman held captive, and you just held her hand?" she said, her voice dripping incredulity.

She asked where he got his idea for the head box.

He claimed he just made it up.

And the rack? "Did you get the idea from a magazine or a video, Mr. Hooker?"

"No, I did not."

She asked about Colleen's second meal, when Hooker hung her up and whipped her for not finishing two egg salad sandwiches.

He denied this, saying, "I didn't care if she ate."

She questioned him about the use of the bedpan.

Hooker claimed Colleen only had to use it a few days, then they brought her upstairs to use the bathroom.

Turning again to his fantasy, McGuire asked if he had discussed it with Jan.

"Yes."

"Did you discuss it with Elaine Corning?"

"No."

She asked whether he practiced bondage on Jan while she was pregnant.

He said he'd practiced bondage, but never hung her up.

Here, McGuire produced several pictures of Janice, seven or eight months pregnant, hung on what Hooker called the "X."

"She's standing," he protested.

Didn't you strike a deal with Janice, McGuire asked, that she could get pregnant if you could have a sex slave?

"No," he said, but his previous cockiness was gone. He seemed quiet and confused.

She harped at him about *The Story of O,* pointing out the similarities between the treatment of O and his treatment of K. Then she reviewed some of the evidence with him. Mentioning the photograph of Colleen being hung, she said tauntingly, "You forgot about that, didn't you?"

McGuire asked if the head box were insulated with foam.

"Yes."

"With carpet?"

"Yes."

Referring to his testimony about opening the head box

and finding Colleen sweating, she said, "Isn't it true she wasn't going through drug withdrawal, she was going through torture?"

"All I know is what she told me later."

"That first week when Colleen was chained to the rack, blindfolded, was she petrified?"

"Yes."

"Terrorized?"

"Possibly."

"In a state of shock?"

"I don't know. She shook a lot."

"Her attitude got better after six months?"

"After she got over being sick, she got friendly."

"The box opened like a coffin, right?"

"It opened like a freezer."

"Didn't you hold a heat lamp close to her pubic area?"

"She was laying on the table and she said she was cold. I held a heat lamp next to her to warm her, then she said it was getting too hot."

McGuire turned to the contract. Gesturing to the poster-size picture next to him, she said, "Look at the contract behind you. Where does it say that the slave will be given freedom?"

"It doesn't."

"When she signed the contract, it made you happy, didn't it?"

"Yeah, in some ways it did."

"She was afraid of you, wasn't she?"

"I don't know."

"She was a good slave, wasn't she?"

"Yes, she was."

"But sometimes, she wasn't good enough, was she?"

"No, she was a good slave."

Then, showing him a picture of Janice tied and submersed in the bathtub, she asked if that was what he'd done to Colleen.

"Something like that," he admitted.

"Face down?"

"Yes."

"You dunked her?"

"Yes."

"Until she almost drowned?"

"No. When she started blowing out bubbles and she couldn't hold her breath anymore, I'd pull her up."

"Was that 'playing' too, Mr. Hooker?"

"Yes."

"On whose part?"

Softly, he answered, "I don't know."

"You said Colleen's attitude went downhill after she signed the contract."

"Yes."

"You seem surprised."

"I didn't know what to expect."

"You told Colleen your father was in the Company, didn't you?"

"No."

"You told her he had a dungeon under his home?"

"No."

"You told the same thing to Elaine Corning, didn't you?"

"No."

"You whipped Colleen to punish her for breaking dishes, didn't you?"

"Yes."

"With what?"

"A cat-o'-nine-tails."

"Were you playing?"

"No."

"You were serious?"

"Yes."

She asked whether he'd burned Colleen with matches. He denied this, maintaining it was Jan.

"Wasn't that one of your fantasies, Mr. Hooker?" she asked, showing him one of his sketches: a naked woman, handcuffed, being threatened by a flame. "Isn't that a match?"

"No, it's a torch."

Putting the sketch away, she said, "You loved Colleen?"

"Yes."

"But you didn't tell her the truth about the Company?"

"No."

"And you kept her under your bed in a box?"

"Not in 1980."

"Or you had her sleeping in the back bathroom with a chain around her neck, like a dog?"

"No."

Turning to the trip to Riverside and its detour to Sacramento, she asked, "Hadn't you told her on prior occasions that Company headquarters was in Sacramento?"

"Earlier, I may have."

"And you told her neighbors were with the Company?"

"I told her they were everywhere."

"And she believed that?"

"Yes."

"You told her the Company had tapped the phones?"

"No."

"You had her say good-bye to the Coppas, the Deavers, and your daughters a week before she left."

"She was leaving."

McGuire reviewed Colleen's return to Red Bluff, the rape on the floor (which Hooker had called "making love"), and her three-year return to the box. Coming to the end of her biting cross-examination, she recounted Colleen's increased freedom, her job with King's Lodge, then listed the amounts of Colleen's paychecks, which Hooker had deposited into his account.

A few jurors studiously took notes. The judge sometimes raised his eyebrows or scowled so deeply it seemed his face was made of rubber. Papendick perched on his chair, seeming irritated.

"Jan moved back in because you promised to get counseling and give up bondage, didn't she?"

"Yes."

"And you didn't give up bondage?"

"No."

McGuire suddenly asked: "Jan hung you up once, didn't she?"

"Twice," he said.

"It was pretty painful, wasn't it?"

"Yes."

"You didn't enjoy that, did you?"

"No."

It was a significant, if slightly askew, addition.

"In 1980, Colleen still believed you were a member of the Company?"

"Yes."

"And in 1984, Colleen still believed you were a member of the Company?"

"Yes."

With that, McGuire abruptly rested her cross-examination.

Defense Attorney Papendick focused his redirect examination on his strongest evidence: the many calls placed between Colleen and the Hookers after her departure, and the letters that she wrote. Papendick went over these item by item, giving times and dates, driving them home, then rested.

McGuire, on her re-cross-examination, also focused on the calls and letters, though her questions usually revealed more than Hooker's answers.

"You called Colleen because you were afraid she was going to the police?"

"No."

"Didn't Colleen's cousin call you?"

"Yes, and chewed me up very thoroughly."

"Did that make you afraid?"

"I don't believe so."

"So you called Colleen again to make certain she wouldn't go to the police?"

"No."

Her re-cross-examination was brief, and now both counsels had concluded their questions to this witness. But before Cameron Hooker could step down, Judge Knight had a few questions.

He asked about that perplexing trip to Riverside in March of 1981: "On the way to Riverside, did you stop in Sacramento?"

"Yes, I stopped at an adult bookstore."

"Are there office buildings in that area?"

"Yes, near the capitol."

"Why was it that you took Colleen to Riverside?"

"Originally, it was to leave her there."

"Why didn't you send her?"

"We wanted to spend the night together, but we didn't 'cause Colleen got excited about seeing her father, so I took her right there."

"But the purpose of your trip was to spend the night together, and you never did?"

"No, we never did."

34

Out of court—clicking down the hall toward the newspeople in her high heels, so smartly dressed they began to jokingly bet on when she might repeat a suit—McGuire seemed friendly enough. But in court she changed, and after her lacerating cross-examination of Cameron Hooker, some of the press corps wondered if her sarcastic approach could backfire, whether the jury might think she was "bitchy."

Attorneys, like salespeople, have to worry about image. A customer often buys a product less on its merits than the salesperson's personal appeal; and sometimes, more than the strengths or weaknesses of the case, an attorney's charm can tip the scales toward a defendant's acquittal or conviction.

The jury is the major imponderable in any trial. Who knows which attorney they prefer, how the evidence affects them, whether inconsistencies in the witnesses' testimonies strike them as lies or simple errors—indeed, whether they're paying close enough attention to catch inconsistencies at all? These jurors watched impassively—a few took notes, some chewed gum, and one noisily rattled candy wrappers. . . .

A total of eleven witnesses would testify over five days for the defense. Most of these were relatives. It seemed remarkable that if Colleen Stan were held captive, these people had never perceived the least hint of distress or oddity. They consistently portrayed Colleen as "happy" and "outgoing." All agreed she was wonderful with the kids. No one could remember ever seeing any bruises or scars on her.

At one point, Papendick stopped the proceedings to read a stipulation into the record. The telephone calls. Followers of the trial may have thought they'd heard everything possible about the calls placed from Colleen's father's residence to Cameron and Jan. They hadn't.

In a clear voice, the defense attorney read each listing: the date, the time it was placed, the duration of the call, the telephone number. It was an impressive list, covering four months, totalling *29 calls,* and taking several minutes to read. When he'd finished, Papendick had surely emphasized these phone records as much as he conceivably could.

More than phone records had been unearthed by Gary Kelley, the private investigator Papendick had retained to assist with this case. But, unknown to the jury (and to Papendick's intense frustration), most of this had to do with Colleen's past and was therefore ruled inadmissible, so Kelley spent only a short time on the stand.

Defense Attorney Papendick elicited some of the strongest testimony from Cameron's immediate family: his mother, father, and brother.

First, Papendick called Cameron's mother, Lorena Hooker, a nervous, quiet woman, who tentatively took the stand. She answered the defense attorney's questions with a distinct country twang and the kind of concern only a mother can convey.

Papendick established that Cameron's parents lived only six or seven miles from his mobile home, then zeroed in on Mrs. Hooker's knowledge of "Kay." "How often did you see her from the time you met her to March of 1981?"

"I saw her a lot of times," she said, "at their trailer, and she was out at our place quite often." Cameron and Jan came to their place about every other week, and "Kay" came with them about half the time.

On one occasion, she'd come to their home by herself. The well had gone out, and she'd asked a neighbor to take her and the kids to fetch Cameron, who was helping his dad thresh wheat.

"Did it ever appear to you that 'Kay' was a servant?"

"No," she replied. In fact when "Kay" came to dinner she didn't even help with the dishes.

Saving this most damaging bit for last, Papendick asked if Mrs. Hooker remembered a particular conversation with Janice shortly after Cameron's arrest.

She did. Jan and her father had come over to their trailer and, Mrs. Hooker asserted, "Jan said she knew for a fact that 'Kay' wasn't raped."

Here it was: the other side. If anyone still needed a reason to distrust Janice Hooker, Papendick had supplied it.

Ending on that note, he turned the witness over to the prosecutor.

After McGuire's pointed cross-examination of Cameron, her treatment of his mother was almost startlingly gentle. In a soft voice she asked, "Mrs. Hooker, you love your son very much, don't you?"

"Yes, I do."

The question was disarming, and at the same time established her undeniable bias. Then McGuire asked a list of questions: Did you ever meet "Kay" while Cameron lived on Oak Street? Did you know she was kept in the basement? In a box? In a hole?

To all of these, Mrs. Hooker could only answer no.

Cameron's father, Harold Hooker, walked to the witness stand with a slow gait, turned, and took the oath looking like a farmer right out of the famous painting "American Gothic"—tall and gaunt, with a weathered face.

He'd known Colleen as "Kay," he said, and thought she was a "pretty pleasant kinda girl."

"Was she afraid of you?" Papendick asked.

"I didn't think so."

The defense attorney asked if Mr. Hooker recalled a time after Cameron's arrest when Jan came over with her dad and made a comment about the rape charges against Cameron.

"She said it was a bunch of hogwash. He didn't rape her," Mr. Hooker said bluntly. When Jan had learned there were thirteen rape counts against Cameron, he went on, "She said, 'They cain't do that,' that he didn't rape her."

During her cross-examination, McGuire steered wide of

this whole business about Jan. She wasn't as gentle with Mr. Hooker as she'd been with his wife, but she kept it brief.

"Do you understand that your son admitted to kidnapping Colleen in 1977?"

"That's the way I heard it."

"And that she was kept in a box on Oak Street?"

"I don't know all that he's admitted to."

"Were you ever down in the basement at Oak Street?"

"One time."

"Did Cameron show you the box?"

"No."

"Did he build a waterbed?"

"I don't know."

"Did you know he kept Colleen in a box?"

"Just hearsay."

"Did you ever see 'Kay' show affection to your son?"

"No."

(After Mr. Hooker testified, McGuire privately commented to Papendick that it would have been a kindness to inform him what Cameron had testified to. Papendick said he had, but Mr. Hooker apparently didn't want to hear it.)

When the defense called Dexter Hooker everyone expected a younger version of his brother. But though he was also tall and gangly, Dexter was better looking, with a Sam Shepard-ish quality to him.

Dexter claimed that he'd visited Cameron's trailer "almost every weekend" in 1978 and saw Colleen "every time I was there." After his divorce in 1980, Dexter spent about thirty or forty hours a week at the trailer, making him the only person outside the immediate family to spend a great deal of time around Colleen. Often, he was there with "Kay" and the kids while Jan and Cameron were at work.

"How did she appear to you?" Papendick asked.

"Normal."

"Depressed?"

"No, she was always smiling, always easy-going."

Like most of the witnesses, Dexter confirmed that Colleen was "real good" with the kids, but unlike the rest, he had a critical piece of corroboration for his brother's story: For a while, he said, the girls referred to Colleen as "Mommy."

This wasn't what McGuire had expected. During her cross-examination, she did her best to demonstrate that, as close to the situation as Dexter claimed to be, he knew little of what was actually going on.

" 'Kay' never told you her last name?"

"No."

"And she never told you she was kidnapped?"

"No."

"Did Cameron ever show you the basement at Oak Street?"

"No."

"Did he ever show you the rack?"

"No."

"Did he ever show you the box beneath the waterbed?"

"Yes."

"Did you know Colleen was kept under there?"

"No."

"Did Cameron ever show you the hole underneath the shed?"

"No."

McGuire also tried to elicit testimony about Colleen's slavelike behavior, but got mixed results.

"You saw Colleen working in the garden?"

"Yes."

"She worked hard, didn't she?"

"Pretty good, yes."

"And she worked real hard around the house, didn't she?"

"Oh, about normal."

"You saw her cooking, preparing lunch, washing dishes— pretty much like a household servant?"

"Yes."

"Was 'Kay' reserved around you?"

"What do you mean?" Dexter countered. "She was quite friendly. She seemed to talk all the time."

The only way McGuire could contest his most damaging comment was to ask: "When you spoke to Officer Shamblin, you didn't tell him the girls called Colleen 'Mommy,' did you?"

He admitted he had not.

Papendick had presented another view of the private lives of the enigmatic threesome who had lived together so quietly for so long and were now on such public display. Layer after layer had been peeled away, but the whole picture had yet to emerge. Now Papendick called his expert witness to put it all into context.

Like McGuire, Papendick had saved his big punch for last. In this "battle of experts," Dr. Donald T. Lunde's testimony would be the final bout.

Papendick asked Dr. Lunde, a plain, slightly pudgy, soft-spoken man, to tell the court of his credentials. This took some time.[1]

As a clinical associate professor of psychiatry at Stanford University Medical School, Dr. Lunde taught psychiatry at the medical school and engaged in clinical work. He also had a private practice in psychiatry. Having done most of his training at Stanford as well, Dr. Lunde was thoroughly a Stanford man.

His specialization was forensic psychiatry—"the interface between law and psychiatry"—and he'd authored about forty articles and about eight books on this subject. He'd received various honors and awards, including one from the California District Attorneys' Association for outstanding service. Some of the cases he'd been involved in relating specifically to captivity included the Jonestown case (United States v. Larry Leighton), the Patty Hearst case, and the U.S.S. Pueblo case, regarding a captain captured by North Koreans in the late 1960s.

---

1. Lunde's association with the defense of Dan White did little for his credibility. Dan White, the man who murdered San Francisco Mayor George Moscone and Supervisor Harvey Milk in 1978, had received a scandalously light sentence, which was blamed on the notorious "Twinkie defense"—a diet of junk food. Recently out of prison, White had committed suicide just four days earlier, putting his name back in the news. When asked about working on the case, Lunde said: "Right. I didn't say anything about Twinkies, though."

Lunde testified that, since being retained by Mr. Papendick,[2] he had prepared for his evaluation of this case in much the way Dr. Hatcher had, except that Hatcher had interviewed Colleen and Janice, while he had interviewed Cameron Hooker.

Having established his expert's credentials, Papendick asked the same question he'd asked Dr. Hatcher: "What's the difference between a psychologist and a psychiatrist?"

Dr. Lunde gave a lengthy answer, concluding: "Psychologists do not have the same kind of background. They are not qualified to diagnose physical ailments or physical effects of psychological distress. They are not able to, or allowed to, prescribe medications and so forth. And basically, psychiatry is a medical specialty. Psychology is more of an academic, nonmedical field."

Next, the defense attorney inadvertently sparked a courtroom squabble by asking the seemingly benign question: "Could you please define the term *coercion?*"

"Coercion exists in a situation where any reasonable person would be in imminent fear of being killed or of suffering serious bodily injury," Dr. Lunde began. "To put it in even plainer language, coercion is a psychological phenomenon that is present when someone has threatened someone else directly with death."

Dr. Lunde went into detail about what he meant about a "reasonable person," then added, "Furthermore, the threat has to be to the person themselves. It cannot be a threat to somebody else. This was an issue in the Patty Hearst case. She claimed, among other things, that the SLA, the Symbionese Liberation Army, was threatening to harm her parents and members of her family. And in that case, as in all of these in the field of forensic psychiatry, the law simply does not allow for threats to other people."

Judge Knight's hackles went up. "Just a minute," he said, turning to Papendick. "The doctor is testifying, counsel, as to the law. What he is testifying to is not accurate."

---

2. McGuire couldn't shake a feeling that it was vaguely unethical that Lunde, who many months prior had indicated he was willing to work with the prosecution, was now about to testify for the defense.

Papendick reframed the question, trying to limit Dr. Lunde to the definition of *coercion* within the field of psychiatry, but again the doctor ventured off into a legal interpretation.

McGuire curtly objected that Lunde's answer was prejudicial to the jury, and moved that his answer be stricken.

Judge Knight granted the motion, ordering the jury to disregard Lunde's definition of *coercion*.

(While the judge may have been piqued that this witness was presuming to define the law, McGuire was alarmed at hearing, as she had feared, that dreaded comparison between Colleen Stan and Patricia Hearst. And Lunde, who had been retained by Hearst's lawyers to conduct some examinations, though not to testify in court, seemed all too eager to make those comparisons.)

Papendick now directed Dr. Lunde toward the term *coercive persuasion,* which Dr. Hatcher had said had no accepted definition within the field of psychology. Papendick asked Lunde to define the term as accepted within the field of psychiatry.

" 'Coercive persuasion' refers to a condition where a person does things they would not otherwise do which are, in fact, possibly contrary to their own belief systems, because of a situation of total captivity and control over their environment and, to a great extent, control over their behavior on a twenty-four-hour-a-day basis." This would have been sufficient, but, again, Dr. Lunde hazarded a legal definition of *coercion*.

Again, McGuire objected.

By now Judge Knight was clearly unhappy with this witness. "Mr. Papendick," Knight said hotly, "he is a medical expert by his own definition. The court neither desires nor needs his definition of legal terms unless they are appropriate and correct. It's up to the court to instruct the jury as to what the law is, not up to this witness."

Again, the jury was instructed to disregard Lunde's comments on legal definitions.

Papendick led his expert witness back to "coercive persuasion," and the doctor explained: "The kinds of things that accompany coercive persuasion are: physical captivity

—being held against one's will for the period in question— that's the first and foremost requirement for this condition; then there are a variety of other conditions that have to do with control over the person's environment and an attempt to indoctrinate them—deprive them of sleep, of food, control their bodily movements, when they can move, other bodily functions such as bladder and bowel functions, and so forth."

(Dr. Lunde spoke to the jury, which usually adds to a witness's impact, but he also had the disturbing habit of frequently licking his lips, a nervous tick.)

Now Papendick outlined a hypothetical situation, based on Hooker's testimony, designed to match Colleen Stan's first year of captivity. He asked Dr. Lunde if, based on these hypothetical facts and his own training and experience, the victim would have been subjected to coercive persuasion.

McGuire shot out: "Objection, Your Honor. Lacks foundation; and the hypothetical is not in line with the facts as they have been elicited."

Judge Knight conceded that the hypothetical was incomplete, but overruled the objection—this time.

Dr. Lunde gave the opinion that, indeed, the victim would have been under the influence of coercive persuasion.

Papendick proceeded, setting forth the next set of hypothetical facts. This time, however, he meant to outline the next *three years* of captivity.

When he concluded McGuire promptly objected: "Misleads the factual basis."

"Sustained."

Papendick took a moment, added another batch of details, and again put the hypothetical to his expert.

Again, from McGuire: "Objection, Your Honor."

Again, McGuire's objection was sustained.

This was embarrassing for Papendick. He asked to speak to the judge outside the presence of the jury.

With the jury excluded, McGuire and Papendick argued over his hypothetical. She claimed it was incomplete; he claimed a hypothetical did not need to include all facts.

The judge listened and finally concluded: "It's not incumbent upon him to frame the hypothetical question in accordance with the prosecution's testimony, but he has to frame it at least in conformity with his own testimony. And while it does not have to have every single detail, it must have every material or important detail. There is no sense in getting an answer to a hypothetical that is incomplete, and certainly a hypothetical that lacks substantial information is incomplete."

"I assume we are talking about the Company," Papendick said.

"That's one of the things," the judge agreed.

The jury was called back, and with this rebuke in mind, Papendick resumed his hypothetical, adding several details about the Company from the defense point of view: "After a period of time, the person is told they have been bought out of the slavery contract and the person is going home within a three-month period of time. Further, assume that the husband and female spend time together cutting posts. That, after the three-month period, the female tells the husband she desires to stay."

McGuire promptly objected that the hypothetical was incomplete.

The judge agreed. Turning to the jury, almost as an apology for the stop-and-go proceedings, he explained: "When you ask an expert witness something from a hypothetical question, you have to present sufficient facts that are encompassed by the evidence for the witness to be able to give an intelligent opinion. Therefore, the hypothetical question is not an easy thing to draw."

Papendick was encouraged to try again. He added several more details to his hypothetical, asked Dr. Lunde if he could render an opinion, and again McGuire objected that the facts were incomplete.

Judge Knight sustained the objection.

"Your Honor," Papendick protested, "the facts that I have presented are the identical facts the prosecution presented for their expert on direct examination."

"No, they are not," Judge Knight asserted, "not to my recollection. I find them lacking as to rather material points."

Now Papendick had reached the point of exasperation.

Thoroughly frustrated by this line of questioning, he abandoned the hypothetical completely, much to the relief of the courtroom, and turned to other issues.

"Doctor," he asked Dr. Lunde, "in your opinion, can you have coercive persuasion without captivity?"

"No, you can't," Dr. Lunde stated. "Continuous physical captivity is a requirement."

"And in your field of psychology and psychiatry, how is physical captivity defined?"

"It's defined as either being locked up in a prison or a cage or whatever kind of device in which somebody has no reasonable chance of escaping; and/or being held continuously under armed guard. That is, somebody with a lethal weapon, usually a gun."

"What is the significance of the Patty Hearst case in your evaluation of this case?" Papendick asked.

"The significance," Lunde began, "is that there are a lot of similarities in that she was also a white female in her early twenties at the time she was kidnapped; that she was subjected to confinement at first—threats, sexual abuse, deprivation of various sorts—and was, at least for approximately five weeks, subjected to the conditions we have talked about as under the rubric of coercive persuasion. On the other hand, after approximately five weeks of captivity she was free to leave and—"

McGuire interrupted Dr. Lunde with an objection: "The Patty Hearst case has nothing to do with this case."

After some bickering between the counsels, Judge Knight sustained the objection, saying, "The Patty Hearst case is dealing with the question of whether Patty Hearst was responsible for her actions. We are not dealing with that question here."

Again having had his line of questioning frustrated, the defense counsel turned to Dr. Lunde's area of expertise: the physical effects of captivity. The court learned that suspending someone by the wrists more than about twenty minutes can cut off the circulation. "Beyond that period," Dr. Lunde said, "there can be physical damage to the limbs and also damage to the cardiovascular system."

"At what point would you expect to see damage occurring?"

"In a period of an hour, in terms of the limbs, the arms in particular. It takes a matter of several hours in a person, who is otherwise healthy, for cardiovascular problems to show up. That is, fluids actually accumulate in the lungs. It's a method effected in crucifixion, simply to hold somebody still."

"If a person were confined in a box for twenty-three to twenty-three and a half hours a day for three years, what physical problems would that person suffer?"

"Persons confined in a close space, whether it's a box or even a hospital bed, for that amount of time, would suffer very serious muscular damage and skeletal damage," Lunde said. "The muscles, within a matter of about six weeks, will start to lose mass—wasting of the muscles as they start to shrivel up and get smaller. There is decalcification of the bones, so that the bones become more and more brittle. A person in a matter of months, much less years, would have serious and visible muscular and bone damage. And in the period of time you speak of—years—such a person would have great difficulty walking, maintaining an upright posture, maintaining balance. There would also be some horizontal dysfunction, probably. That would be quite visible."

"Would the person's speech be affected?"

"Probably, yes."

"In what way?"

"Well," Lunde continued, "a person confined in a box for three years on end, separated from contact with other people, whether it's in a box or an isolation cell, usually begins to hallucinate at some point, so their speech might reflect them talking to imaginary people. It might reflect the hallucinations. If they actually don't do much talking, after a period of time, you would probably notice some speech impediment, some difficulty simply with normal speech because, like any other complex learned activity, if you go for several years without using it, you lose the skill, the complex brain-to-muscle kind of skills that are involved in simply forming words. Memory might be affected as well."

"What is the physical effect of electric shock administered

to the human body from house current attached to a person's thighs?" Papendick asked.

McGuire objected that it hadn't been established that it was house current Colleen was shocked with, but she was overruled. The court listened closely to learn why Papendick had questioned Colleen so rigorously on this point.

"Shock of house current can cause contraction of the muscles around the thigh area, the quadriceps or hamstring muscles, and this can be painful," Lunde said. "It doesn't cause permanent damage. Once a person is grounded, which in a usual house is carpeting or floor or something which doesn't conduct electricity, it simply causes contraction of the muscles, you know, a feeling, literally, of shock. But that's about it."

"What exactly do you mean by contraction of muscles?"

"The muscles go into spasm, involuntary spasm."

"What effect does whipping have on the physical body?"

"Well, people I have seen who have been subjected to actual whipping, usually on the back, have visible scars from the lacerations, usually vertical scars."

During Lunde's testimony, McGuire kept watching the jurors for reactions. If they believed the Stanford psychiatrist, they believed Colleen had lied. Except that they were attentive, she couldn't read them.

Papendick took the noon recess to reframe his hypothetical. When court reconvened, he addressed the witness: "Dr. Lunde, I would like you to assume, in addition to all the facts I have previously given you, the following facts." With that, in a slow, steady voice, Papendick added a lengthy list of various incidents—from the shotgun "obedience test," to the water-skiing trip. At its conclusion Papendick asked the doctor to render an opinion.

As everyone expected, McGuire again objected.

A discussion ensued among both counsels, the judge, and the witness.

Looking vexed, the judge asked Dr. Lunde: "Doctor, do you really think you can answer that question from the hypothetical given you?"

"I think so."

"Wouldn't you have to know which time the questions referred to?"

"To my understanding, the question began sometime ago with an assumption that we were talking about the time period of the spring of 1978 to 1981."

Still, the judge remained unconvinced that a responsible witness could answer the question as it was framed. With the judge's permission, Papendick added several time elements to his hypothetical question.

When Papendick finished, McGuire objected, prompting another discussion.

Judge Knight turned to the witness. "Do you mean, Doctor, that you can tell this jury, based upon the hypothetical given you, whether or not, during that whole period of time, this person was subjected to coercive persuasion; or whether, during any part of that time she was subjected to coercive persuasion?

"Part of the time," Dr. Lunde replied.

"That's the problem," said the judge. "It's so broad that it's almost meaningless. Do you understand, Mr. Papendick?"

"I understand what the court is getting at," Papendick allowed. Still, he maintained: "The witness understands the question and is able to answer it."

Judge Knight, looking annoyed, finally relented, overruling McGuire's objection and allowing Dr. Lunde to give his opinion.

Dr. Lunde dove in: "My opinion is that during those periods of time when this person is not in a state of captivity as I defined it earlier—either confinement or being directly held at gunpoint or knifepoint—one of the essential conditions for coercive persuasion does not exist.

"It would be different if you were talking about a child, if you were talking about a mentally retarded person, a seriously mentally ill person, somebody continuously under the effects of certain drugs. But I believe that, when this all started, you asked me to assume a person of at least average intelligence.

"Somebody who goes jogging for fifteen minutes out on the road without the presence of an armed guard is not in [captivity]. Surely somebody who goes home to meet with her family and is not in the presence of the captor is not in a condition where they would be subject to this kind of phenomenon.

"The safest place, psychologically, for human beings, is the family," the doctor explained. "Even if you believed in the existence of the company—which is not something that a person of normal intelligence in this society would be likely to believe—here, you are at home. You could write them a note and say: 'Help. I am being tortured. I am being held captive.'

"I don't know of anybody who, if given the opportunity to go home and spend twenty-four hours, would have returned to the place of captivity, whether you are talking about a prisoner in North Korea or the settlement in Guyana in Jonestown or the SLA headquarters in Berkeley. It is simply not consistent with everything we know about human behavior in psychology and behavior of people in captivity who don't want to be there."

Having finally succeeded in getting his expert witness to render an opinion on his hypothetical question, Papendick turned Dr. Lunde over to the prosecutor.

Deputy DA McGuire opened her cross-examination by attacking Dr. Lunde's familiarity with the case.

"Besides interviewing the defendant, Doctor, who else did you interview?"

"I did not personally interview anybody else."

"You have never been to Red Bluff for the purpose of this case, have you, Doctor?"

"No."

"And you haven't been to the basement on Oak Street?"

"Well, I have seen the photos, but I have never been there."

"You have never seen this box before today?" she asked, gesturing to the waterbed which still stood before the jury.

"It was disassembled when I saw it last."

"And you have never been to the mobile home on Pershing, have you, Doctor?"

"No."

"And you have never been inside what has been referred to as the 'hole' under one of the sheds?"

"No."

McGuire established that when Dr. Lunde reviewed the evidence, he hadn't bothered to open several boxes.

"I think it's true that some boxes contained magazines and certain things we did not go through," he said.

"Handcuffs?"

"Right."

"You didn't see any of those?"

"No, because there were photographs of some of them, and I looked at the photographs."

"You haven't seen the photographs of Janice being hung in various positions, have you, Doctor?"

"No. Mostly, they were destroyed, I understand," he answered.

"You reviewed Dr. Hatcher's report, correct?"

"Yes."

"Did you prepare a report?"

"No."

McGuire had made some points, but at times she completely lost control of the witness, who went off on long narratives expounding the very theory she wished most to avoid.

In answer to a question concerning the influence of the Company in keeping Colleen from leaving, the psychiatrist said: "Based on the evidence I have seen, which includes reading Colleen Stan's statements, listening to hours and hours of tape-recorded interviews, and seeing letters written by her, given what I know, and having read statements of Janice Hooker and Cameron Hooker as to jealousy between the two women and the attachment of the children to Colleen, I think the more likely explanation is that Colleen fell in love with Cameron Hooker, became attached to the children, and that subsequently this created your basic triangle situation where you have two women very angry at each other or vying for the attention of some man in the household, who happened to be Cameron Hooker. I think that's why she returned to him from her family."

"Are you telling me, Doctor, that given the hypothetical

this morning, that person was not, to use the lay term, 'broken'?" McGuire asked.

"No. I don't know what that means," Dr. Lunde said. "I've heard of horses being broken, or dishes being broken, but people . . . people may become depressed. That's a clinical term, and maybe it's closest to what you're trying to describe.

"People who [believe that]their situation is hopeless—and I have seen some people who have been held prisoner for a long time—may become depressed, and the symptoms of that include certain patterns of sleep disturbance, feelings of hopelessness, worthlessness, and eventually suicidal thoughts, and sometimes an actual suicide attempt.

"This person may or may not have become depressed. I don't know of any evidence that she became suicidal or even entertained thoughts of suicide, which would tend to indicate to me that she did not become that depressed or 'broken,' if you want to use that term."

McGuire was incensed. "So what you are telling us, Doctor, in a nutshell, is: Given all the torture, the isolation, and the result of the techniques employed, all we have is a depressed person. Is that what you're telling us?"

"Oh, I don't even know," he answered nonchalantly. "As I say, we don't have a lot of evidence she was profoundly depressed."

McGuire asked if it would make a difference in his opinion if the victim were subjected to "attention drills."

Dr. Lunde compared this to his own basic training in the Marine Corps in the fifties, saying he "would have traded places."

"Were you stripped naked and forced to stretch your arms to the top of an archway and then whipped until you finally admitted to something you didn't do?" she demanded to know.

"No, but just about," he said, his chin in his hand, talking into his fingers. "Certainly there were obstacle courses and things of that sort one had to go through and underwater situations that were life-threatening. And then, in between, one had to run in pretty hot summer Virginia weather to the point of exhaustion, and then people were, in fact, struck by the drill sergeant if they stopped or fell down."

McGuire asked if it would make a difference in the doctor's opinion if the victim were placed in a bathtub and repeatedly had her head forced under water.

"Actually, as I say, it's somewhat similar in terms of underwater escape training." Dr. Lunde was intractable.

But McGuire did manage to make a little headway regarding Lunde's testimony on the physical effects of captivity.

"Doctor, isn't it a fact you wouldn't expect to see [serious] damage if the person, who is being kept in the box, is mobile in the box?"

"Well, no. You would see the damage because the variable is they have to get into an upright position. The human cardiovascular system is designed to work in a vertical position with muscles moving at least a certain number of hours a day."

"If a person is taken out to cut posts, that's exercise?"

"Right, sure."

"Taken out to dig out a hole underneath a shed, that's exercise?"

"Sure."

"You wouldn't expect to see any permanent physical damage under those circumstances, would you, Doctor?"

"No. The opinion I gave was in response to the hypothetical question that assumed the person was in the box twenty-three plus hours a day. If they are out cutting fence posts, as I believe she was, that's a whole different story. You wouldn't expect the problems," he conceded.

"Now this spasm caused by shocking you referred to—that would be painful, wouldn't it, Doctor?"

"Sure."

"Very painful, wouldn't it?"

"Sure."

"There are occasions, Doctor, when some kind of electric shock would leave burn marks, isn't that correct?"

"Sure, if you suffered a high voltage or a certain kind of grounding," Lunde said.

"Whipping doesn't always leave a permanent scar, does it?"

"No. Depends upon the type of whip and how hard you use it."

"It might leave red marks?"

"Sure."

"And those marks will go away?"

"Sure."

Dr. Lunde's first day on the stand came to an end, and the cross-examination would be resumed the following day. This wouldn't be worth noting, except that the next morning he was late.

The jury waited. The judge waited. The press and spectators waited. Both counsels waited. Cameron Hooker and the bailiffs, the court reporter and the court clerk waited. After about five minutes, people began to titter. Some of the jurors looked amused; the judge did not.

Astonishingly, when Dr. Lunde bustled in and took the stand ten minutes behind schedule, he did not apologize to anyone.

Lunde's answers to McGuire's first questions would surprise even Mr. Papendick. "Dr. Lunde, you are being compensated for each day that you testify in court, aren't you?"

"Sure. All the time."

"And at what rate, Doctor, are you being compensated?"

"A hundred dollars an hour for my time outside of the courtroom; three thousand dollars a day for testifying in court."[3]

McGuire resumed her line of questioning, but Lunde steadfastly held to his views, restating that a reasonable person would never believe the story of the Company and that Colleen only stayed because she'd fallen in love with Cameron Hooker.

It began to look as if McGuire would never break free of this deadlock. Then she suddenly asked, "You wrote an article entitled 'Brainwashing as a Defense to Criminal Liability' in 1977, is that correct?"

---

3. Papendick told McGuire later that he hadn't realized his expert was charging so much.

"Yes."

"Doctor, yesterday I used the term *broke,* do you recall that?"

"Yes, sure."

"And you have indicated that was an inappropriate term?"

"Not a scientific term."

"Didn't you, on page 351 of your article, write: 'The North Koreans simply broke Bucher and his men by torture and threats to the point where further resistance seemed ridiculous.' Do you recall writing that?"

"Oh, I think the sentence is there," Dr. Lunde said, unfazed. "I may have used the word elsewhere in the article in that some people 'broke' their word. The term has a meaning similar to what we were talking about yesterday."

McGuire continued, "The article also contains on page 349:

> The control of all communication in the environment is not only an important step, it is the basis for the whole process. In other words, the captors, those that are performing the process of coercive persuasion, control everything the victim sees, feels and experiences, and the reason why this is so basic to the full process is that the victim begins himself to feel totally controlled by his captors and they become omniscient to him, that is, they become all-knowing people who understand him, who know things about him that he never dreamt of, who simply have total access to everything about him. And in that sense he begins to feel inwardly controlled. And that's reflected in a process by which, even after he may no longer be in direct control of his captors, when they become his former captors, he still feels their presence inside of him."

"Sure," Lunde responded, "taken in that context, yes."

Both counsels finally exhausted their questions of this witness, and then Judge Knight asked a few.

"You didn't intend to equate what happened here to Marine Corps boot camp training, did you?"

"No. It was a specific aspect, namely, the attention drills, being called to attention and having to hop to a stand-up-straight position."

"I think you also referred to it in connection with the attempted drowning of Colleen Stan. Do you equate that with Marine Corps drills?"

"No, I don't equate the overall experience. Obviously, there are significant differences between Marine Corps training and this experience. There are some similarities, such as the indoctrination, the control of what time you go to bed and what time you get up, bodily functions, those types of things. Those are similarities. But there are differences. You are in the hands of what you know to be government, society-sanctioned agencies. You know the time in which you are getting out. Those are differences."

Judge Knight asked, "You do equate it to a certain degree?"

"There are similarities, sure."

"There is one other thing I do not understand," Judge Knight said. "In regard to this business of Riverside, is it your testimony that a captor, who imposes coercive persuasion and threats on a victim, could never, ever let that victim go home and expect to retrieve her twenty-four hours later?"

"I don't think that's inconceivable," the doctor said, "depending on the reasonableness of what has been told to the person, the basis for their believing or not believing certain things—"

"Well, Doctor, what may appear to be reasonable to a person would depend a lot on what they are told, isn't that true?"

"Yes. But if this person in the hypothetical had twenty years of experience in this society and schools and so on, versus a much lesser number of years with the captor (presumably absent the conditions I mentioned of mental illness or something), those things would stand them in good stead in terms of having some awareness that there are agencies, police and so forth, that represent the law and are here to protect me and, if I ever get a chance to tell somebody or get to a phone, I will make use of it."

"So every rational victim would immediately call the police regardless of the threats that were made?"

"Oh, I think, if they want to get away, sure."

"How rational would you expect a person to be after a period of torture?"

"I have seen many subjected to much more severe torture than these," Lunde declared. "Skin and bones, scarred from head to toes, and who were still resisting and still jumped at the first chance to get away when it arose."

"Were their families threatened?"

"No."

Judge Knight suddenly switched gears, asking a question that went right to the heart of the matter: "What is altruistic love?"

"Altruistic love is love given with no expectation of return," Lunde replied.

"Basically," the judge mused, "it puts the person's life beneath that of the person loved, is that true?"

"Sure."

"For instance," Knight went on, "the parent who sacrifices his life to save a child is an example of altruistic love?"

"Sure."

"Wouldn't it be an example of altruistic love if someone decided not to risk the lives of their family and sacrifice themselves?"

"I am saying it could be. I am saying, in the situation presented to me, I don't think . . ." Dr. Lunde sputtered another long-winded answer that added very little. It didn't matter. The judge had made his point.

The Stanford psychiatrist was excused, and the defense rested.

35

Before closing arguments, the prosecution has the opportunity to call rebuttal witnesses; McGuire called only one. The jury had heard her name during Cameron Hooker's cross-examination. The state called Elaine Corning.

Heads turned as a tall, willowy blonde entered the courtroom, and reporters buzzed with curiosity as the surprise witness settled into the witness stand.

McGuire asked a few preliminary questions, establishing that Corning knew Cameron when she was sixteen. Then she asked: "Did Cameron ever relate a fantasy to you?"

"It didn't come up as a fantasy," Corning replied. It was just a friendly conversation, and somehow he'd come around to telling her "either that he had, or that he wished he had a dungeon under his parents' place."

"Did he tell you the purpose of this dungeon?"

"To keep women there."

This was the court's first glimpse of Cameron's past. Everyone expected more, but now Papendick cut McGuire's questions short with an objection. Both counsels approached the bench for a quick consultation with the judge, and then McGuire abruptly turned her witness over for cross-examination. After a few quick questions by Papendick, Corning was excused.

That was that—a rather anticlimactic conclusion to the surprise witness's testimony. Corning exited the courtroom, leaving everyone wondering what else she might have revealed about Hooker's youth if the defense attorney hadn't objected.

Before closing arguments, the jury was excused while a few final motions were heard. All the false imprisonment charges, counts twelve, thirteen, and fourteen, had already been dropped on technicalities. Papendick now moved to dismiss counts fifteen and sixteen, both charges of abducting to live in an illicit relationship, contending that the law, written in 1905, was unconstitutionally vague. Judge Knight agreed that in 1985 it seemed impossible to define an "illicit relationship," and these two counts were dropped as well. Eleven felony counts remained, and five of these had to be amended.[1]

The jury was brought back in, and the press and spectators perked up: It was time for closing arguments, the grand finale, when both attorneys attempt to sway the jurors by stressing their best evidence and waxing eloquent about the iron boundaries of the law while playing upon sentiments.

The prosecution's closing argument is first, the defense's second, and then the prosecution gets a parting shot, a rebuttal. With this in mind, McGuire's strategy was to give a brief and simple summary the first time around, saving her best for last.

After a few words of thanks to the jury, she said that her mother, who had sat on a jury, told her the instructions were the most confusing part. So, though the judge would be giving them instructions later, McGuire reviewed a few points to help make them clear. For instance, she discussed the meaning of "reasonable doubt," saying there was a natural human reluctance to sit in judgment, yet cautioning them not to mistake a feeling of queasiness for reasonable doubt.

---

1. When the charges against Hooker were filed, no one in the Tehama County DA's office realized that the extraordinary time-span of this case presented an unusual problem: The sexual assault laws had changed in 1981. Some of the counts against Hooker occurred before the change and so would have to be charged according to the old law. The more recent counts stayed the same. Making this case even more complex, the jurors would be given different instructions for judging sexual assaults occurring in different years.

She mentioned that direct and circumstantial evidence were to be given equal weight, and here she gave her favorite example. She had a fifteen-month-old daughter, she told them. Now, if she'd just frosted a chocolate cake, left if for a moment to answer the door, then returned to find a chunk of the cake gone and icing on her daughter's mouth and fingers, *that* was circumstantial evidence. She hadn't actually seen her daughter eat the cake, but it was clear what had happened.

Several jurors smiled.

McGuire then emphasized that the jury must weigh the testimony and credibility of each witness and summarized the important points of several testimonies, spending a good deal of time on the two expert witnesses. She also highlighted some of the physical evidence, which the jury would later have an opportunity to review for themselves.

Finally, after detailing the legal elements of all the crimes, she held up a verdict form, explaining that one would accompany each of the eleven counts,[2] and quickly concluded her remarks. Thanking the jury for their time, she sat down, giving the floor over to the defense.

Papendick also thanked the jury for their attentiveness, then began his summation with the comment: "This is the best part of the case for the attorney because it signifies the end. The attorney is done. Your job is just beginning."

The defense attorney said the key issues were: whether there was forcible, continuous detention; whether Colleen consented to the alleged acts; and whether Cameron had a reasonable belief of consent. (This was the first time the jury heard that Hooker's perception of consent was at all an issue.)

Resistance, Papendick pointed out, was a subissue of consent. He explained that the legal definition of rape had changed, so that before 1981 the victim was required to re-

---

2. If they found the defendant guilty, the jury then needed to deliberate over "special findings" to determine whether the defendant had used force, violence, duress, menace, or threat of immediate and unlawful bodily harm in committing the crime.

sist, and her resistance had to be overcome by force or threat of great and immediate bodily harm.

Throughout the trial, Rolland Papendick's courtroom manner had been straightforward, sometimes agitated, rarely dramatic, but during his closing argument, he was friendly, confident, now subtle, now bold. He raised fresh legal questions, demonstrating his skills as an advocate.

In an affable tone, he said: "Lawyers like to give examples. The prosecutor gave an example of chocolate cake; I like to give an example of lasagna. It contains certain ingredients, but if you take ten chefs, the recipe turns out a number of different ways. It's the same with testimony. All the witnesses add their own spices."

These spices the attorney equated with "questionable exaggerations," and then went on to cite several.

Colleen had testified that she was kept in a box every day from March of 1981 to May of 1984, for example. She also said that during that time, she read the Bible. How could she read the Bible in the box? There was no light, it was dark: she couldn't.

This was a point where things were being exaggerated.

The jury had also been told that Colleen had been hung and whipped more than ninety times—whipped even to unconsciousness—yet there was no physical proof, no scars on her back. Colleen's testimony, Papendick contended, was misleading.

In jury selection, he reminded them, they'd said they wouldn't hold Cameron Hooker's sexual preference for bondage against him. Bondage was not a crime, yet several pieces of bondage equipment had been entered as evidence against his client. Even the prosecution's own expert, Dr. Hatcher, had explained that for couples involved in dominant and submissive roles, bondage creates a degree of tension and excitement, and a number of magazines cater to those with bondage as a sexual preference.

"If that's not enough evidence that bondage is alive and well," Papendick declared, flourishing several photographs, "we have Janice Hooker!"

The essence of the case, Papendick said, was what three people did behind closed doors. Their relationship was private. The box was a complete secret. The bondage was a complete secret. It was probably the "best kept secret in Red Bluff," he said.

"The prosecutor has attempted to present a horror story that would cause you to act without thinking," Papendick continued. "The defense asks you to think before you act." He asked the jurors to put aside their prejudices and apply their common sense. It was simply common sense, he contended, that some people would put up with seemingly horrible conditions to keep a relationship, and "Janice Hooker is exhibit number one!"

Colleen knew the relationship with Cameron involved bondage, yet she stayed, Papendick posited, because she found things she wanted. What? No drugs, a family relationship, a spiritual reawakening, and children she loved.

"I think it's clear that Colleen Stan was in love with Cameron Hooker," he said. As proof, he quoted from his trump card, the Christmas letter: ". . . I don't know the right words to describe how much I love you, but I seem to be falling deeper and deeper in love with you with each passing day. I find love hard for me to express with words. But you bring the passion out in me and it's a way of expressing my love for you. . . ."

Papendick again advised the jury that they would have to decide whether it was reasonable for Cameron to *believe* that Colleen loved him.

Dr. Hatcher had given sixteen sophisticated techniques which were employed against Korean POWs. It had been established that Cameron could scarcely read. How could he have read and understood sufficiently to plan out sixteen techniques employed by the North Koreans?

The police and the district attorney had spent hours combing through Hooker's magazines, trying to find those having any connection with slavery and bondage. Dr. Hatcher reviewed them, they were sent to Colleen Stan, "and *then,*" Papendick said, with a lilt of incredulity, "she testified that she found sections in those magazines that were *exactly* what Cameron had done to her!"

The prosecutor had described a horrendous story of torture, isolation, and sexual abuse, yet none of the witnesses had testified to Colleen having bruises, a speech problem, or anything unusual about her appearance.

Bonnie had testified that her sister was dirty and unkempt, yet by everyone's agreement, Colleen could bathe during this period. More inconsistency! More exaggeration!

Papendick compared these exaggerations to "a snowball coming down a hill," getting bigger and bigger all the time.

It all came down to credibility, he said. In determining a witness's credibility, the jurors had to consider demeanor, attitude, consistent and inconsistent statements, and memory. He challenged: "How many times did Colleen tell you, 'I can't recall'?"

And the phone calls. She knew Jan had gone to stay with her parents, yet she called on August 13, at 12:11 A.M., and talked for *seventy-six minutes*. Again, with that tone of disbelief, Papendick said: "She wants you to believe she talked to Janice!"

Holding up the picture taken of Colleen and Cameron in 1981, Papendick charged that Colleen had denied talking about the picture, denied sending it, yet it was taken by her *parents*. How else would Cameron have gotten it, unless she'd mailed it to him?

Regarding the snapshot in his hand, Papendick remarked: "Look at the smiles!"

He reminded the jury of the worst moments of Colleen's testimony. She had written of love in her letters, writing that it was "a climate of the heart." "But more than what this expression of love meant to Cameron," Papendick said, "think about this in terms of Colleen's credibility when she said: 'I may have written it to Jan.'"

The defense attorney raised an interesting point: During the entire time Colleen was with Cameron and Jan, there wasn't one slip up, not a single occasion when she accidentally called Cameron "Master" or Janice "Ma'am" in front of others. With raised eyebrows, he said: "I submit that's rather amazing."

Interestingly, Jan had corroborated the kidnap and initial isolation on Oak Street, yet she couldn't corroborate any of the sex charges except for the eighth count, which she said didn't appear to be forced. Rather, she reported that Colleen had asked: "Is it okay?"

Further, Jan had testified that she started seeing affection between Cameron and Colleen in 1982, hugging four or five times a week in 1983, and nearly every day—sometimes in front of the children—in 1984. Papendick added that it was "real interesting that at that time, Colleen was supposed to be in the box."

"I can't tell you what happened," Papendick declared, "except that Janice wanted Colleen out—and she succeeded."

Papendick mocked the prosecution's contention that fear of the Company kept Colleen from leaving. Dr. Lunde, the defense psychiatrist, had explained that coercive persuasion *requires* captivity. "Keep in mind, we're dealing with an adult," Papendick said, "not a child or a retarded person. You saw her testify; she's at least of normal intelligence."

Her greatest fear, the prosecution claimed, was for her family, yet the single person she'd met who was with the Company, Cameron, she took to meet her family. She told the jury she'd been hoping and looking for a way out, but why hadn't she written a note? She hadn't used the phone, she hadn't even whispered to them.

In 1984, after Colleen had left Red Bluff, she was threatening to return. And, the defense attorney reminded them, Jan had testified that she was afraid "it would start all over again."

If Colleen wanted to stay, have Cameron's baby, and force Jan out, why would she come into court and tell this tale? Papendick posited at least three reasons:

One: personal embarrassment and humiliation. She was, no question, a victim of kidnapping. Jan decided to go to the police, and at that point Colleen became a victim. Would she say, "Yes, he did kidnap me, chain me, et cetera, but I fell in love with him?" Or would she say, "I had no choice, I was a slave?" It would be less embarrassing to say the latter.

Two: love and jealousy. Colleen loved Cameron, but he didn't kick Janice out, he didn't go to bat for her; she was a woman spurned.

Three: financial gain. Colleen had already filed a lawsuit

against Cameron Hooker. And although she'd denied on the stand that she wanted to sell the rights to her story, her truthfulness was open to question.

(Now coming to the end of his remarks, Papendick noted there were only ten sex charges over a seven-year period, and made an aside to the jury: "The press has been calling this the 'sex slave' case. Why were there long periods with no sex? It's the *sexless slave* case.")

Sex charges require force, menace, duress, or threats of great bodily injury, he pointed out. And in order to find the defendant guilty of kidnapping, the jury needed to find there had been continuous, forcible detention. "Even if you find that," he cautioned, "you cannot conclude from this alone that she did not consent to the sexual acts." It was incumbent upon the jury to determine not only whether she did or did not consent but also whether the defendant, in good faith, had *believed* she had consented.

There was no question, Papendick concluded, that Cameron Hooker believed Colleen loved him.

He beseeched the jury: "Look at the facts. Read these letters. And think about what the contents meant to Cameron Hooker."

As Papendick returned to the defense table, Cameron looked up at him and smiled.

McGuire, who had some stunning moments during the trial, seemed tired as she began her summation in a thin, cheerless voice.

Responding to Papendick's comments about Colleen's credibility, she pointed out that Colleen had to remember facts that happened over a number of years and that she had no motive to lie. Rather, in bringing Hooker to trial, Colleen subjected herself to an emotionally wrenching process.

The defense attorney claimed that Colleen had been a member of the family, that Hooker had provided her with security, a drug-free environment, and spiritual reawakening. "If Colleen were a member of the family, why did the defendant go to such great lengths to disguise her identity?"

Further, outside of the defendant's testimony, there hadn't been the least indication that Colleen was a drug user or addict. McGuire confided to the jury that defense attorneys, when they have no defense, often throw in a red herring: "That's all that's being done here."

The prosecutor then asked: Why didn't the defense attorney ask Dr. Vovakes about Colleen's physical condition? Why? Because Dr. Vovakes would have given answers the defense didn't like. Instead, Papendick had asked Dr. Lunde, a man who had never even seen Colleen, to speculate on her health.

And what about Colleen's physical condition? Bonnie had the strong white teeth and thick hair Colleen no longer had. By the testimony of the defense counsel's own expert, Colleen wouldn't have skeletal damage because, thank God, she was out of the box every day, did knee bends, could stretch or curl up in the box, was out cutting posts, and digging the hole; she was not immobile.

McGuire heaped scorn on Dr. Lunde's testimony. He wouldn't stoop to render an opinion on Hooker's collection of publications, merely calling them "trashy." He could claim little experience with cases involving sado-masochism, coercion, and slavery. And he'd testified that coercion couldn't exist without captivity, yet he'd described that very circumstance in an article he'd written.

Dr. Lunde had said it was not *reasonable* for a person to believe in the Company, but, McGuire said, it was up to the jurors, not Dr. Lunde, to decide whether Colleen's fear was reasonable.

The prosecutor mentioned *The Story of O,* and the defense attorney quickly objected, but was overruled. She drew numerous comparisons between Hooker's favorite film and his treatment of his slave—life imitating art.

Hooker had a continuous plan, McGuire contended: A plan he began to formulate even in high school, a plan he'd shared with Elaine Corning, a plan to take sex slaves.

The defense attorney had contended that Hooker was "just a millworker" and that devising a plan and applying coercive techniques was beyond him. But it was evident, McGuire said, that Hooker had learned those techniques through his collection of magazines and publications. "He didn't even have to read them," she declared, "all he had to do was look at the pictures!"

The defense attorney claimed there was no corroboration for much of Colleen's story. "Look at this courtroom," McGuire demanded, gesturing toward the boxes and displays. "There are over one hundred and forty pieces of physical evidence to corroborate the testimonies of Colleen and Janice."

"The only thing I've heard the defense counsel raise again and again is a seventy-six-minute phone call," she scoffed. Dr. Hatcher had explained that the phone calls were a way for Colleen to confront her captor without fear of retaliation.

For a time, the prosecutor seemed to lose the thread of her summation. Countering the defense's closing argument in a piece-meal fashion, her own deteriorated, and for several minutes she seemed to get caught up in random and sometimes trivial points.

Papendick listened, playing with a pen, while Hooker sat calmly at his side, rarely even glancing at the jury.

Switching to points of law, McGuire pointed out that the statute of limitations prevented her from charging Hooker with sexual assault crimes occurring before 1979, and commented that it was interesting that Hooker admitted to crimes occurring before that time.

While there was a three-year statute of limitations on the charge of kidnapping, McGuire explained, an exception existed if the kidnapping were continuous—in other words, as long as the person was detained by force or threats of force. Guilt on count one, she asserted, had already been proved beyond a reasonable doubt.

Launching into a long discussion of rape, she again reviewed the instructions for both the old and new laws. And she mentioned there needn't be overt resistance, since rape was also committed if the victim submitted because of threats of great and immediate bodily harm.

"But what of resistance?" she asked rhetorically. After being "broken," how could Colleen resist? How could she resist on a stretcher? How could she resist when tied to a frame? How could she resist when hung from the rafters of the shed?

Countering Papendick's claim that Hooker believed Colleen loved him, and in good faith believed she had consented, McGuire asked, "How can a person who detains another person against their will believe they are consenting?"

The defendant didn't want a consensual relationship, the prosecutor maintained; he already had that with Janice. But that wasn't his fantasy. He wanted a woman who couldn't say no.

"The defense attorney tried to make an issue out of the fact that Colleen had access to phones that *we* know were not bugged; but *she* didn't know." Papendick said Colleen had several opportunities to escape, but didn't. The truth was that she *did*, but only when she could believe it was possible.

Hooker had even admitted that Colleen believed in the Company, that he'd made her sign the slavery contract, that she was his slave, that she was kept in the box. "Most of us have trouble imagining this happening," McGuire said, coming to the end of her remarks. "It's hard to imagine being hung, having a head box snapped over our heads."

"You can try it on," she challenged the jurors. "Put that head box on for one minute and feel the terror—yet you know it's only temporary; Colleen knew it was for real. Climb into that box and behold the perspective it contains, feel that box close in on you—even knowing that it isn't locked. Multiply your fear by a thousand!"

In conclusion, McGuire said: "The state has proved the defendant guilty beyond a reasonable doubt. It is now your duty to apply the law to the facts and arrive at the only verdict possible: I ask you to find the defendant guilty on all counts."

Closing arguments had gone on all day. It was nearly four P.M. when Judge Knight put on his spectacles and began to explain the instructions for evaluating evidence and judging testimony. As he read, the jury of eight women and four men appeared studious; several took notes.

The judge reviewed each count, defined "threat of great bodily harm"; "a deadly or dangerous weapon"; and "consent." He further explained that it was also a defense if the defendant "reasonably and in good faith believed Colleen voluntarily consented."

He explained that "reasonable doubt" must not be fanciful or imaginative, but must rest in the evidence.

He instructed the jurors that they were the sole judges of the believability of the witnesses and the weight to be given the testimony of each.

He advised that they should give the weight they deemed appropriate to the elements of detention and slavery.

He informed them that their decisions must be unanimous.

At the conclusion, the judge advised the jury to disregard anything that he had said or done and to form their own opinions. Further, they were not to discuss sentencing.

With all the necessary details taken care of, Judge Knight removed his glasses, the jury was put in the bailiff's custody, and the wait began.

When deliberations started the next morning the commotion that had accompanied much of the trial slowed to a Sunday afternoon shuffle. The hallways were quiet, the courtroom was empty.

Unhappy about seeing her daughter only on weekends, McGuire had brought her down from Red Bluff. With her dark curls, Nicole was her mother in miniature, and she toddled up and down the corridors, collecting admirers.

At about four P.M., the jurors asked for the legal definitions of "duress" and "menace." Both counsels were called; Papendick rushed over from the nearby apartment where he was staying; McGuire asked one of the journalists in the hall to babysit for a moment. The defendant was brought up from the jail, the jury filed in, and Judge Knight read legal definitions from the bench: "Duress: unlawful confinement of victim and property. Menace: violent threat of unlawful confinement of victim and property."

Their questions answered, the jury filed back out and the courtroom emptied. A nonevent.

Afternoon slid toward evening and the jurors adjourned—
some taking with them a gnawing fear that they were going
to end up a hung jury.

The second day of jury deliberations, more media people,
expectant of a verdict, lined the halls and filtered in and out
of the courtroom. Judge Knight had decided to lift the ban
on cameras for the verdict, and camerapersons negotiated
angles with the bailiff and each other. With little to do but
wait, newspeople argued about the case, the men tending to
lean in Hooker's favor, saying Colleen had stayed because
she'd fallen in love, the women generally convinced that
Hooker was guilty.

The day dragged by with no news. The jurors broke for
lunch. No verdict.

At two-thirty, word got out that the bailiff had gone to get
the defendant and optimism rose. The prosecutor arrived
and chatted with reporters in the hall, waiting for the defense attorney. The cameras in the court were readied.
Papendick arrived, and the judge asked to see both counsels
in chambers. After several minutes, Papendick came out
smiling.

Hooker sat at the defense table, and the jury was brought
in.

With everyone assembled, Judge Knight said that, going
over the instructions, he had found an error. He reread
count ten, changing the instruction slightly for penetration
by a foreign object.[3]

The jury had no questions, and they were excused.

On his way out of the courtroom, Hooker smiled boyishly
at the bailiff and said: "I know I'm going home tomorrow."

The morning of October 31, the third day of deliberations,
Mr. Hogan, the jury foreman, was the object of considerable
speculation. He arrived wearing a tie.

At ten-thirty, the jury asked to see the exhibits, and the

3. The previous instruction did not apply; penetration need not be
committed with a "criminal intent," but, rather, "for the purpose of
sexual arousal, gratification, or abuse."

court was cleared of journalists and cameras. The jurors spent about ten minutes going over items they had viewed for weeks but hadn't touched.[4]

Lunchtime came and went and with still no hint of a verdict. Then, at two P.M., court was reconvened, and Judge Knight announced that he'd received two notes from the jury.

The jury was brought in and seated. Camera tripods bristled behind the railing, and followers of the trial seemed to lean forward in their seats, eager for some news.

The first note was a technical question on count ten.

The second note from the jury jolted the courtroom: "If we are a hung jury on one or more counts, how do we decide?"

Judge Knight explained that each count was separate. If they couldn't reach a unanimous decision, they would be hung on *that* particular count only, as each count is a distinct offense.

One juror, Mrs. King, took notes, then spoke up and thanked the judge.

The jury filed out and the waiting resumed.

Frustrated journalists spilled out into the hall, making bad jokes about a "hung" jury. Papendick walked over and stood alone at a window toward one end of the hall, smoking and gazing out at Redwood City. McGuire conversed with a spike-haired, orange-jacketed sketch artist who sat painting watercolors into her morning's work.

About forty-five minutes later, Crystal Davis, the court clerk, came out into the hall to tell the attorneys, "It won't be long now."

The crowd hustled back into the courtroom, and Judge Knight came in to quiet them. "Let me tell you what's happening," he said. The jury had sent him a note saying they'd reached a verdict, but were hung on one count. He said he intended to bring them in to see "just how hung they are—and if it's truly hung."

---

4. Three of the jurors tried on the head box, and one of the jurors, Mrs. King, climbed into the box beneath the bed.

Cameron Hooker was brought in, the attorneys took their places, and the jurors resumed their seats in the jury box.

"Ladies and gentlemen," the judge said, "the bailiff has informed me that you are hung on one count. I don't want you to tell me the number of the count, or the number of votes for guilty or not guilty, but I want to know the numerical count."

Mr. Hogan replied that the jury was hung six to six.

"Is there any chance of resolving it?"

"No, Your Honor."

Judge Knight said the alternate juror would be called, and when she arrived, the verdict would be read.

Again, the players in this drama dispersed. The judge and jury disappeared. Hooker was taken out. Both counsels left.

Meanwhile, with the verdict at hand, more people filed into the courtroom, bringing more television cameras, more photographic equipment. All the seats filled, and the noise level rose. The atmosphere was almost festive.

Mrs. Sater, the alternate juror, arrived in a proper white suit.

This was it.

The players reassembled. Papendick and McGuire took their seats, both apparently nervous. The bailiff brought in Cameron Hooker, and a hush fell across the courtroom.

At three twenty-five the jury took their seats in the jury box, and Judge Knight addressed the foreman: "Mr. Hogan, I've been informed you've reached a verdict."

"Yes, Your Honor."

The bailiff carried a stack of verdict forms over to the court clerk, Crystal Davis, who stood and read: "Count one: guilty of kidnapping. Special allegation [of having used a knife], true. Count two: guilty of rape. . . . Count three: guilty of rape. . . . Count four: guilty. . . ." Over and over, the court heard the word *guilty*. Cameron Hooker had been found guilty of ten felony counts.[5] The eighth count[6] was hung.

Hooker, as usual, showed no emotion.

5. There were some special findings, including use of force, violence, duress, menace, and threat of immediate and unlawful bodily injury, on

With the verdict in, Judge Knight ventured to make some extraordinary comments from the bench. After thanking the jury, he said: "I want to particularly commend you for having the intelligence to reject the testimony of Dr. Donald Lunde, the defense psychiatrist. I think witnesses like that are a real menace to the criminal justice system. They come in here posing as objective scientists, when, in fact, they are nothing but paid advocates." Jaws dropped, but the judge continued, "I'm happy that you had the good sense to see through him, because one Dan White case is enough."

Further, Judge Knight said: "I would like to say that I know what a terrible emotional strain it must have been for all of you to go through this. Looking back on it, you can say that in a way it's a happy ending, because faith and love —and I mean Colleen Stan's faith in God and her love of her family—did triumph over evil. You have done justice, and I certainly agree with your verdict."

The judge wished the jury a Happy Halloween,[7] and court was adjourned.

Moved and deeply relieved, Deputy DA McGuire had tears in her eyes. She looked over at one of the jurors, Mrs. Rhodes, and saw that she was teary-eyed too, then noticed that most of the women jurors' eyes were moist. Some stepped from the jury box to give the prosecutor a farewell hug. Out in the hall, others were besieged by reporters scrambling for quotes.

A few shied away, others, finally able to talk to faces that had become familiar during the long course of the trial, were accommodating:

Mrs. King told of climbing into the box: "I didn't believe that someone could turn around in it." She tried it; she could. "It was a scary feeling," she said. "I have an inordinate fear of the dark, anyway."

---

all the rape counts. Special findings determine whether a full, separate, and consecutive term shall be served for each sex offense.

6. Half the jury felt the evidence indicated that the sexual encounter in 1984 was not technically rape, since Colleen had apparently first asked Janice if it was okay.

7. Janice Hooker later said she thought it was appropriate that Cameron was convicted on his favorite holiday, Halloween.

Mrs. Slattery, the graphics designer whose husband was a psychologist, said Dr. Hatcher "very definitely pulled a lot of it together as far as the state of mind of the victim." Asked about Dr. Lunde's contention that Colleen had fallen in love, she responded, "Well, a different kind of love, like an abused child, seeking attention and affection after being abused."

"What made the victim convincing?" someone asked.

She replied: "Her deadness, her stillness."

In the courtroom, Christine McGuire was meanwhile calling Colleen Stan with the news.

Reporters crowded around as the call went through and McGuire told her: "The jury just came back with the verdict. Guilty on ten counts! Do you have any comment for the press?"

Colleen replied: "Praise the Lord, justice is done!"

EPILOGUE

The sentencing of Cameron Michael Hooker was scheduled for nine A.M., November 22, in the court of the Honorable Clarence B. Knight.

It was a sunny, breezy day. The cast from the Hooker trial reassembled in the eighth floor courtroom, with a slightly effervescent feeling of reunion. Several of the jurors sat behind the railing. (Unusual—jurors rarely choose to attend sentencings, yet seven had come to Hooker's.)

Cameron Hooker was brought in wearing the orange jumpsuit issued to convicts. His mother sat just behind him.

Colleen Stan entered the room for the first time since her testimony. She and her attorney sat just in front of the railing, near Christine McGuire. Colleen seemed tense.

Court was called to order and Judge Knight ascended the bench. The first order of business jolted the courtroom: The judge addressed Defense Attorney Rolland Papendick's eleventh-hour motion to disqualify him.

Papendick claimed Knight had been prejudiced against Hooker, basing his claim principally on statements he said the judge had made in chambers or in the hallway (such as, that Hooker would have felt at home with the Spanish Inquisition, that Hitler would have liked the defendant, and that the "most sadistic thing" Hooker ever did was force Papendick to try this case).

Judge Knight, plainly affronted, told Papendick that he believed comments made in chambers were confidential, and rather hotly denied making any reference to Hitler or the

Spanish Inquisition. He concluded that any remarks made outside the presence of the jury "had no effect whatever on my position as judge." The motion was denied.

A few technical matters were considered, then Hooker's sentencing was at hand.

According to state law, the victim has an opportunity to make a statement, and Colleen asked her attorney to read one on her behalf. Barrett stood and read a long, eloquent plea, asking that Hooker be locked away as long as possible, so that what happened to Colleen Stan would never happen to anyone else.

When she resumed her seat, all turned toward the judge expecting that he would pronounce the sentence.

Judge Knight obliged: "I consider this defendant the most dangerous psychopath that I have ever dealt with, in that he is the opposite of what he seems. He will be a danger to women as long as he is alive, and I intend to sentence the maximum possible." Citing Hooker's "pattern of violent conduct," and "high degree of cruelty and callousness," Judge Knight sentenced him to consecutive sentences for the sex crimes, totalling sixty years. He then imposed indeterminate sentences of one to twenty-five years for the kidnap, plus a five-to-ten-year sentence for the use of a knife. If the California Board of Corrections chose to apply the full terms, Hooker would serve a maximum sentence of one hundred four years.

Hooker was expressionless, except for a slight smile when the judge also fined him fifty thousand dollars.

(At the end of the hearing, Hooker turned to Papendick and said: "I want you to thank the judge for me. I have a library, a gym, and time to enjoy them, and it's better than living with those two women.")

Court adjourned, and McGuire announced that Colleen wished to personally thank the jurors, asking them to step out into the hall. She requested that the press wait, promising that Colleen would come back in to make a statement.

After listening to her testify for days on the stand, the jurors now met the woman whose ordeal had occupied their thoughts for so many weeks. They clustered around her in the hallway in an almost protective fashion. Colleen beamed, her cheeks matching her pink suit, her eyes moist. The jurors seemed equally emotional. They'd scarcely met, yet in some ways they were already bonded, having been drawn together by this draining and exhausting trial.

They shared a rush of questions, words of support, and a few shy hugs, but soon reporters and photographers, eager for their chance with Colleen, were spilling out into the hall. The sheer crush of expectation forced an end to their meeting.

Colleen took a seat at the prosecution's table, a battery of microphones before her. She seemed both nervous and happy as she told the crowd that she was "very glad that [Cameron] won't ever be able to hurt me or anyone else again."

Colleen was asked what kept her going while she was confined in the box.

"It was very hard," she said. "At times, I'd come to a point where I couldn't take it anymore, and I'd just want to let go."

The gathering learned that Hooker had phoned Colleen from jail just three days after his conviction. At first, she didn't recognize his voice. Then he said, "This is Cameron, and I just called so that you can chew my butt out or say whatever you want to me."

Colleen replied: "I have nothing to say to you," and hung up. (Upset, she then called McGuire, who contacted the San Mateo County Jail, asking that they prevent Hooker from placing any more calls to Colleen.)

Asked about her plans for the future, she said, "Just to go on with my life."

"What was the first thing you did when you got back home?"

Colleen smiled. "I went shopping and bought some clothes," she said, and everyone laughed.

With a few final comments, she concluded her statement to the press, said good-bye, and escaped into the hall. Several jurors followed to wish her well, and after a few more hugs and tears, Colleen Stan turned and walked away.

* * *

The jurors for *People* v. *Hooker,* united by their emotional six weeks together, have kept in touch. Shortly after the sentencing, eight of them met for dinner with Judge Knight and Gordon Campbell, the bailiff. They still have occasional get-togethers.

(The judge, by the way, reported that he received nothing but positive feedback about his unorthodox castigation of the defense's expert witness Dr. Lunde.)

It seems somehow poetic justice that Cameron Hooker, the sex criminal, was prosecuted by an attractive young woman. But this case took its toll on Deputy DA McGuire. By the trial's conclusion she had lost eight pounds, and her hair was touched with gray.

Perhaps the Hooker case took its toll on her private life as well. She and Jim Lang divorced.

Now remarried, Christine McGuire lives in Santa Cruz County with her husband, Richard. She works in the District Attorney's office, heading up a special task force on the prosecution of rapes and homicides.

She found prosecuting the Hooker case the most involving and most challenging case of her career—rewarding, but also wearing. Once was enough. With a half-smile she says, "I hope I never have to prosecute a case like that again."

Though she was only there a fraction of the time, the trial wasn't easy on Colleen Stan. Following the proceedings in the news, then nervously awaiting the verdict, she lost fourteen pounds from sheer anxiety.

Colleen will carry the taint of those seven years forever. Her physical health may never be the same. She has poor teeth, and it will be a long time before her hair grows back— if it ever does. She has chronic back problems and can't sit up straight for long without support. The scars on her body have healed and faded; it will take longer for the scars on her memory to fade.

Some effects are less noticeable—a fear of going out alone, for instance, a fear of crowds. And she dislikes going out to dinner because, she says, after all those years of eating just one meal a day, never knowing when she would eat again, she feels compelled to finish everything on her plate.

Colleen remains close to her family and continues to work and reside in Riverside. She is religious—still more inclined to go to church than to therapy—subdued, passive, and fairly private. (At this writing, she may have already changed her name.)

Colleen is determined to live a full and rich life, despite what has happened to her. "I just decided that I'm going to do my best to put it behind me," she has vowed to herself. "I'm not going to let them keep me from doing what I want with my life."

Money will surely help, and Colleen has sought and found some financial compensation. California's Victim Witness program awarded Colleen more than $20,000, and her civil suit against Cameron Hooker reached an out-of-court settlement with the Puritan Insurance Company (the insurers of Hooker's mobile home), who agreed to pay her a total of about $150,000.

Having children has been Colleen's long-held desire, and on April 23, 1987, after a risky and difficult pregnancy, she gave birth to a healthy baby girl. "She has a little worried look," Colleen says, "like me."

Janice Hooker filed for divorce on January 28, 1986, and has taken back her maiden name. Today she is a much stronger, more independent woman than the one who gave statements to police in the fall of 1984. She is more sure of her own decisions and has gone back to school.

Janice dotes on her children—who are, indeed, lovely daughters. (People often asked why the state hadn't taken the girls away from Janice, but McGuire observed her to be an excellent mother. The daughters had been shielded from the unsavory truths at home, and anyone could see that they were well-adjusted, healthy, polite, and delightful girls.)

Jan goes to counseling and thinks deeply about how she ended up in such a strange and toxic situation. She believes she and Colleen were both brainwashed. "It can be done to anyone," she says.

Still, she feels Colleen's personality made it easier for

Cameron to dominate her. He is very perceptive, Janice believes, and he picked a victim who was submissive, compliant, someone who tended toward destructive relationships.

Reflecting on the changes she has made, Janice says, "I chose not to be a victim. I hope Colleen makes that choice. Not to just walk out but to make a total change, to become an unvictim, to take charge."

The grapevine around the San Mateo County Jail has it that Cameron Hooker told Jan that his big mistake was that he didn't kill Colleen while he had the chance.

After sentencing, Hooker was shipped to California Diagnostic Center at Vacaville for evaluation. Now he is serving time in Folsom Penitentiary.

Rolland Papendick, who has given up smoking, filed an appeal. It was denied on March 8, 1988.

What quirk of nature results in a Cameron Hooker? It would be easy if we could simply say that he was abused, therefore he abused others. It's often the case, for example, that victims of child abuse become child abusers themselves or that sons of wife-beating fathers become wife-beaters, too. But Hooker took great pains to shield his daughters from the darker side of his personality, and no evidence of familial abuse during Cameron's childhood emerged. If there was domestic violence, it was kept very quiet.

If anything, people who knew them were in remarkable agreement that the Hooker family was a fine, upstanding, and welcome addition to the Red Bluff community. "Honest" and "hardworking" were the adjectives almost unanimously used to describe Cameron's parents. They were salt-of-the-earth types, and no one had anything but good things to say about them. The investigation turned up no evidence of a violent homelife, only that Harold and Lorena Hooker were devastated by the charges against their firstborn son.

More likely, Cameron Hooker is, himself, an aberration, not the product of an aberrant childhood.

Why? The question reverberates . . . and remains, always, unanswered. Cameron Hooker doesn't know, and science can't tell us—beyond speculating about infinitesimal chemical exchanges within the brain. Lawyers, mere public servants, handle the legal questions, but evil is left, ultimately, for philosophers to weigh and debate. Whatever the verdict, the complete truth lies always beyond our grasp, outside the courtroom, unknowable.

One person close to the case who wished to remain anonymous made perhaps the most enlightening comment not just on Cameron Hooker but on certain types of criminals in general:

"People like to believe in an Einstein or a Beethoven— geniuses—but they hate to believe in their opposites. A genius is a mutant, something unnatural. But just as some people are born with extra intelligence, others are born without much intelligence or without fingers or limbs or consciences.

"The human body is phenomenally complex, with trillions of cells, and trillions of things can go wrong. Cameron Hooker is a fluke, an accident of internal wiring. His instincts are simply the opposite of yours and mine."